The Book of Health & Care Cost Management

© Copyright 2024

All rights reserved. No part of this publication may be reproduced, distributed or transmitted in any form or by any means, including photocopying, recording, or other electronic or mechanical methods, without the prior written permission of the publisher, except in the case of brief quotations embodied in critical reviews and certain other noncommercial uses permitted by copyright law.

Although the authors and publisher have made every effort to ensure that the information in this book was correct at press time, the authors and publisher do not assume and hereby disclaim any liability to any party for any loss, damage, or disruption caused by errors or omissions, whether such errors or omissions result from negligence, accident, or any other cause.

Adherence to all applicable laws and regulations, including international, federal, state and local governing professional licensing, business practices, advertising, and all other aspects of doing business in any jurisdiction is the sole responsibility of the reader and consumer.

Neither the authors nor the publisher assumes any responsibility or liability whatsoever on behalf of the consumer or reader of this material. Any perceived slight of any individual or organisation is purely unintentional.

The resources in this book are provided for informational purposes only and should not be used to replace the specialised training and professional judgment of a health care or mental health care professional.

Neither the authors nor the publisher can be held responsible for the use of the information provided within this book. Please always consult a trained professional before making any decision regarding treatment of yourself or others.

For more information email colin.lewry@carados.com

ISBN: (print only): 978-1-9196304-2-7

Cover Design: Lucia Hawe - design.luciahawa.com

Contents

Introduction   3

About The Authors   7

Chapter One: An Introduction to Managing Cost   11

- What Is Cost Reduction?   13
- Organisation Vs. System Cost Control   17
- What Do We Call it?   21
- The Trouble With Money   23
- The Trouble with Finance Departments   25
- Obvious vs. Hidden Costs   27
- Spend to Save   29
- Useful Skills For Cost Control   31

Chapter Two: Barriers to Cost Control   35

- Complexity Of Health & Care Transformation   37
- Inherent Resistance To Change   41
- Fragmented Nature of Health & Care Systems   45
- Financial And Resource Constraints   49
- Unforeseen Consequences And Unintended Outcomes   53
- The Evolving Nature Of Health & Care   57
- Conclusion   61

Chapter Three: Approaches to Managing Cost   65

- Turnaround   67
- Value-Based Health & Care   71
- The Organisation Wide Project   75
- Organisational Focus On Quality   77
- A Focus On What Is Important   79
- Service Line Management   81
- Transformation   85
- The Model Organisation   87

Chapter Four: The Approach — 89

- Overview — 91
- Phase One: Scope & Mobilise — 97
- Phase Two: Generate Ideas — 109
- Phase Three: Develop Future State — 125
- Phase Four: Plan & Implement — 133
- Phase Five: Sustain Success — 137

Chapter Five: The Ideas — 143

- The Headings — 145
- Tactical Cost Review — 149
- Grip Operations — 157
- Plan Workforce — 165
- Manage Non-Pay Spend — 193
- Improve Efficiency — 207
- Align The Back Office — 239
- Transform — 253

The Bit at the Back — 261

- Glossary — 263
- Abbreviations — 267
- Links — 271

Introduction

Improving the health of the world's population is a great enterprise, but there can be little doubt that it is an expensive one, and potentially limitless in scope. This creates a challenge for health & care systems and organisations across the world. Whatever our goals and whatever our strategy, we need to consider the cost of providing health and care support.

This book is about that cost – what it is, how we control it, how we reduce it. We do that within the context that cost is only part of health and care provision – and the staff that provide health and care, and the populations that those staff serve are just as important, if not more so.

The trouble is that writing a book on the topic of cost of provision is not easy. There are at least five reasons that make it a complex undertaking, which we need to understand before we start:

1. Variable reasons for reducing cost

The reason for addressing this topic is variable, both between and within countries. Some organisations are interested in profit (some in the short, and some in the longer term) and generating organisational value. Others are more interested in the overall health of their populations and service-users, and do not have a profit motive, although they still want to stay within budgets. These reasons give us a different lens on how we control cost, require or allow different ideas to be used, and may necessitate different approaches. So, we need to consider the different reasons, and the impact that they have on approach, and the ideas we use.

2. Variable levels of maturity

The level of maturity of organisations and their commissioners / payers / purchasers / funders, is also variable. Some actually care (and are incentivised to care) about the overall health of the country, others are much more focused on short-term political goals and targets. Some worry about cost, whereas others worry about value. This level of maturity has a significant impact on the approach, and on the ideas that will make up a cost reduction programme.

3. Different types of organisation

If we want to be specific about how to address the problem, we need to get into the detail. We don't want to just give some high level principles, we want to dive into the ideas that will help you reduce cost in your organisation. The trouble is that the health & care sector is a disparate mix of organisations and systems. This leads to a problem, because the ideas that are core to some organisations (for example, improving theatre utilisation) might be completely irrelevant to others. A mental health provider will have different needs to an orthopaedic hospital - and both will have wildly different requirements to a charity supporting trauma survivors, a residential care home or a dental practice.

Throughout this book, we will be providing approaches and ideas for cost management - many of which will be irrelevant for some organisations. We won't be getting too detailed here (e.g. we might not talk about the cost management implications of specific medicines) but we will be getting detailed enough to build relevant plans no matter what your organisation. We have also tried to create general rules for as many organisations as possible, with specific focus areas for staff groups (e.g. nurses) or process areas (e.g. theatres) that some organisations need, and others can comfortably ignore.

4. Variable amounts of and approaches to money

Some organisations and systems have lots of money, and some have very little. Approaches to controlling cost and addressing demand can be very different depending on the availability of money in the short and longer term, and on whether profit is important, or whether it is just the amount that you spend. In this book, we must therefore set out the different approaches and styles to cost management and their impact on the sorts of ideas that you can countenance in a cost management plan or strategy.

5. Variable histories and contexts

Different health systems, usually because of a combination of the above, have their own unique histories, contexts, problems and approaches when it comes to health and care, and addressing the cost of it. The culture of the country and its health and care systems will have a significant impact on, for example, the level of change management that will be required in a cost management programme. If organisations have been through cost reduction or "turnaround" before, the approach may been to flex to bring people with you on the journey - or it might not. You are a better judge than we are of what should work, and what will definitely not work, in your organisation. So we've set out flexible approaches, and a lot of ideas, which we hope you will choose from wisely…

Reflecting all of these variances in one book, and ensuring that everyone finds this book relevant to them is therefore not an easy task. But whether you've got lots of money or very little, you are worried about budgets or value, you are in a hospital group in Singapore, a mental health charity in England, running a care home in the United States or a private clinic in France, the one thing everyone should care about is efficiency: getting the right amount of work for the resources invested. Getting bang for your buck, as it were. The more efficient we are, the more choices we have – whether that's to provide more and better care, or to hand dividends to shareholders.

So, this book focuses on that core element of efficiency, and on where we think that everyone should aim to be - which is value-based health and care.. We should be concerned about generating value - not slashing costs. We should be ensuring that we are efficient and that we are in control of costs, but not destroy value by cutting deep.

However, because some systems and organisations are not as mature as others, or because there are short-term issues that force people to compromise on the best interests of their population's long-term health and care, we will also talk about suck things as "turnaround" and "cost-cutting". We just don't like these approaches very much.

The authors work across the world but spend most of their time in the United Kingdom and the Middle East. In England, we work across all areas of Integrated Care, but know that a lot of the focus is on hospitals. This version of the book will try to approach the problem in a way that is as widely applicable as possible, but it won't all be relevant all the time. So, if you read about medical efficiency, and you don't have any doctors working for you, just ignore the section – it will hopefully be relevant to someone one else; or maybe even you at another stage in your career. And if we're talking about income generation, and you can't do that - move on to something you can do.

The book is aimed at anyone who needs to consider the cost of health and care, so it is very relevant for any manager or leader in any aspect of health and care in any organisation in any country. You might be in the organisation or you might have been asked to help it – either as part of the overall health system or as an external advisor / management consultant.

It is in three key parts. In part one we start by considering the concepts involved in cost and its management, in part two we set out a core approach and tools to cost management, and finally we set out a whole list of ideas and areas to reduce cost. Hopefully, this should provide everything you need to manage cost in your team.

About The Authors

Colin Lewry

In his heart, Colin Lewry is a workforce planner, with over 25 years' experience in developing workforce models, building workforce hubs and writing and implementing workforce plans. It all started in retail (rebuilding someone else's workforce models for branches of Martin the Newsagent) and culminated in him writing "The Bumper Book of Health & Care Workforce Planning".

As part of that career, Colin worked for PricewaterhouseCoopers in England and Europe developing cost reduction plans for over fifty different teams and organisations mainly in hospitals – staff represent around 70% of all cost (and value) so it made sense.

In 2014, after moving to another consultancy, Colin worked with Craig Barratt and Frances Bazire at Lancashire Care NHS Trust, assisting in delivering cost control work, and developing the Workforce Repository and Planning Tool – a workforce model still used across the UK National Health Service today.

Eventually he escaped from his third management consultancy and now runs Carados Ltd, a training and development company that aims to build the skills of managers in health and care across the world in the ares of Workforce Planning, Customer Service and (of course) Cost Management.

At time of writing, he is the Director of WRaPT in the UK and the TAQAA Workforce system in Saudi Arabia, founder of the Association of Health & Care Workforce Planning, and a Visiting Fellow of the University of Suffolk.

Craig Barratt

As a lawyer by qualification (College of Law), an accountant by qualification (Fellow of CPFA) and experience, and now a management consultant, it is often claimed that Craig doesn't actually have a heart. In reality, he cares deeply about health and health care, and has spent many years as an Executive Director within the English National Health Service.

He is a seasoned management consultant and executive healthcare leader specialising in strategy, finance, and transformation. With over 25 years of dedicated service in health and care, Craig has built a reputation for leading transformative change and driving strategic innovation across global healthcare systems. His academic background in law and accountancy, complemented by a Postgraduate Diploma in Program Management, has provided a robust foundation for his diverse roles in healthcare leadership and consultancy.

As a leader in global strategy consulting firms, Craig has been at the forefront of developing and implementing health practices that emphasise sustainability and value. His work has consistently focused on integrating digital innovations, improving financial models, and fostering effective governance structures within health systems. These initiatives have often resulted in policy adaptations and strategic overhauls that significantly impact health service delivery and patient outcomes on a national and international scale.

Frances Bazire

Frances has been working with process and pathways efficiency, quality, and citizens experience for 24 years.

In 2000, as a young graduate she volunteered to attend the inaugural Lean rapid improvement event at the UK Legal Aid Board, an early adopter of continuous improvement in Whitehall. She had found her path - spending 9 years working in central government bringing Lean to the public sector from prisons to court rooms with a focus on preventing our hard-earned dosh being wasted on activities that add no value.

Frances then moved into the NHS, had her eyes really opened to the impact of fragmented care, and set about building a team and using these skills to improve healthcare pathways where she then met Craig and Colin. At this point she was seduced by the dark side (private sector) and joined a global management consultancy working with private healthcare providers, MedTech companies and Pharma.

She now runs Fadefain Limited a management consultancy focused on bringing industry and healthcare together to accelerate access to healthcare, reduce failure demand for services and building tools, games and models with Colin, to support the sustainable redesign of pathways and the elimination of waste!

CHAPTER ONE

AN INTRODUCTION TO COST MANAGEMENT

This chapter considers some cost management concepts and definitions that you need to know before you get started. It includes definitions and information that should give us a basis on which to start, but its main aim is to make you think hard about what you are trying to achieve, and to consider the power you have, and the skills you need, to manage costs.

1.1 What is Cost Management?

Cost Management, Cost Reduction, Cost Control, Efficiency - these are all things we want to talk about in this book, and they are all connected. We nearly used "Cost Reduction" in the title of this book, because that is what people often first think about, but the reality of the situation is much more complex than just reducing costs. As we will see, Cost Management is the key here - which may very well include cost reduction.

But, let's start with Cost Reduction. In its simplest case, this is really easy to define. At the moment, you are spending money, so if you spend less money, you are reducing costs. Cost reduction is about spending less money.

Great.

But why do you want to do it? Reducing costs for its own sake doesn't make any sense, there has to be a reason, which might include:

- "I want to make more profit" – for shareholders, to make the organisation safer, etc.

- "I want to be more efficient"– so I can deliver more for the same amount of money, so I can make more profit, or so I can get my product/service into the market cheaper than other people can (to do more good, so I can make more profit, or so I can increase the value of my company).

- "I've been told to", or "I am getting pressure from above to do it" – from your manager, regulator, directors, investors, shareholders, etc.

- "It will look better for investors" – I need to show "the market" that we are a company that isn't afraid to make hard decisions.

- "The organisation is running out of money" – If we don't stop spending at this rate, we're going to go out of business or face massive lending costs. This is where you may face insolvency and where the concept of organisational "turnaround" comes from. More on that later.

- "I want to protect the organisation (or myself) from some other threat" – there might be a takeover threat, the Board are thinking of firing me, etc.

- "I just love reducing cost" – for some reason. Hey, if that is where you get your kicks, who are we to judge?

- Other reasons – sometimes, you are looking to be more efficient because something has changed – for example, you can't get enough social workers, so you are looking to be more efficient with what you have got. That's not cost reduction per se, but it is efficiency. Increasingly there is a recognition in the world of value based health and care that resources = carbon and that carbon feeds global warming, so your motivation might be environmental. In which case, this book could actually save the planet.

We can see that most of these are not about reducing cost - they are about making more money and/or creating more value, with a focus on cost.

We separate all of these different reasons into two groups – what we characterise as the rational and the irrational.

- **The Rational** – It makes perfect sense to want to be more efficient. If your organisation is spending more than it needs or more than its income, then it will make less profit, be at risk of censure/closure or be able to deliver less. It won't be the best organisation it can be and may therefore not attract the best staff.

    So, efficiency we understand – it is rational. But efficiency isn't necessarily **REDUCING** costs.

    Efficiency is about getting more for your money, so in the rational case, there are other options than just to reduce cost. You can increase income, or you can increase the number of people that you serve (if not in an income-generating group). And part of being efficient is **OPTIMISING** your costs for the outcome you want to achieve. That will almost certainly mean **CONTROLLING** or **MANAGING** your costs and it **MAY** mean reducing your costs.

- **The Irrational** – Sometimes, to make someone look good or to follow a mandate from on high (regulators, head office, "The market") you must reduce cost.

    This happens in both the public and the private sector, but in different ways. In the public sector, when you are a part of a big organisation, you sometimes get told to reduce staff or control other costs, even when it will make your organisation or team less efficient by:

    - Making good staff redundant;

    - Annoying good staff;

    - Making short term procurement deals that will be more costly in the long-term; or

    - Pulling out of deals that will be profitable long term but costly short term.

    It may be rational to the "higher-ups" (spoiler: It probably isn't, even to them), but to you, it makes little sense. But you have to do it anyway.

So, it is worth considering a few things when you consider cost reduction:

- **Understanding costs** - you cannot control what you cannot measure (or at least it is much more difficult)

- **Controlling costs** - making sure that you don't spend money you shouldn't spend, thus ending up either over budget, less efficient, or both.

- **Efficiency** - getting more income, or delivering more activity/service, for the same amount of cost. You can split this into three groups:

- **Increasing efficiency while increasing costs** - for example, adding new equipment without reducing the staff, but delivering much more activity with current levels.

- **Increasing efficiency while maintaining costs** - for example, replacing staff with new equipment, and delivering more activity as a result.

- **Increasing efficiency while reducing costs** - for example, replacing staff with new equipment and delivering the same amount of activity, taking the benefit as reduced cost/more profit.

- **Reducing costs** – bringing overall spend down – either whilst improving efficiency (as in the last option above) or while not caring about efficiency.

Depending on your reasons, any of these may be appropriate. In most cases though, the question is:

How can the team or organisation become more efficient and at the same time, how can I control costs so that I spend what I expect to spend and don't end up with nasty surprises?

And this, for us, defines Cost Management

This is important – If you are going to do this properly, you need to understand why you are trying to do it right from the start.

1.2

Organisation vs System Cost Control

Health & care organisations are not working in isolation, they are part of a system of organisations that help manage and improve the health of their populations. In almost all cases, the country is interested in ensuring that their population remains well, so there is real interest in making sure that the health & care system is working.

The trouble is that not all organisations are interested in ensuring that the system is working well. In many systems around the world, organisations are incentivised differently to the system.

In England, for example, Integrated Care Systems are relatively new, and few have managed to reach the level of maturity that is needed to work together effectively and efficiently for the long term, in the face of incentives that often force them to focus on their own performance first.

This situation creates a couple of problems that you should be aware of when looking to manage costs.

Problem 1: A focus on the big health providers

One set of organisations are the large providers of secondary and tertiary health and care (physical and mental), many of which also provide community care. These organisations are what we call "noisy": They are obvious - when something goes wrong in health and care, these big organisations are the ones where you see the problems most obviously – waiting lists, queues at Emergency Departments etc – you notice when these go wrong. Which means that they get a lot of attention and focus, including from national governing bodies where they exist (like NHS England).

There is a lot of cost tied up in these big providers: In England, for example, the Department of Health and Social Care (DHSC) has a budget of about £200 billion of which £160 billion goes to NHS England (according to a recent King's Fund report) . About £100 billion of this goes to the big providers, with about another £20 billion going to Primary Care and £27 billion spent in adult social care. Social Care expenditure comes from another budget, and isn't the full cost as social care isn't free at the point of delivery for everyone – but in terms of government money, and attention, you can clearly see that the focus is on the "noisy" big providers.

When you look at our list of detailed ideas for cost reduction later, that means that the vast majority of them relate to these "noisy" (largely secondary care) organisations. Whilst the essence of these ideas are relevant to all, there is much more information on reducing cost in these organisations than in primary care, social care or the Voluntary, Community, Faith & Social Enterprise (VCFSE) sector.

And it is really important to focus on cost management in these big health providers, but the reality is that, for system cost management and efficiency, there are very strong arguments that we should be focusing on keeping people well earlier in the system, if we want to be more efficient (and create better health outcomes for the population for less or the same money without stressing our staff).

Problem 2: Systems don't work together to reduce cost

In the detailed list of ideas (that we will finally get to in this book, we promise), the really important ones are those that focus on addressing population need through integrated working across systems. The trouble is, that this doesn't happen. Organisations are too often forced to (or just do) act to ensure that their own organisation is financially viable, and there is less incentive to solve issues as a system. In England, the reasons why are legion, but it starts with the political structure that separates Social Care funding and governance via local authorities and healthcare funding and governance via NHS England.

Then the lack of clarity and alignment over systems actually being in charge mean that it takes a lot of consistent effort from a lot of people over a lot of years to focus on costs as a system. Few organisation leads are happy handing money over to other parts of a system.

Thus, cost control is often done in the easier and more comfortable area of the organisation rather than the harder and often less controllable system environment. The reality is of course that we need both: Organisations need to be efficient and control their costs and the system needs to ensure that the system is targeting the resources at the most effective and efficient areas.

There are two issues though – first, systems are not targeting resources at the most effective and efficient areas – they are just not driven to effect the transformational change needed and instead are dealing with budget shortfalls in organisations – organisations that can't balance their books because (among other reasons) demand is outstripping budgets. Secondly, organisations are making cost decisions that actually reduce system efficiency by acting in their own self-interest.

This is central government's doing (with a bit of human nature thrown in) rather than the fault of the hard-working organisation and system staff, but nonetheless, you will find that system cost control is focused on the big health organisations, and that these organisations are not yet driven to make the right decisions for systems.

This book is aimed primarily at managers in health and care organisations, so is by its nature pragmatic. It includes ideas that you can use on the ground in organisations and systems, picking what is most appropriate for your circumstances. So it includes lots of ideas for the big "noisy" organisations as well as the large-scale ideas that will align costs more closely with the service users and really start to improve efficiency within national health and care systems.

The Efficiency Triangle

Whenever we undertake any management training, we introduce the concept of the Efficiency Triangle to help people navigate the tricky world of management. We believe that three things need to be in balance for everyone to be happy:

- The Staff need to be happy - they have reasonable workloads and salaries, a fulfilling role, development, respect, etc.
- The Service-User or Customer needs to be happy - everyone needs to be dealt with, and the organisation should spend as much time with them as they expect or need.
- The Organisation needs to be happy - which in this case we define as "making enough money", although it can be much wider than that.

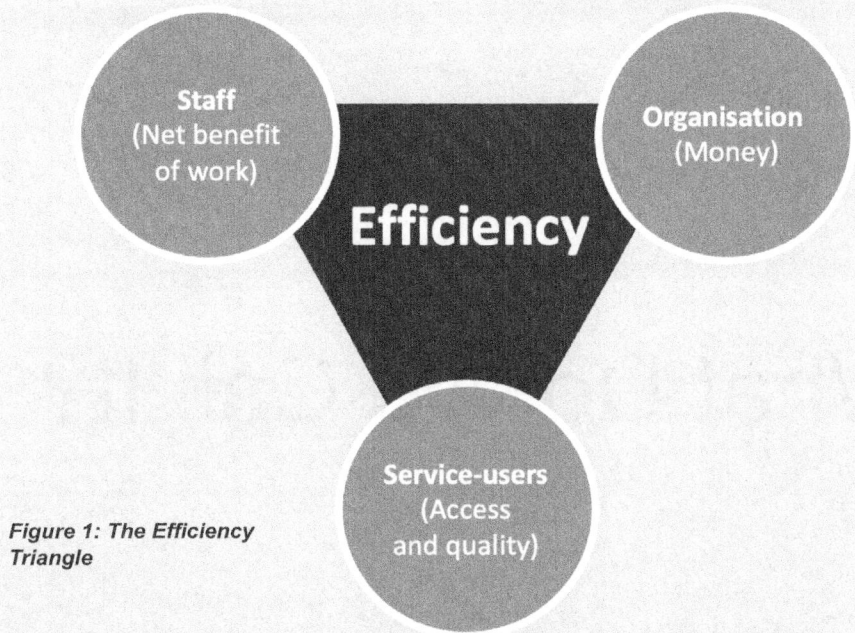

Figure 1: The Efficiency Triangle

The requirements for each of these groups can vary, and one of these circles can dominate the rest (which could be different for each organisation). But, in almost all cases, these three are in conflict - staff leave because the work is not what they expected, service-users don't get seen or the quality of their service is poor, or budgets get breached and the organisation doesn't make money.

The point of this section is not that you can avoid conflict between the circles - this conflict is part of life, and expectations grow. The point is that it is efficiency that reduces that conflict. If you cut costs, without improving efficiency, you will damage your staff and/or your service-users (AND almost certainly the organisation). If you focus on EFFICIENCY, then you stand a chance of controlling costs long term.

1.3

What Do We Call It?

As well as a lot of Britney Spears, the late 1990's were characterised (in the UK anyway) by cost reduction plans.

They were everywhere – and still make a comeback occasionally (like Britney herself).

In the big UK NHS Organisations, the financial year end is the end of March. Quite often, everyone is happy at the start of the year, because finances will only be a little bit adrift, and there is plenty of time to get back on track. Uneasiness builds in the boardroom every month as the finances get worse and the time to deal with it is ticking away.

Normally, there was uneasiness around August when month four's figures came in and showed that costs were more than expected, more concern in September when it became clear things were getting worse, and then a sudden panic to either develop a plan - or hire management consultants to develop a plan.

These plans had quite a few names including:

- CIPs - Cost Improvement Plans.

- CRES - Cost Reduction and Efficiency Schemes

- CRPs - Cost Reduction Plans

- Turnaround Plans

- P&E - Productivity & Efficiency Plans

It was always interesting to see what the organisation was calling them - with CIPs being the clear favourite. Between us, we've worked on more than a hundred of these plans. Whilst the aim of these was pure, the short-term nature of them and the lack of time and effort in engaging the whole organisation in the task, meant that their effectiveness was patchy.

Some worked, some didn't. Some worked well, some worked a little, and a few were a pointless waste of money and effort.

The key word used almost every time is "plan". Later we will discuss how to go about cost reduction as a planned programme in "The Approach" section.

1.3

The Trouble With Money

'Money, money, money, Must be funny In the rich man's world", wrote Benny & Bjorn of ABBA – and they knew what they were talking about.

Money is funny. Money isn't real. Well, coins and notes are actually things, but these days, who sees many of them? Money is a concept – an agreement that we will exchange it for different types of money or for goods, services and other things. Governments can just print more of it (or just add more zeroes to electronic accounts). Some people have just made up digital versions of it. If enough of the right people decide that it isn't worth anything, then it isn't.

We're often told that there isn't enough money for something. We can't afford a new scanner or a drug or more staff. But that's not true - there is enough money. It is just that enough of the right people haven't decided that we can spend it for that purpose. And people worry about money a lot. They say that we don't have the budget for health and care - but if we spent more money on health and care, then people would be healthier, would pay more taxes, and there would be more money to spend on health and care.

The point of this unnecessarily confusing section is to point out that people can get a bit obsessed about something that isn't real, and isn't the real problem. The problem that we face is rarely that we don't have enough money, it's much more complicated than that.

Sometimes it is about money - in the private sector, then money is represented either by cash flow (how much ready money we have), by profit (how much more money we make in income above costs), or by the value of the organisation (share price etc). Each of these things can drive different cost reduction behaviours - if we are running out of cash then a turnaround approach may be needed, for profit we need to consider efficiency, and for organisational value … well, who knows - but that is usually about size rather than costs.

Public sector organisations' problem with money is more about prioritising costs in the face of an almost limitless amount of demand. There is a lot of money in a system or an organisation, but it is tied up in the way things are already done - although it's possible there still isn't enough. Sometimes governments want to send a message that they are tough on public sector spending, at other times they are more worried about waiting list impacts on their election chances. So money is sometimes restricted and sometimes made so available that you'd think we'd discovered a magic money tree. The point here, is that you need to look at money from a different angle. Don't believe the narrative and don't just keep the status quo. This can include:

- Challenge budgets where they aren't high enough, and continue to compare what you are allowed to spend with what you need to spend to meet demand.

- Ensure we talk about efficiency rather than (or alongside) money.

- If balancing budgets is impossible (e.g. because cost improvement plans will take time) - be honest. This is important at all levels of health and care - sometimes, it is just impossible to balance the Efficiency Triangle to any extent - and if we don't raise a chronic lack of money as a problem, then we will end up with poor services that few people can access. We already have that in lots of cases.

1.4

The "Trouble" With Finance Departments

One of the issues that we face constantly when considering cost control or cost reduction is the influence of finance. We get told that "finance have said that we can't have more staff" or, "finance's staff model is different to ours". Some health systems seem to be in the thrall of this finance behemoth.

As some health care systems demote human resource / human capital / Organisational Development Director roles to non-Board / non-voting status, Finance Directors continue to sit at the centre of power for most.

As we have said in the "Efficiency Triangle" section, any organisation needs to consider the needs of its service-users, its staff and itself. Finance, in this case, represents a facet of the organisation's own needs - the need to make money or at least not to break it's centrally-set budgets.

As the champion of the organisation, the finance department can be very efficient - it can be well resourced, it has a simple mission, and it has the attention of some very powerful stakeholders. But left to itself, it can end up damaging the very thing that it is trying to save - by creating a situation where costs spiral out of control and efficiency worsens.

But in itself, the finance agenda is not either evil or the most important thing for an organisation. It is merely one of the most important things and it needs help to keep itself in balance. There needs to be voices for the service-user, voices for the staff and other voices for the organisation – these voices are typically provided by a strong operations team.

Finance are not the arbiters of all that is right in an organisation – they should be one voice in a dynamic discussion about the needs of all stakeholders. But neither are they the enemy - much of their reaction is due to a lack of any real belief that operational staff are capable of managing costs, or even want to,

The only way to create that belief is to actually care about cost as part of the equation and to speak the language of finance - if we want a certain amount of staff, then we should build a workforce model that shows them why we need that level. If we want investment, we should build a business case that is based on good evidence.

We need to learn to speak the language of finance, and we need to challenge them to see that what is needed is not cost cutting but a focus on efficiency and value – in balance with the needs of the team and the service-users.

The reality is that finance departments are not the trouble. If we didn't have them, we would run out of money very quickly (and they do a lot of very boring stuff that we REALLY don't want to have to do).

The problem is that we, as managers, are not balancing the needs of all of our stakeholders properly, and we aren't engaging finance in the right way. We need to speak their language and help them to meet their objectives - whilst continuing to fight for all stakeholders to be fairly treated. We need to engage them in integrated planning, or use Service Line Management (SLM - see later) techniques.

1.5 Obvious vs. Hidden Costs

In the last section, we spoke about the need to build a workforce model to engage finance in our thinking about why we need the staff that we need.

Colin builds a lot of workforce planning spreadsheets. These usually add up all the tasks that people do, and calculate how many people you need for different amounts of activity. He builds in time for development and redesign and for downtime. Then - well, then people generally ignore the results and set lower staffing levels because of, well, money. See earlier.

Lots of times people just make up staff numbers without even bothering with the spreadsheet stage. It leads to a reality gap between what is needed and what is costed - we actually need more people than we have in our establishments.

Assuming that budgets are not breached, or that the cost pressure doesn't suddenly create more efficient working, then this reality gap will be filled by staff working harder or by some service-users not getting the service. In the case of the staff, Frances calls this Fried Egg Economics, where the yolk is the effort you pay for, and the white bit is the extra work that people do beyond their contract.

When people look to improve efficiency or reduce costs, this reality gap can cause a real problem. People identify efficiencies that can be made – but they are often made in this reality gap area, which means that you can't monetise the savings. All you are doing is reducing the extra work that staff have been doing for free. So that means that benefits cases don't stack up, and the efficiencies aren't made. In reality, all efficiencies should be made, as the savings in the white bit of the egg are as worthwhile as reduced cost.

Another similar hidden cost is the massive amount of demand that we are sometimes not addressing. Colin has seen clinicians in workforce planning redesign programmes identify some truly dazzling efficiencies, but they don't actually "save" any money, they "merely" allow 30% more patients to be treated for a little more money - but they didn't get resourced because they are "only" addressing the needs of more patients rather than reducing cost. It's crazy, but it's true.

All efficiencies should be made, even if they don't reduce cash spending. If you hide costs, then it is difficult to convince people to do anything to address them.

To solve this, you need to consider measuring this hidden cost. It might be more or less scientific, but the level of additional stress you are putting staff under should be measured. One way of doing that is to use a workforce model that actually shows the additional time that people are asked to absorb into their role. Another is to measure it qualitatively through surveys or observation. The level of lost service to service-users should also be monitored - as it is these two groups that suffer when we focus only on money.

However you do it, do it. Hiding things is making us less efficient - we need to balance the needs of the organisation, the service-users and the staff (as we may have mentioned once or twice already…).

1.6

Spend to Save

While we are talking about cost management concepts, let's consider another fun element of cost reduction, the "spend to save" scheme.

These are ideas that cost money to implement, but will create a saving. They could include buying a new computer system, or adding a new staff member to save costs elsewhere. And when we say they cost money to implement, what we mean is that the finance department need to authorise more expenditure somewhere.

Typically these schemes are seen as "second-class" schemes compared to ideas that just reduce cost without having to spend any money. The main worry being that it is easy to spend more money, but it is a lot less easy to realise the benefits.

We think the concept of the spend to save scheme is wrong. In reality, almost all schemes are "spend to save" - you have to expend something to make a change happen. An intervention or change needs to be made to reduce cost - it doesn't just happen by magic. You will need to spend something - even if it is "just" the time of staff that are already in the budget. It's just that some of them don't require the numbers on a spreadsheet to change (you can just make busy people do more work – see Fried Egg Economics in the previous section).

When these schemes suddenly require the sort of spend that finance people notice then all hell breaks loose and everything becomes much harder.

As we said, the reality is that all cost reduction or efficiency schemes have a cost, and that cost should be recognised. Any cost reduction scheme should be treated as an intervention, a change, a project. Every change aimed at reducing cost should be evaluated to understand its cost and its benefits. We need to know what the plan is, how we will know it has been successful and what the impact will be on staff and service users (as well as the impact on budget that is the focus of the change). Make sure that you do an equality impact assessment on all schemes as well.

Where that cost is particularly large, then, of course, the controls around that change need to be stronger, and the bureaucracy around them will increase. More detailed benefits cases are needed, more people need to assess and sign off the extra cost, and, if agreed, the implementation of these schemes needs to be monitored and assured by senior people.

But, in reality, all schemes are spend to save schemes, and we should ensure that all schemes make sense before we do them, and that they are implemented. It's just that scale generally brings more risk, and thus greater support and focus is needed for larger schemes.

.

1.7

Useful Skills for Cost Control

As a manager, we think you need skills in all areas of management - which we broadly split into skills concerning customer/service-user service, workforce planning and cost control, all while considering your own needs.

A balance of these skills is needed to be great, as all of these are needed to manage the conflicting pressure between the wants and needs of the organisation, the service-users and the staff.

In terms of cost management, the skills that we think that you need can be split into four themes:

1. Front-line cost control.
2. Developing a cost-control project.
3. Redesigning for efficiency.
4. Governing for cost control.

We'll look at each of these in turn.

1. Front Line Cost Control

These skills are those that are needed when you are the manager of a team. They include a large range of individual sub-skills that help you to control costs. Front-line cost control skills include:

- **Budget awareness and control** - you need the skills to be able to know how much you can spend, to make sure that you aren't exceeding it unnecessarily, and to bring things back into line when necessary.

- **Developing capacity and demand models** - or at least understanding the balance between service-user need or activity and the staff and equipment needed to meet that demand.

- **Scheduling and rostering** - allowing you to efficiently target resources to match the needs of service users. If you have people sat around doing nothing one day, and queues out the door the next, then you aren't being efficient.

- **Job planning** - specific skills to be able to translate service-user needs into clear workloads and plans for staff.

- **Leadership & management skulls** - in the context of cost control, this includes a wide set of skills that allow you to create a team that is interested in managing cost as part of their role, that performs at their best (efficiently), and that is building for the future.

Across the Internet, there are a vast amount of free and paid resources to help you build your skills in these areas, and your organisation should be able to offer a lot of them to you.

Otherwise, they aren't investing in their managers very well. And, of course, Colin run's a training company, so send him an email...

2. Developing a cost-control project

These skills are relevant to front-line managers who want to change their approach to cost, or need to develop a cost improvement plan. They are also needed for those project staff that have responsibility for a cost improvement project across the entire organisation. They include:

- Developing a plan.

- Documenting a plan.

We will cover these skills later in the approach section

3. Redesigning for efficiency

These skills are system redesign skills used with a focus on cost control rather than on workforce planning, quality, or customer service. They include:

- Project management - delivering the plan.

- Process redesign.

- Programme Management Offices (PMOs).

Again, these are skills that you can build through self-study, or you can access a whole range of training both free and paid for. This is also a skill that is one that larger organisations will have specialists for - if you have a need for redesign, then you can often engage these experts to help.

4. Governing for cost control

These skills are relevant for executives who want to make sure that they have their hands on the levers for cost, so that they never get caught out needing to suddenly create a cost reduction or turnaround plan. These skills include:

- Managing cost improvement metrics.

- Leadership for cost control.

We touch on the elements of these skills in the approach and specific ideas sections later in this book.

Building Your Skills

The approach we use to develop executive, managerial and front-line team skills is the same across all the domains we operate in, including workforce planning, customer service and cost control .

We see development as a pyramid (or is it a tetrahedron?), with three elements on the base, and one at the pointy bit.

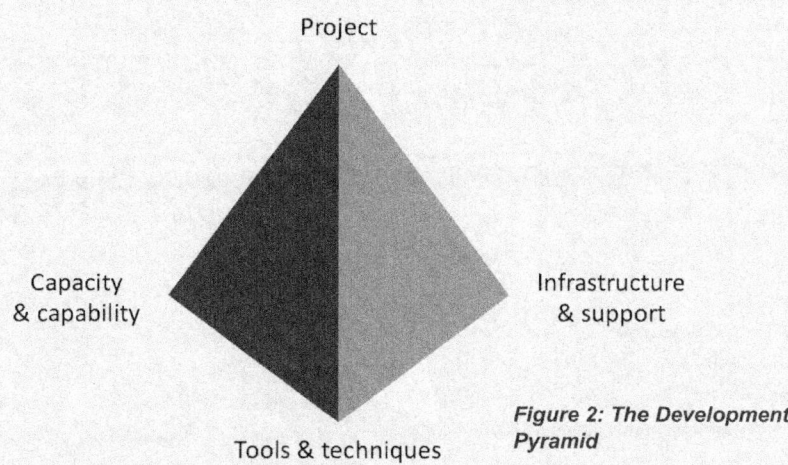

Figure 2: The Development Pyramid

The three elements of the base are:

Building Capability and Capacity Through Training: Knowing how to do it is a basic part of doing something. But on its own it isn't enough. You also need the time to do it.

Tools and Techniques: Training needs a base approach to form a shared language for those doing it, and to provide something concrete to go back to when you haven't used your training for a while.

Embedding in Your Organisation: The first two are surprisingly easy. Now it jumps to 'very hard' very quickly, as you need to ensure that the approach is embedded into the organisation in which you work, otherwise you won't be able to start it, complete it or maintain it into the future. The approach builds in how this is going to be sponsored, maintained, refreshed and celebrated, to reduce the chance of failure or atrophy.

Then we get to the last one. Every pyramid needs a point, and in this case the point is actually doing something useful (**The Project**) with all of the above. Preferably this should be something really important to the organisation or system (because that really helps with embedding it).

In a later section, we will focus on this - the project approach that you can consider to undertake a project to control cost in your organisation or system.

CHAPTER TWO

BARRIERS TO CONTROLLING COSTS

Health & care cost management is impossible. Sorry about that, but it is true. Every programme that any of us has been involved in hasn't solved the long-term control of cost.

None do.

And for three reasons:

Continuous Evolution of Health and Care Needs

Health and care systems must constantly adapt to the evolving needs of their populations. As demographics shift (e.g. ageing population), diseases change, and new health challenges emerge, the goals and strategies of health system transformation also need to evolve. This continuous change means that there is always something new to address or improve upon, preventing the achievement of a final, unchanging state of success.

Technological and Pharmaceutical Advancements

The rapid pace of technological and pharmaceutical innovation in health and care constantly alters what is possible in diagnosis, treatment, and service-user care. As innovations emerge, they not only provide opportunities for improvement but also create new benchmarks for what constitutes a successful health system. This ongoing technological evolution means that health systems must continually integrate new tools and approaches to stay current and effective, indicating that transformation is an ongoing process rather than a completed task.

Shifting Societal Expectations and Standards

Public expectations and global standards in health and care are continuously advancing. What is considered excellent health and care today might be seen as average in the future. As societies develop, their expectations around health and care access, quality, and patient experience evolve. Health & care systems, therefore, need to constantly improve and innovate to meet these rising standards and expectations, implying that the journey towards transformation is perpetual, with no definitive endpoint of complete success.

So, cost management is a journey, not a destination - because that destination moves and we are forever having to manage the balance between service-users, staff and money. Just like keeping people well, it's an impossible task to do it all the time, and there are a huge array of barriers in our way to make it harder.

This section considers those barriers, and what can be done to address them as you start the journey towards health & care cost management.

2.1

Complexity of Health and Care Transformation

Transforming health and care is an effort that operates within a complex adaptive system, involving an array of stakeholders, each with their unique perspectives and interests. This complexity emerges from the interplay of social, economic, political, and technological factors. Socially, diverse cultural beliefs and values shape health and care practices, adding variability that challenges the use of standardised approaches. Economically, the interplay between funding mechanisms and resource allocation necessitates balancing cost-effectiveness with equitable access. Politically, health and care policies and regulations are continuously shaped by diverse interests and ideologies, shifting with changes in parties, leaders, and mood. Technological advancements bring potential for innovation but also complexities like interoperability, data privacy concerns, he necessity for continuous adaptation, and large shifts in patient flows across systems.

The inherent complexities of this adaptive system hinder the full realisation of transformation goals, requiring collaboration, negotiation, and the even rarer compromise among stakeholders. Provider dynamics, payer systems, regulatory environments, and service-users contribute to these challenges. Providers grapple with balancing operational costs and quality care in the face of fluctuating, unclear and mis-aligned reimbursement models. Payer systems, including insurance companies and government health payers, influence care accessibility and affordability through their financial policies and use of contractual levers. The regulatory environment, aiming to ensure patient safety and quality care, often adds layers of complexity and administrative burden. Furthermore, service-users, as central stakeholders, have diverse needs and behaviours influenced by their socio-economic status and health literacy, influencing the effectiveness of any transformation initiative. To effectively navigate this landscape, visionary leadership, effective communication, and a deep understanding of these dynamic interactions are crucial.

To illustrate the complexity of health and care transformation, let's consider the implementation of electronic health record (EHR) systems. Despite the potential benefits of EHRs in improving patient care coordination and reducing medical errors, their implementation has faced many challenges. One notable example is the implementation of the National Health Service (NHS) electronic patient record system in the United Kingdom. The project, known as the National Programme for IT, faced significant challenges due to its scale and complexity. It experienced delays, cost overruns, and failed to deliver the intended benefits. The case study of the NHS electronic patient record system serves as a cautionary tale of the complexities involved in health and care transformation.

Another example is the implementation of new clinical guidelines or protocols. Health and care organisations often introduce new guidelines to improve patient outcomes and standardise care practices. However, the complexity of health and care, including variations in patient populations, health and care settings, and provider preferences, can make the implementation challenging. A case study is the implementation of new sepsis management guidelines in hospitals. Sepsis is a life-threatening condition that requires prompt and standardised care. Implementing new sepsis guidelines involve educating health and care providers, updating clinical protocols, and integrating decision support tools. However, the complexity of sepsis management, including diagnostic challenges and variations in patient presentations, can hinder the successful implementation of the guidelines

So how can we solve this? Well, we have a few suggestions...

Action 1: Foster Collaboration and Stakeholder Engagement

Establish a culture of collaboration and engage stakeholders from various departments and levels within the organisation. Encourage open communication, active participation, and shared decision-making to ensure all perspectives are considered.

Outcome: Improved coordination and alignment among stakeholders, leading to more effective transformation efforts.

Things to Watch Out for: Resistance from stakeholders, conflicting priorities, and challenges in maintaining sustained engagement.

Action 2: Develop a Comprehensive Transformation Strategy

Create a comprehensive transformation strategy that outlines clear goals, objectives, and a roadmap for implementation. Ensure the strategy aligns with the organisation's mission and vision, and involves input from key stakeholders. Regularly review and update the strategy to adapt to changing needs.

Outcome: Clear goals, objectives, and a roadmap for transformation, ensuring a systematic approach.

Things to Watch Out for: Lack of strategic alignment, inadequate resource allocation, and difficulties in adapting to evolving needs.

Action 3: Invest in Change Management and Leadership Development

Recognise the importance of change management and invest in developing leaders who can effectively navigate and lead transformation efforts. Provide training and resources to enhance change management skills, foster a culture of innovation, and empower leaders to drive change.

Outcome: Enhanced change readiness, effective leadership, and a culture that embraces transformation.

Things to Watch Out for: Resistance to change, leadership gaps, and insufficient investment in change management resources.

Action 4: Leverage Technology and Data Analytics

Embrace technology solutions and leverage data analytics to drive decision-making and improve operational efficiency. Implement electronic health record systems, telemedicine platforms, and other digital tools to enhance patient care. Utilise data analytics to identify trends, measure performance, and drive quality improvement initiatives.

Outcome: Improved decision-making, operational efficiency, and patient outcomes using technology and data-driven insights.

Things to Watch Out for: Data privacy and security concerns, interoperability challenges, and resistance to technology adoption.

Action 5: Promote Continuous Learning and Knowledge Sharing

Foster a culture of continuous learning and knowledge sharing within the organisation. Encourage employees to share best practices, innovative ideas, and lessons learned from successful transformation initiatives. Establish knowledge sharing platforms, conduct regular learning sessions, and recognise and reward innovation.

Outcome: Cultivate a learning culture, foster innovation, and share best practices across the organisation.

Things to Watch Out for: Lack of knowledge sharing platforms, resistance to change, and difficulties in capturing and disseminating lessons learned.

2.2

Inherent Resistance to Change

One of the primary challenges in health and care transformation is the inherent resistance to change, an issue deeply embedded in the culture and operations of health & care institutions, their employees and the people they serve. Typically, and often understandably, only a minority of health and care workers are inclined to embrace changes, with many meeting changes with distrust, doubt, and even outright rejection.

This resistance is often rooted in a deep-seated preference for the status quo, where workers are more comfortable with known practices and are apprehensive about exchanging them for unfamiliar, unproven alternatives. Resistance to change in health and care is influenced by a range of factors, both psychological and structural.

- **Psychologically,** resistance is often a reaction to perceived threats. These threats need not be real or significant; the mere perception of a threat can trigger resistance. This resistance can manifest in various forms, from the effective and pervasive passive inaction to the more rare overt refusal or even aggressive opposition. As one of the authors can attest to when seeking to change a 24hr emergency department to a 12hr minor injuries unit, opposition can quickly turn heated.

- **Structurally,** it is said that systems are perfectly designed to get the results that they get. In the case of health and care, the equivalent is that they are designed to achieve no change from the results currently being delivered. High levels of legislation and regulation, which are essential for maintaining standards and patient safety, also make rapid adaptation and change challenging. These regulations often take years to modify, creating a lag between emerging health and care innovations, needs and system response. Additionally, the layered bureaucracy in large health and care organisations can slow decision-making and impede the implementation of innovative ideas.

The intricate interplay of various stakeholders - from hospital administrators to commissioners or insurance companies - further slows the path to change. Each group, with its vested interests and perspectives, can inadvertently reinforce the status quo, making systemic transformation an arduous task.

Moreover, the necessary focus on service-user safety in health and care, often acts as a double-edged sword in the context of change. The liability borne by health and care professionals, institutions and their leaders for safety can create a risk-averse culture. This cautious approach, while safeguarding patient well-being, can also deter the adoption of innovative practices and improvements. Employees, wary of the consequences of errors, may prefer to adhere to established, familiar methods rather than venturing into new, albeit potentially more efficient, practices.

Additionally, psychology and structure can combine. Organisations, including medical institutions, must continually adapt to external changes. However, if the period of change is prolonged, employees may experience 'change fatigue,' leading to psychological uncertainty, emotional exhaustion, and an increased resistance to further change. This phenomenon can significantly impede the process of transformation within health and care systems. It is important to recognise, however, that psychological and structural resistance to change is not solely negative. It can serve functional purposes, such as maintaining system stability and preventing hasty or ill-conceived changes. Critical views on proposed changes can initiate constructive debates, leading to improved outcomes. Effectively managed resistance can be a catalyst for positive transformation, forcing a re-evaluation of the objectives and methods of change.

To demonstrate this, a survey conducted by the American Medical Association found that physician resistance to change is a significant barrier to the adoption of new health and care technologies. The survey revealed that 45% of physicians cited resistance to change as a major obstacle to implementing EHR systems. The implementation of telemedicine services provides a relevant case study for understanding resistance to change. Despite the potential benefits of telemedicine in improving access to care and reducing health and care costs, its adoption has been slow. A study published in the Journal of Medical Internet Research found that both patients and health and care providers expressed concerns about the quality of care, privacy, and the lack of in-person interaction. These concerns highlight the resistance to change and the need for effective change management strategies in health and care transformation initiatives.

Again, we have some solutions to consider.

Action 1: Create a Compelling Vision and Communicate the Need for Change

Develop a clear and compelling vision for the transformation and communicate it effectively to all stakeholders. Clearly articulate the reasons for change, emphasising the benefits and positive impact on patient care and outcomes. Engage in open and transparent communication to address concerns and build support for the transformation.

Outcome: Increased understanding and buy-in from stakeholders, leading to a more receptive environment for change.

Things to Watch Out for: Lack of clarity in the vision, ineffective communication, and resistance due to fear of the unknown.

Action 2: Involve and Empower Frontline Staff in the Change Process

Engage frontline staff in the planning and implementation of change initiatives. Seek their input, involve them in decision-making, and empower them to take ownership of the transformation. Provide training and support to enhance their skills and confidence in adopting new practices.

Outcome: Increased staff engagement and commitment to the change.

Things to Watch Out for: Lack of staff involvement, resistance from staff due to perceived lack of support, and challenges in balancing operational demands with change efforts.

Action 3: Address Concerns and Provide Support for Health and care Professionals

Proactively address concerns and resistance from health and care professionals by providing support and resources. Offer training programs, workshops, and coaching to help them adapt to innovative technologies, workflows, and care models. Create forums for open dialogue and feedback to address individual and collective concerns.

Outcome: Reduced resistance and increased acceptance of change among health and care professionals.

Things to Watch Out for: Lack of support and resources, inadequate training, and challenges in managing individual resistance.

Action 4: Communicate the Benefits and Impact on Patient Care

Clearly communicate how the proposed changes will improve patient care, outcomes, and experiences. Share success stories and case studies that demonstrate the positive impact of similar transformations. Engage patients and their families in the change process, seeking their input.

Outcome: Increased understanding of the benefits of change and improved patient satisfaction.

Things to Watch Out for: Lack of patient engagement, resistance from patients, and challenges in measuring the impact on patient outcomes.

Action 5: Celebrate Successes and Recognise Change Champions

Celebrate milestones and successes throughout the transformation journey. Recognise and appreciate individuals and teams who embrace change and contribute to its success. Share success stories and lessons learned to inspire others and create a positive culture that values innovation and improvement.

Outcome: Increased motivation and engagement, and an improved culture.

Things to Watch Out for: Lack of recognition and celebration, failure to acknowledge the efforts of change champions, and challenges in sustaining motivation over time.

2.3 Fragmented Nature of Health & Care Systems

As well as being wickedly complex, health and care systems are often plagued by fragmentation, characterised by multiple stakeholders operating independently, leading to significant challenges in successful transformation.

This fragmentation hinders the coordination and integration necessary for effective health and care delivery. Fragmented care occurs when health and care is spread across an excessively large number of poorly coordinated providers, pervasive in systems like the US and UK health and care systems. The implications of this fragmentation are particularly evident in the difficulties primary care providers face in coordinating care among specialists, leading to redundant and unnecessary care.

The causes of fragmentation can be attributed to evolving organisational structures, diverse payment models, and the absence of standardised practices. Fragmentation leads to inefficiencies, redundant care, and compromised patient outcomes. Factors, such as different service levels, varying legislation between services, and diverse digital systems, exacerbate these challenges, making it difficult for providers to share information effectively and coordinate patient care. A lack of cohesive collaboration between various health and care actors and services, such as general practitioners, emergency services, and mental health services, also contributes to the fragmented nature of health and care, posing significant barriers to the delivery of person-centred care.

In health and care systems, there's a persistent tension between centralisation and localisation in decision-making and control. Centralisation aims for uniformity in standards and efficiencies at scale, potentially simplifying nationwide health strategies and policies. However, it often overlooks local nuances and specific needs, leading to a one-size-fits-all approach that may not be effective in every context. Conversely, localisation empowers individual entities to tailor health and care delivery to specific community needs, fostering innovation and responsiveness. Yet, this can lead to inconsistent care standards and fragmented systems, as localised entities may lack the resources or overarching coordination to effectively manage complex health and care challenges. Balancing these two approaches is key to addressing the inherent fragmentation in health and care systems, ensuring both standardised quality of care and adaptability to local needs.

The challenge lies not in the rightness or wrongness of either centralisation or localisation, but rather in the continual oscillation between these two models. This constant shifting back and forth creates a cycle of disruption and readjustment that hinders sustained progress and long-term planning in health and care systems. As priorities and strategies continually change, it becomes difficult for health and care providers to adapt and for systems to evolve cohesively, ultimately impeding effective health and care transformation.

Fragmentation can be observed in the lack of interoperability between electronic health record systems, siloed health and care delivery models, and misaligned incentives among different health and care providers. These barriers hinder the seamless exchange of information and collaboration required for comprehensive transformation. The integration of care across different health and care settings provides a relevant case study for understanding the fragmented nature of health and care systems. Accountable Care Organisations (ACOs) aim to improve care coordination and reduce costs by integrating care delivery across hospitals, primary care providers, and specialists. However, the success of ACOs has been limited due to challenges in aligning incentives, sharing data, and coordinating care effectively.

Options to address these, include:

Action 1: Establish Collaborative Partnerships and Networks

Foster collaborative partnerships with other health and care organisations, community providers, and stakeholders. Develop networks that facilitate information sharing, care coordination, and seamless transitions across different health and care settings. Establish formal agreements and protocols to ensure effective collaboration.

Outcome: Improved coordination and integration of care, leading to better patient outcomes and experiences.

Things to Watch Out for: Resistance to collaboration, challenges in aligning incentives, and difficulties in maintaining effective communication.

Action 2: Invest in Interoperable Health Information Systems

Implement interoperable health information systems that enable the seamless exchange of patient information across different health and care providers and settings. Ensure compatibility and standardisation of data formats, protocols, and interfaces. Promote the use of health information exchanges and electronic health record systems that support interoperability.

Outcome: Enhanced information sharing, care coordination, and continuity of care.

Things to Watch Out for: Technical challenges in achieving interoperability, data privacy and security concerns, and resistance to adopting new systems.

Action 3: Implement Care Pathways and Care Teams

Develop care pathways and multidisciplinary care teams that span across different health and care settings. Define standardised care protocols, roles, and responsibilities to ensure coordinated and patient-centred care delivery. Foster effective communication and collaboration among care team members.

Outcome: Improved care coordination, reduced fragmentation, and enhanced patient outcomes.

Things to Watch Out for: Resistance to standardised care pathways, challenges in aligning care team members' schedules, and difficulties in maintaining effective communication.

Action 4: Align Incentives and Payment Models

Align financial incentives and payment models to promote collaboration and integration among health and care providers. Explore value-based payment models, accountable care organisations, and bundled payment arrangements that incentivise coordinated and high-quality care. Foster shared savings and risk-sharing arrangements to encourage collaboration.

Outcome: Increased collaboration, improved quality of care, and cost savings.

Things to Watch Out for: Misaligned incentives, challenges in measuring and attributing outcomes, and resistance to changes in payment models.

Action 5: Advocate for Policy and Regulatory Changes

Advocate for policy and regulatory changes that support the integration and coordination of health and care services. Engage with policymakers, regulatory bodies, and industry stakeholders to address barriers to collaboration and promote system-level reforms. Participate in policy discussions and contribute to the development of guidelines and standards.

Outcome: Improved policy environment, reduced regulatory barriers, and enhanced support for integrated care.

Things to Watch Out for: Slow pace of policy change, competing interests among stakeholders, and challenges in influencing policy decisions.

2.4

Financial and Resource Constraints

Setting aside complexity, resistance to change and fragmentation, in order to transform system, and even to reduce costs, investment and strategic resource allocation is needed.

Yet, health and care organisations often face budgetary pressures that limit their ability to support large-scale transformation efforts. As we discussed earlier, the idea that you need to spend in order to save is not a welcome concept in most health and care organisations where there is a need to justify all spending in the equivalent number of nurses that could have been paid with it instead.

The challenge lies not only in securing sufficient funds but also in effectively prioritising and managing these investments. Factors contribute to this financial constraint. Economic fluctuations, changing health and care policies, and competing priorities within the health and care sector often divert funds away from transformation initiatives. Furthermore, the cost-effectiveness of innovative technologies or practices is a crucial consideration, as health and care managers must weigh the potential benefits against the financial implications. Sometimes the evidence to support this just isn't available and there remains resistance from organisations and suppliers to explore outcome based payment models.

In addition to financial constraints, a shortage of qualified human resources (or "people" as we sometimes call them) at the local level significantly impacts the ability to undertake health and care transformations. Regions, especially those in developing areas, often face challenges due to a limited pool of trained health and care professionals. This shortage is exacerbated by the migration of skilled workers to more affluent areas and the global mismatch between the supply of, and demand for, health and care professionals. In some cases new models of care, even if leading to cost reduction, require roles and skills that do not currently exist in the right numbers. The time to train qualified health and care professionals in new and innovative roles can take many years and requires significant national level investment and co-ordination.

For health and care managers, this means grappling with not only the implementation of new systems or practices but also ensuring that there are enough trained personnel to manage and sustain these changes effectively even when the money is available to pay them.

The implementation of electronic prescribing systems provides a relevant case study for understanding financial constraints in health and care transformation. Electronic prescribing systems have the potential to improve medication safety and reduce costs. However, the upfront costs of implementing these systems, including software, hardware, and training, can be substantial. Health and care organisations face financial constraints that limit their ability to invest in such initiatives, resulting in incomplete implementation or delayed adoption.

You might address these through:

Action 1: Conduct a Comprehensive Financial Assessment

Conduct a thorough assessment of the organisation's financial landscape, including revenue streams, expenses, and budgetary constraints. Identify areas of inefficiency and opportunities for cost savings. Analyse financial data to prioritise transformation initiatives and allocate resources effectively.

Outcome: Improved financial sustainability, optimised resource allocation, and cost-effective transformation efforts.

Things to Watch Out for: Incomplete financial assessment, challenges in obtaining accurate financial data, and resistance to reallocating resources.

Action 2: Seek External Funding and Partnerships

Explore opportunities for external funding and partnerships to support transformation initiatives. Identify grants, government programs, and philanthropic organisations that align with the organisations goals. Collaborate with other health and care organisations, research institutions, and industry partners to leverage resources and share costs.

Outcome: Increased financial resources, expanded capabilities, and enhanced collaboration.

Things to Watch Out for: Limited availability of external funding, challenges in establishing partnerships, and potential conflicts of interest.

Action 3: Prioritise Transformation Initiatives

Prioritise transformation initiatives based on their potential impact, feasibility, and alignment with organisational goals. Conduct a cost-benefit analysis to assess the financial implications of each initiative. Consider short-term and long-term returns on investment, as well as the potential for cost savings and revenue generation.

Outcome: Focused resource allocation, targeted transformation efforts, and measurable outcomes.

Things to Watch Out for: Lack of alignment between prioritised initiatives and organisational goals, challenges in estimating costs and benefits, and potential resistance to deprioritised initiatives.

Action 4: Optimise Operational Efficiency

Identify opportunities to improve operational efficiency and reduce waste within the organisation. Streamline workflows, eliminate unnecessary processes, and automate manual tasks where possible. Implement lean management principles and continuous improvement methodologies to drive efficiency gains.

Outcome: Increased operational efficiency, reduced costs, and improved resource utilisation.

Things to Watch Out for: Resistance to change, challenges in identifying inefficiencies, and potential disruptions to established workflows.

Action 5: Develop a Business Case for Transformation

Develop a compelling business case for transformation initiatives, highlighting the potential return on investment, cost savings, and improved patient outcomes. Quantify the budgetary impact of the proposed changes and align them with the organisation's strategic objectives. Present the business case to key stakeholders, including executive leadership, board members, and financial decision-makers.

Outcome: Increased support and buy-in for transformation initiatives, secured funding, and sustained commitment.

Things to Watch Out for: Insufficient data to support the business case, challenges in quantifying budgetary impact, and potential skepticism from stakeholders.

2.5

Unforeseen Consequences and Unintended Outcomes

Health and care transformation initiatives, while aiming to improve systems and outcomes, can often result in unintended consequences. These consequences can range from positive additional benefits to negative impacts that inadvertently harm those involved, either directly or indirectly. In some cases, unintended effects can be predicted, but often they arise from complex interactions within the dynamic health and care environment, making them unforeseeable

Reducing costs in one area can lead to increases in another, within the same organisation or in another one, sometimes this might go undetected or the impact may not be fully felt for many years.

As we said previously, health and care system complexity is a barrier to change. It also contributes to producing side-effects when change does occur. Interventions developed for specific contexts fail to translate into meaningful whole health system improvements when applied elsewhere. This issue partly arises because these interventions are context-specific and cannot be generalised across different settings. This complexity is further compounded by the integration of sophisticated technologies like genomics, precision medicine, Artificial Intelligence (AI), and advanced pharmaceuticals, which, while beneficial, add layers of complexity and necessitate improved coordination. The failure to anticipate and account for this complexity can result in interventions that do not achieve the desired transformative impact.

Failure to put in place and effectively track Key Performance Indicators (KPIs) can lead to unintended outcomes going unnoticed, as can poorly designed transformations that lack a comprehensive understanding of underlying issues.

Additionally, a scarcity of data on what drives success and failure in health and care transformations hinders the ability to replicate successful initiatives or avoid past mistakes. Rapid implementation of changes, without adequate planning and assessment, can also exacerbate existing issues rather than resolving them.

Addressing these challenges requires an integrated approach that considers the complex, adaptive nature of health systems. An effective methodology for large-scale health system transformation must harness systems thinking to understand and anticipate emergent behaviours within these systems. It should also contextualise interventions to account for the unique characteristics of each health system, including the hierarchy of systemic and organisational structures. The challenges in a competitive system with no national health strategy will be very different to one with a hierarchical and government-funded monopoly system.

It is not just technology transformation that go wrong in health. The implementation of pay-for-performance programs provides a relevant case study for understanding unintended consequences in health and care transformation. Pay-for-performance programs aim to incentivise quality improvement by linking reimbursement to performance metrics. However, studies have shown that these programs can lead to unintended consequences, such as cherry-picking patients, focusing on specific metrics at the expense of overall quality, and creating additional administrative burdens for health and care providers.

Some more solutions...

Action 1: Conduct a Comprehensive Risk Assessment

Conduct a thorough risk assessment to identify potential unintended consequences and mitigate associated risks. Analyse the potential impact of transformation initiatives on various stakeholders, processes, and outcomes. Develop risk mitigation strategies and contingency plans to address unforeseen challenges.

Outcome: Proactive identification and management of risks minimised negative consequences, and enhanced adaptability.

Things to Watch Out for: Incomplete risk assessment, challenges in predicting all potential consequences, and resistance to acknowledging risks.

Action 2: Engage Stakeholders in the Change Process

Engage stakeholders, including health and care professionals, service-users, and community members, in the change process. Seek their input, perspectives, and feedback to identify potential unintended consequences. Foster a culture of open communication and continuous learning to address concerns and adapt to emerging challenges.

Outcome: Increased awareness of potential consequences, improved stakeholder engagement, and collaborative problem-solving.

Things to Watch Out for: Limited stakeholder involvement, challenges in managing diverse perspectives, and potential resistance to change.

Action 3: Monitor and Evaluate Transformation Initiatives

Implement robust monitoring and evaluation mechanisms to track the progress and impact of transformation initiatives. Continuously assess outcomes, processes, and unintended consequences. Collect and analyse data to identify trends, patterns, and areas for improvement. Use feedback loops to inform decision-making and make necessary adjustments.

Outcome: Timely identification of unintended consequences, evidence-based decision-making, and continuous improvement.

Things to Watch Out for: Insufficient data collection and analysis, challenges in measuring intangible outcomes, and resistance to evaluation efforts.

Action 4: Foster a Culture of Learning and Adaptation

Foster a culture of learning, adaptability, and innovation within the organisation. Encourage staff to share lessons learned, best practices, and insights from transformation initiatives. Establish mechanisms for knowledge sharing, such as regular meetings, forums, and communities of practice.

Outcome: Enhanced organisational learning, increased agility, and improved ability to address unintended consequences.

Things to Watch Out for: Lack of knowledge sharing platforms, resistance to change, and difficulties in capturing and disseminating lessons learned.

Action 5: Communicate and Engage with External Stakeholders

Communicate openly and transparently with external stakeholders, including regulatory bodies, policymakers, and the public. Share information about transformation initiatives, potential consequences, and mitigation strategies. Seek feedback and input from external stakeholders to ensure a comprehensive understanding of potential unintended outcomes.

Outcome: Increased trust, collaboration, and alignment with external stakeholders, leading to better decision-making and reduced unintended consequences.

Things to Watch Out for: Challenges in managing external expectations, potential conflicts of interest, and resistance to transparency.

2.6

The Evolving Nature of Health & Care

In the whirlwind of modern medicine, health and care stands at the forefront of evolution, driven by relentless advancements and societal shifts. This dynamic field continuously reshapes itself, responding to the expanding horizons of medical knowledge, technological innovation, and evolving societal expectations. The need to integrate new medical discoveries and technologies often necessitates significant restructuring of established practices and policies. This restructuring is not just a matter of technological upgrades; it can demand a comprehensive paradigm shift in patient care and operational methodologies.

A key challenge in this evolution is the strain it places on health and care organisations. They must merge these cutting-edge advancements with the imperative of maintaining exceptional patient care and operational efficiency. This dual objective becomes even more complex in the context of large-scale cost reduction programs. These programs aim to streamline operations and reduce expenditures, but the rapid pace of change in health and care can render cost-saving strategies outdated almost as soon as they are implemented. For instance, investing in a particular technology might seem cost-effective today, but rapid advancements could soon make that technology obsolete, leading to further investment and adjustment costs.

The evolving societal expectations and regulatory landscapes add layers of complexity. Informed and empowered by digital advancements, today's patients demand higher quality care, personalised treatments, and increased accessibility to services. Simultaneously, regulatory changes, aiming to enhance patient safety and quality of care, often mandate new compliance measures. Implementing these measures can be both resource-intensive and time-consuming, challenging health and care organisations to balance external pressures with internal capabilities, especially when operating under the constraints of cost reduction programs.

The pace at which these changes occur can sometimes outstrip the ability of health and care organisations to adapt effectively. Initiatives designed with current knowledge and technology in mind may quickly become outdated or misaligned with emerging practices and standards. This lag in adaptation can lead to initiatives that fail to meet their objectives or miss new opportunities for improvement, thus complicating large-scale cost reduction efforts. A World Health Organisation report highlights this rapid pace of change in health and care and the ensuing challenges for health and care systems worldwide, emphasising the need for adaptive and flexible approaches in health and care transformation.

The adoption of precision medicine provides a relevant case study for understanding the evolving nature of health and care. Precision medicine aims to tailor medical treatments to individual patients based on their genetic makeup, lifestyle, and environmental factors. However, the implementation of precision medicine faces challenges in terms of data integration, privacy concerns, and the need for new clinical decision support systems. These challenges highlight the need for health and care transformation initiatives to adapt to the evolving landscape of health and care.
.

While health and care transformation is a critical goal for improving patient outcomes and health and care delivery, the hypothesis that no large-scale attempt ever fully succeeds holds merit. The complexities inherent in health and care systems, resistance to change, fragmentation, financial constraints, unforeseen consequences, and the evolving nature of health and care contribute to the perceived incomplete success.

However, it is important to note that despite these challenges, considerable progress has been made in health and care transformation. By acknowledging the barriers and learning from past experiences, health and care leaders can continue to strive for meaningful and sustainable improvements in health and care delivery.

Action 1: Foster a Culture of Continuous Learning and Adaptation

Foster a culture of continuous learning and adaptation within the organisation. Encourage staff to stay updated on the latest advancements in medical knowledge, technology, and health and care practices. Provide opportunities for professional development, training, and participation in conferences and workshops.

Outcome: Enhanced knowledge and skills, increased adaptability, and improved ability to keep pace with health and care advancements.

Things to Watch Out for: Resistance to change, challenges in allocating time and resources for learning, and potential information overload.

Action 2: Embrace Innovation and Technology

Embrace innovation and leverage technology to stay ahead of evolving health and care trends. Explore emerging technologies, such as telemedicine, artificial intelligence, and digital health solutions, that have the potential to improve patient care and operational efficiency. Foster a culture that encourages experimentation and the adoption of innovative practices.

Outcome: Improved patient outcomes, enhanced operational efficiency, and increased competitiveness in the evolving health and care landscape.

Things to Watch Out for: Resistance to technology adoption, challenges in integrating innovative technologies with existing systems, and potential privacy and security concerns.

Action 3: Engage in Strategic Planning and Scenario Analysis

Engage in strategic planning exercises that consider different future scenarios and their potential impact on the organisation. Conduct scenario analysis to identify potential challenges and opportunities arising from evolving health and care trends. Develop contingency plans and strategies to adapt to different scenarios.

Outcome: Enhanced strategic foresight, improved preparedness for future changes, and proactive response to evolving health and care needs.

Things to Watch Out for: Over-reliance on a single scenario, challenges in predicting future trends accurately, and potential resistance to change.

Action 4: Foster Collaboration and Partnerships

Foster collaboration and partnerships with other health and care organisations, research institutions, and industry stakeholders. Engage in knowledge sharing, joint research projects, and collaborative initiatives to leverage expertise and resources. Collaborate with external partners to stay informed about emerging trends and best practices.

Outcome: Access to diverse perspectives and expertise, increased innovation, and improved ability to navigate the evolving health and care landscape.

Things to Watch Out for: Challenges in establishing and maintaining partnerships, potential conflicts of interest, and difficulties in aligning goals and priorities.

Action 5: Engage in Advocacy and Policy Development

Engage in advocacy efforts and contribute to policy development to shape the evolving health and care landscape. Participate in industry associations, professional organisations, and policy forums to influence health and care policies and regulations. Advocate for policies that support innovation, patient-centred care, and the integration of innovative technologies.

Outcome: Influence over health and care policies, improved alignment with regulatory requirements, and enhanced ability to adapt to changing health and care regulations.

Things to Watch Out for: Challenges in navigating complex policy environments, potential conflicts of interest, and resistance to policy changes.

2.7 Conclusion

While the challenge of transforming health and care is formidable, it is not insurmountable.

By understanding and addressing the complexities, resistance to change, fragmentation, financial constraints, unforeseen consequences, and the evolving nature of health and care, we can chart a path to success. Collaboration, stakeholder engagement, change management, and leadership development are crucial in navigating the complexities of health and care transformation. Interoperability, care coordination, and alignment of incentives can help overcome the fragmented nature of health and care systems.

Comprehensive financial assessments, external funding, and resource optimisation are essential in addressing financial constraints. Risk assessment, stakeholder engagement, and continuous monitoring and evaluation can mitigate unforeseen consequences. Finally, fostering a culture of continuous learning, embracing innovation and technology, and engaging in strategic planning and advocacy can help navigate the evolving nature of health and care.

By implementing these strategies and embracing the lessons learned, we can pave the way for a more successful future in transforming the cost and efficiency of health and care. It is through collaboration, innovation, and a relentless pursuit of excellence that we can achieve remarkable progress in improving patient outcomes, health and care delivery, and cost reduction.

However, large-scale health transformations are about making ongoing improvements, not reaching a final goal. Success in this field means constantly adapting to new health and care needs, technologies, and what people expect from health and care services. It involves finding ways to get better health results for patients, make their experience smoother, and run health and care services more efficiently. The idea that these transformations are never fully achieved comes from the fact that health challenges and opportunities keep changing. For example, as people get older, diseases change, and new medical technologies are developed, the goals and methods in health and care also need to evolve. This means health systems must always be ready to change and improve, keeping up with both current and future needs.

Ref	Action	Check
1.	**Complexity of Health & Care Transformation**	
1.1	Foster collaboration and engage stakeholders.	
1.2	Create a clear transformation strategy with goals and a roadmap.	
1.3	Invest in change management and leadership development.	
1.4	Embrace technology and data analytics for decision-making.	
1.5	Promote a culture of continuous learning and knowledge sharing.	
2.	**Inherent Resistance to Change**	
2.1	Communicate a clear vision for change.	
2.2	Involve and empower frontline staff in the change process.	
2.3	Address concerns and provide support to health and care professionals.	
2.4	Communicate the benefits of change for patient care.	
2.5	Celebrate successes and recognize change champions.	
3.	**Fragmented Nature of Systems**	
3.1	Establish collaborative partnerships and networks.	
3.2	Invest in interoperable health information systems.	
3.3	Implement care pathways and multidisciplinary care teams.	
3.4	Align incentives and payment models.	

| 3.5 | Advocate for policy and regulatory changes. | |

4. Financial and Resource Constraints

4.1	Conduct a comprehensive financial assessment.	
4.2	Seek external funding and partnerships.	
4.3	Prioritize transformation initiatives based on impact and feasibility.	
4.4	Optimize operational efficiency.	
4.5	Develop a business case for transformation initiatives.	

5. Unforeseen Consequences and Unintended Outcomes

5.1	Conduct a comprehensive risk assessment.	
5.2	Engage stakeholders in the change process.	
5.3	Monitor and evaluate transformation initiatives.	
5.4	Foster a culture of learning and adaptation.	
5.5	Communicate with external stakeholders.	

6. Evolving Nature of Health & Care

6.1	Foster continuous learning and adaptation.	
6.2	Embrace innovation and technology.	
6.3	Engage in strategic planning and scenario analysis.	
6.4	Foster collaboration and partnerships.	
6.5	Engage in advocacy and policy development.	

CHAPTER THREE

APPROACHES TO MANAGING COST

Before you do anything, there's a whole style thing to think about.

There are lots of ways to go about managing cost – we'll set out eight in this section:

- Turnaround.

- Value Based Health & Care .

- The Organisational Wide Project.

- Organisational Focus On Quality.

- A Focus On What Is Important.

- Service Line Management.

- Transformation.

- The "Model Hospital".

Some of these include approaches, others are more of a mindset, but they all include some useful things to think about, and help you to set the tone for your particular cost control approach.

And then in the next section, we will consider the "nuts and bolts" of an approach that you can use, consider, or adapt to help you solve your particular issue.

3.1

Turnaround

"(Turn around), Every now and then I get a little bit angry and I know I've got to get out and cry. (Turn around) Every now and then I get a little bit terrified, but then I see the look in your eyes..."

Jim Steinman (performed by Bonnie Tyler) – Total Eclipse of the Heart

I bet you didn't realise that Bonnie Tyler was such a big fan of cost reduction? I bet half of you don't even remember the song, which isn't going to help the undeniable comedy of the moment. Why did the Welsh songstress espouse this particular approach to bringing costs under control?

Well, it has been quite a popular approach. We've used it ourselves many times - both in health & social care and outside it - although we would argue that, except in certain very specific circumstances, it isn't one that should be used in health & social care.

So, what it is? Turnaround is an approach used when an organisation is about to fail. Typically, experts are brought in to help the company stop going in the destructive direction it is going, and to "turnaround" its fortunes.

In the English NHS in the early 2000's, following significant growth in funding over the previous 10 years, the national leadership viewed any 'failing' NHS trusts as entirely to blame for their own problems. Any level of understanding of how NHS services operated was seen as a disadvantage, and teams of so-called private sector insolvency experts were drafted in to 'fix' these organisations with all their wisdom and expertise gained from stripping-out factories and turning around retailers.

In one instance, at a previously successful Foundation Trust in a poor region of the North East of England, Craig found himself sitting on a swivel chair in the middle of a room of junior insolvency practitioners who had last seen the inside of a hospital when they left the warmth of their mother's womb. He became dizzy after a week of spinning around answering the well-meaning questions: 'what is an outpatient?'; 'why can't I close the A&E?'; 'operating theatres are expensive; how many can we get rid of?'; 'how much more can we charge for these treatments that are losing money?'. It was an extreme example, but its safe to say its better to not assume that anything is obvious - as Frank Lloyd Wright said, 'there is nothing so uncommon as common sense'.

When Colin was doing turnaround, he was working for a management consultancy and was brought in, as part of a team, to bring some focus to the cost control of the organisation - in his case, he used to develop workforce planning models for retail branch operations, so you could see where stores were overstaffed for the demand, and to redesign processes to reduce the number of staff needed. Other experts were brought in to control the spend on equipment, reduce the price of products, consider whether such a big back office staff was needed etc. He did also ask what "GP" stood for in one meeting, proving that he's not half as clever as he things he is...

The trouble is that, at its heart, you can see what the plan is here – reduce staff, reduce spend, reduce costs. Control, control, control. Cut, cut, cut.

You see, the reality of cost reduction is that there are really only two ways to save money: Pay staff less and pay suppliers less. That's it.

The other ways to improve the fortunes of a business are to make more money, to control unnecessary costs and to generally become more efficient – and they are generally a much better way to do things.

There is nothing in this approach that we won't consider in our book, because lots of the elements make sense.

These include:

- Capacity and demand modelling.

- Process improvement to improve efficiency.

- Budget controls.

- Procurement contract reviews.

- Programme Management and Programme Management Offices

- Executive responsibility and monitoring.

- Operational grip.

But it is the ethos that we don't recommend using. Turnaround tends to include:

- Top-down control, rather than looking to create an organisation that cares about finance alongside its staff, service-users and quality.

- Cutting costs in the short term, rather than investing for efficiency.

- Spend controls – like "vacancy review panels" that can drive inefficiency.

- A view that the organisation has somehow "failed".

All of this just isn't very inspiring…

As an approach it has merits. In a private sector organisation, that has lost control and is heading for oblivion because it is running out of money, it is probably the best place to start. The organisation faces an existential threat – and that threat is generally caused by the money running out – cash gets too low, payments need to be made which can't be made, and the company heads into administration. There are elements of it that are really useful in this situation. Tightly manage costs, improve the efficiency of processes, consider the staff that you need, and remove the rest. To be honest, this should have been happening anyway – but for whatever reason, it wasn't happening, and now this approach is needed.

The problem we have with it, is its use in health and social care. And we've used it a lot in health and care – Colin was involved in the almost national-scale turnaround in the early 2000's in England, where the NHS was going to be £1.5 billion in debt and a national Programme Management Office (PMO) was put in place to "encourage" hospital and primary care trusts to reduce their deficits. A little later, councils went through the same thing – although much harder and much faster.

The issue that we have with it in health & social care – in PUBLIC health and social care – is that the organisation is generally not "failing" because it has lost control of its finances. It is overspending on budgets because those budgets do not reflect what is needed to deliver the expected care. AND it's probably lost control of its finances…

There are two sub-approaches to turnaround that are worth considering;

- **The External Project** – As described, getting a team of turnaround experts (and preferably health and care specialists) in to undertake a turnaround is one approach that was used a lot at some point, and we are sure will come again..

- **"Turnaround Tim"** – The board hires a director to deliver the agenda, who marshals internal and external resources and activity to "turn the organisation around".

We wouldn't use turnaround as the approach in any but the most existential of crises. Cutting may work in the short term, but it isn't the way to run organisations in the long term and will likely create issues for the future. But there are many elements from it that should be included – just included in a much more positive way, and in a way that reflects the root cause of the issue.

And to be fair to many Turnaround Directors, management consultancies, and ourselves – most of the time we weren't really just doing cost cutting in these public bodies – we were helping put in place the elements of control and planning that the organisations needed.

Or at least trying to...

3.2

Value-Based Health and Care

Value-Based Health Care (VBHC) has emerged as a transformative approach in modern health and care, shifting the focus from volume to value. It emphasises patient outcomes relative to the costs of care delivery, addressing critical challenges such as escalating costs, variable quality, and access disparities in global health systems.

By focusing on outcomes that matter most to patients, VBHC aims to optimise resource utilisation, fostering more sustainable and effective health and care systems.

Implementing VBHC requires a strategic framework that aligns the incentives of various stakeholders, including providers, payers / commissioners, and service-users. This alignment involves cultivating a health and care ecosystem where outcomes and cost-efficiency are paramount, fostering a collaborative environment that rewards improvements in patient outcomes while promoting cost-effectiveness. Aligning these incentives is crucial to transition successfully from traditional fee-for-service models to value-based models.

In addition to strategic frameworks and stakeholder alignment, non-financial incentives play a critical role in the successful implementation of VBHC. These include provider satisfaction, service-user engagement, and a culture of continuous improvement and innovation. A shift towards patient-centric care, which lies at the heart of VBHC, requires a transformation in health and care culture and practices. This transformation involves embracing a holistic view of care, where the quality of life and service-user experience are as important as clinical outcomes.

Health & care providers are encouraged to adopt new approaches that prioritise service-user engagement and satisfaction. This shift often requires training and development programs to equip health & care professionals with the skills needed to navigate these changes effectively. Such programs focus on communication, empathy, and shared decision-making, fostering a more patient-centric approach to care.

A robust data infrastructure is vital for the effective implementation of VBHC. This infrastructure includes advanced data analytics, health IT systems, and digital tools that enable the tracking of outcomes and costs. Accurate and accessible data is crucial for making informed, evidence-based health and care decisions.

The adoption of health IT systems facilitates the collection and analysis of a wide range of data, from outcomes to satisfaction metrics. These systems can also support the implementation of personalised care plans and monitor their effectiveness over time.

Additionally, the integration of AI and machine learning technologies can provide deeper insights into patient data, enhancing the ability to predict outcomes and tailor interventions.

Examples include:

DigiPROM at Charité Berlin

The DigiPROM project at Berlin's Charité Hospital exemplifies the integration of digital patient-reported outcome measures in oncology. This initiative underscores the impact of VBHC in specialised medical fields, demonstrating improved patient engagement and treatment personalisation.

Ayushman Bharat Program, India

One of the world's largest public health insurance schemes, Ayushman Bharat, embodies VBHC principles. It demonstrates how cost containment can be balanced with improved access to quality care, particularly for marginalised populations.

Dutch Health and Care System

In the Netherlands, the national-level implementation of VBHC has led to more coordinated care, better patient outcomes, and cost reductions. This approach offers valuable lessons for other countries looking to adopt VBHC.

Medicare Program, USA

The U.S. Medicare program's adoption of VBHC principles, evident in initiatives like the Hospital Readmissions Reduction Program, shows the adaptability of VBHC in diverse health and care settings.

Swedish Rheumatology Quality Registry

Sweden's emphasis on patient registries in rheumatology highlights the importance of long-term patient outcome tracking, a key component of VBHC.

Singapore's Preventive Care Model

Singapore's health and care system, focusing on preventive care and chronic disease management, demonstrates the effectiveness of VBHC principles in primary care settings.

Collaborative efforts within and between countries are key to the success of VBHC. Sharing experiences and best practices across different health and care systems can expedite VBHC adoption and refinement. International forums and conferences provide platforms for health and care leaders to discuss challenges, share innovations, and form partnerships, fostering a global community dedicated to improving health and care value.

Challenges in VBHC implementation include aligning stakeholder interests, managing the transition to new care models, and ensuring equitable access to high-quality care. Technological advancements like AI and telemedicine are pivotal in overcoming these challenges, enhancing data collection and analysis for personalised care.

The future of VBHC involves more integrated care models, enhanced patient engagement strategies, and increased use of technology for personalised care. As health and care systems globally adapt to these changing paradigms, the delivery of high-value care becomes increasingly achievable.

VBHC represents a critical evolution in health and care, focusing on patient outcomes and cost-efficiency. For health managers globally, understanding and implementing VBHC principles is key to navigating the evolving health and care landscape. This shift promises not only improved patient outcomes but also a more efficient and equitable health and care system worldwide.

3.3 The Organisation Wide Project

In our humble opinion (and people that know us, know that we are very humble people. Deep down), and as old management consultants, we find that the organisational-wide project is the way to go when you've found yourself in a situation where cost reduction is necessary, and cost-control has gone somewhat out the window.

The organisational-wide project is, in fact, our favourite response to everything. As an ethos, it is about getting the whole organisation to get behind the drive to reducing cost and keeping it under control..

This is the project that was often delivered when doing "turnaround" projects in the public sector. It certainly wasn't turnaround and just cost cutting. It included elements such as:

- Putting in place a programme to understand what the problem is and how it will be addressed.

- Implementation of improved governance for the control of operational costs across the organisation, including new metrics and operating models.

- Engaging teams in the importance of cost control, and why it mattered to them.

- Improvement in cost control and efficiency skills - including budget management, and transformation.

- Building infrastructure for ongoing cost improvement - like transformation teams and ongoing training opportunities.

- The robust identification of opportunities to reduce costs across all aspects of the organisation's operations.

- Targeted action in individual teams and divisions.

At its heart, this is about improving the integration of finance and operations from top to bottom. More on this later on.

3.4 Organisational Focus on Quality

This is less of an approach, but more of a mindset when it comes to controlling cost.

The underlying theory is that quality health and care is efficient health and care. Don't focus on money, focus on:

- Delivering health and care that is genuinely needed.

- Doing it right first time.

- Focussing on getting people well at home.

With a real focus on what is needed for the service-user, the answer will, by its nature, result in efficient health and care.

This isn't a carte blanche to just spend as much money as you want on health and care. It is a mindful approach to delivering patient-focused, quality-care.

In terms of our efficiency triangle, this one is about focusing on the service-user (and often, on the staff) element of the triangle - but it isn't about ignoring the finance one. The aim is to align the finances to the aim of the organisation, not ignore the aims of the organisation to meet the needs of finance.

3.5 A Focus on What is Important

An approach to cost reduction, and one we have used in corporate functions, is sometimes also known as "Priority Based Budgeting".

Under this approach, the plan is to list out everything that needs to be done on one side, and put the amount of money that you are able to spend on the other side.

You then prioritise them using any criteria that you like to understand what is important. Once you've worked out what is most important you start at the top and work your way down, calculating what (and how much money) is needed to deliver them. Once you get to the point where you are just about to run out of money, you stop – and that's all you can deliver.

A similar approach is to do the same from the bottom up. Work out what is least important, and how much you can save if you stop doing it until you've saved enough to meet your budget.

It's far from our favourite approach, but if you are being asked to do more than you can deliver, then it is a logical way to show your stakeholders the impact of that imbalance in a more real way than just going over budget – it shows the human cost of not having enough funding.

3.6 Service-Line Management

Service Line Management (SLM) is an approach that was documented by Monitor, the forerunner to NHS Improvement, now part of NHS England in the English National Health Service. And it was brilliant. It was a business planning approach to management,.

The UK government website describes it thus:

> **"Service-line management is a combination of management and business planning techniques designed to improve the way health and care is delivered.**
>
> **It involves identifying the different business units, or 'service lines', of an NHS foundation trust and understanding how they contribute to the trust's performance as a whole, allowing clinicians and managers to deliver improvements in quality and productivity at the specialty level.**
>
> **Service-line management aims to ensure more effective use of resources to fund better patient care, benefiting both patients and taxpayers. In the longer term, it can contribute to improved quality and patient experience."**

As an approach, it has four main elements:

- **Organisation Structure:** Building individual service lines that operate as autonomous business units with clear decision making and accountability lines. Clinicians have prominent management roles alongside managers to balance the needs of service-users, staff and the organisation (specifically ensuring financial balance).

- **Strategic and annual planning process:** The integrated management teams work to develop plans for the next year and beyond, balancing activity, cost and quality. The annual planning process includes many of the key elements we talk about in the cost control ideas, including developing capacity and demand plans, workforce planning and undertaking reviews of future opportunities and risks.

- **Performance management:** Everyone sets targets and measures as part of the approach, and ensures that they meet them. Organisational management performance manages the units – leading to a culture that is a combination of operational grip and local accountability.

- **Information:** The approach is based on detailed financial and operational information, preferably at a patient level, allowing for real financial mindfulness in the operating units. The team are able to see how their expenditure compares to the income received and can flex how they spend the money accordingly.

The whole thing works to build a culture of cost control (control of everything, really) through a combination of operational grip and team accountability. It stopped being used in hospital trusts in the UK NHS, generally just as it was getting embedded.

The move away from Payment by Results (PbR) to block contracts has meant that there is less clarity around how much income is being generated, and increasing activity is outstripping the available money to match it.

But as an approach, it is really good and we'd recommend it to any health and care organisation as a way of controlling costs into the long term – as well as ensuring that everything is being well managed.

There is a whole host of information available through the link highlighted at the back of this book.

3.7 Transformation

Cost reduction can be tough. If you are working in an organisation looking to reduce costs then everyone sees you as the hatchet-person. You are taking things away from them. Denying them money. Get used to eating alone at lunchtime. It's hardly an inspiring way to get everyone working together to save money.

People want to know – What is in it for me? How can I cope with the change? What is the point? So we need something a bit more exciting, something with a vision. Something bold, something transformational.

The list of ideas that we discuss later in this book includes a whole host of transformational elements that you might want to consider. But a few examples that we have worked on include:

- **Mergers and acquisitions** - completely changing the structure of an organisation and merging teams, can be a destabilising event in its own right, and is a good chance to rethink everything that people do when trying to develop the "new normal".

- **New buildings** - between us we've worked on new hospitals, new community maternity facilities and entire new systems of buildings, and know that these are a great chance to transform the way that services are delivered.

- **Technology** - the introduction of new Electronic Health Records (EHR) or bringing in a Command Centre (as Johns Hopkins did) can completely change the status quo. Technology-led change means that everyone is getting something new and shiny to play with, and there is a real excuse to change.

- **Contract change or lead provider** - not quite as nice as getting a lovely new building, but changing the financial flows can change the status quo and lead to true transformation. If a new private provider was given control of health and care in a system, you can bet that a lot would change very quickly.

When Colin had been working in heath turnaround for a year, slowly building consensus for cost changes to make an organisation more efficient, a council told the health trust he was working for to reduce the cost of its sexual health services by 25% and to keep the same outcomes or it would re-tender the service and probably give it to someone else. Within three weeks the service had been transformed. It showed him that, when faced with an existential threat, people came up with a solution - they were no longer bound by the restrictions they placed on themselves as an organisation and instead they found a way.

But there are many ways that you can start transformation, and the section on transformational cost control ideas will give you some more to think about. The approach to actually transforming requires a well-resourced and properly run programme to succeed. Get the best programme management you can get, align your executive and stakeholders behind it, and get your best people working on it

3.8

The Model Organisation

And finally, a very logical and model-based approach to cost control. You can define your costs based entirely on a model for your organisation set from above.

This is sometimes done when health and care organisations are being set up for the first time and a sponsor is paying for the resources that it needs. How do you work out how many people you need?

The approach you can take is to set your resources based on good practice ratios or similar. By defining the resources needed for each activity, you can build a model that allows you to establish how many people, how many rooms, how much non-pay resource etc you will need in order to deliver the care and build your organisation from this bottom-up understanding.

When undertaking cost control work, you can take a similar approach. In this case you would:

- Build a model organisation (using standard ratios, the UK Model Hospital information, or a more relevant source for your organisation).

- Check that it is affordable (with some contingency for model errors). If it isn't, then you need a good chat with your stakeholders about it, because you can't deliver the service within the cost envelope. Possibly bring in Tom Cruise and the Mission Impossible team at that point.

- Compare it to your current costs to identify where there are differences.

- Examine the differences and then either adjust your model if needed or take out the unnecessary costs.

This is really about having a weapons-grade capacity and demand plan in your organisation – which even if you are going to use other approaches is a really good idea to build.

Such a model helps you break down your costs into individual elements that can be challenged, or will have to be accepted, by customers or commissioners.

We love them as a way of getting proper agreement between finance and operations teams.

CHAPTER FOUR

THE APPROACH

4.1 Overview

As we have seen, there is no one way to undertake cost management in your organisation. There is also so much variation in the way in which health & care organisations operate that providing too much detail for one type of organisation may be largely useless for other types. Cost ideas change regularly, and the reasons for undertaking cost management change just as quickly.

The authors have, however, learned plenty over the years. Most lessons have been painfully earned, so it is only fair that we get to share them here.

What we set out in this section is a generic approach that we think provides the required steps that most people in health & care will need to implement cost management and meet their cost objectives.

When we undertake cost management in health & care, we take the view that implementing an effective long-term programme requires a few things:

- It should be a strategic and inclusive approach that aligns with the organisation's long-term goals, balanced with the needs of staff and service-users. That might sound obvious, but as we've seen from the list of approaches previously, not everyone takes this view.

- Because you don't have cost management fully in place now (otherwise you wouldn't be reading this book), you need to put it in place. This requires a programme or a project to move from one state to another. This programme needs resourcing, managing, monitoring, and supporting. You would therefore benefit from having learned how to manage a project. Whilst our approach includes some project management elements, you can (and should) use this book alongside your knowledge of, and skills in, project or programme management.

- Because there will be a change, you would also benefit from understanding change management as a specific skill set. Our approach includes some of the more standard elements of change management. Look back at our section on barriers to see how important change management is. It is fundamental to success.

- This approach includes a phase by phase, step by step way of managing costs, but as Peter Drucker once said, "Culture eats strategy for breakfast". A key area of focus, alongside this approach, should be the strengthening of your culture and your teams, so that cost management is something that people do well naturally, in balance with the other priorities of the organisation, its service-users, and its staff. Again, some elements of organisational development and organisational design are included in this approach, but skills and approaches in this area would be useful to develop and understand alongside it.

- The approach that we set out, is a considered and step-by-step way of implementing cost management, but as we have seen, cost management sometimes needs to be done very quickly. If your organisation is heading for a financial cliff edge, then action needs to be taken We have split cost management into elements that include everything from long term transformational change to short term cost cutting to save the organisation – but you need to be flexible with the approach, and may have to implement some changes while you are still working out what the complete list of ideas might be.

Cost Management Elements

Our approach to cost management considers four key elements – Save, Grip, Improve, Transform:

- **Save** - cutting costs and doing big things quickly to ensure the organisations survival. This includes addressing known issues, addressing quick opportunities and short-term cost cutting.

- **Grip** - controlling the way cost operates in your organisation - putting in place the tools and processes for control (such as demand and capacity models), and the controls around pay, non-pay, income and demand.

- **Improve** - building greater cost management in your organisation's processes, staffing, estates and technology. It includes workforce planning, managing non-pay and improving efficiency.

- **Transform** - redefining the way you operate to improve efficiency and potentially fundamentally change your cost model

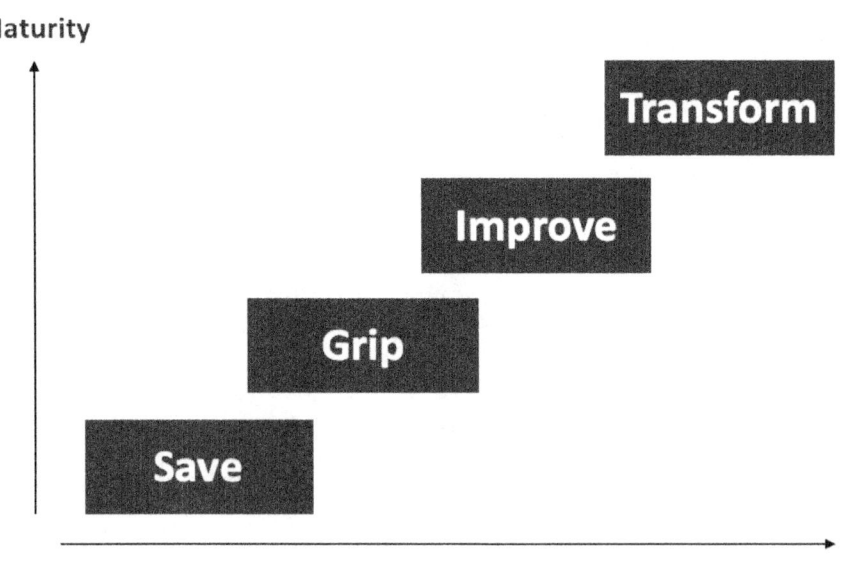

Figure 3: Cost Management Maturity

These represent an increasing maturity in your organisation from a death spiral (practically) at one end, to an organisation that shows world-class efficiency and cost management at the other end. When we talk about maturity, this normally implies a timeline - and it is no different here. We would expect that "save" actions would be done in year (possibly in month, in week or even within a day of starting), whereas "transform" actions may have to wait a few years.

So, when undertaking this approach, we will need to consider that the process may need to be done very lightly and quickly for the first element, and perhaps more comprehensively and slowly for the latter elements. But, hey, we're not your parents (believe us, you wouldn't want that), so you might want to start with quickly and lightly implementing transformational ideas. You do you.

Approach Overview

Right, onto the approach. Whilst they overlap, and the importance of each varies from situation to situation, we consistently see successful programs of cost reduction consist of five key phases.

- Scope and mobilise.

- Generate ideas.

- Develop future state.

- Develop and implement plans.

- Sustain Success.

In summary, each of these include:

Phase 1: Scope and mobilise

This first phase is predominantly about getting set up for success, both for the programme and for cost management in the future. As we said earlier, we believe cost management requires it be aligned with the organisation's strategy, and it is in this phase that we start that alignment. We also make sure that we are very clear why we are doing this work, set clear and measurable objectives, and set the project up correctly. It is also here where we start the engagement will all levels of stakeholders from the frontline to the Executive, service-users, suppliers, and commissioners (if applicable).

Phase 2: Generate ideas

A large part of cost management programmes is the identification, development and prioritisation of ideas to improve cost control, and to reduce expenditure (or increase income). We will again engage stakeholders, this time to leverage a structured process to generate a wide range of cost-saving ideas – encouraging innovation and collaboration across the organisation.

Phase 3: Develop future state

Once the ideas are generated, the future state needs to be developed so we know what the programme is going to include and the impacts it will have. We will look at the operations of the business and a range of changes to improve efficiency. This phase includes engaging stakeholders (again), preparing the information to support developed ideas, developing the changes, and aligning the findings to the challenge to make sure that It is all adding up to a programme that will meet the organisational objectives. If not, it is back around the process again. This phase also includes assessing the impact of changes.

Phase 4: Develop and implement plans

This phase includes writing everything down in a coherent plan and case for change. It includes identifying the resources for delivery and developing detailed action plans for the change. It also includes delivering it, monitoring it, and evaluating its impact – and then adjusting for when things start going off the rails.

Phase 5: Sustain success

The final phase can easily be forgotten – but it is as important as the rest. This is about sustaining the success of the programme over multiple years. It includes ensuring that the governance, from the front-line to the Executive is in place to ensure success and spot where cracks are starting to appear again. It includes having the right long-term metrics in place to monitor cost – including "leading" indicators to let you now when the basics aren't being done. It includes refreshing the programme every year, to allow it to address more transformational elements and build on its successes. It also includes addressing such elements as the culture, the cost management skills of your teams and the resources available to people who want to continue to improve cost control and efficiency. It's a big phase, and one that is worth real focus.

In summary, the approach includes:

Scope & Mobilise	Generate Ideas	Develop Future State	Plan & Implement	Sustain Success
Engage Stakeholders	Engage Stakeholders	Engage Stakeholders	Document Case	Improve Governance
Assemble Team	Collate, Collect, Create	Prepare Information	Plan Actions	Monitor Cost
Understand Challenge	Analyse Data	Develop Changes	Allocate Resources	Refresh Programme
Set Clear Objectives	Theme and Assess	Align Changes to Challenge	Implement	Develop Skills
Agree Project		Assess Impacts	Monitor, Evaluate & Adjust	Develop Culture
Ensure Clear Governance				Build Supporting Teams

Figure 4: Overview of approach

4.2

Phase One - Scope & Mobilise

This first phase is predominantly about getting set up for success, both for the programme and for cost management in the future. Cost management requires that it be aligned with the organisation's strategy, and it is in this phase that we start that alignment. We also make sure that we are very clear why we are doing this work, set clear and measurable objectives, and set the project up correctly. It is also here where we start the engagement will all levels of stakeholders from the frontline to the executive, service-users, suppliers, providers, commissioners, etc (as applicable).

1.1   Engage Stakeholders

We're going to do this a lot throughout this approach. Remember, cost management will only work if it is sold-in, aligns with objectives and if people have the understanding and skills to maintain it. It's all about the people.

Right at the start, you need to work out your stakeholders. Realistically, you have four groups, all of which will have their own engagement needs.

- **Group 1 - The Team:** The people who will be doing the actual work. This includes a core team, plus a set of experts who will be involved in the "doing". This itself can be subdivided into those that are doing the work to set up the programme, and those that lead (and help with) the individual projects once they've been defined. So this can be quite a fluid set.

- **Group 2 - The Steering Group:** The people engaged in the programme, but not actively doing the work on the ground.

- **Group 3 - The Engagement Group:** The people not included above, who will attend the various interviews, workshops, and redesigns.

- **Group 4 - Other Stakeholders:** People who will be affected by the change, but who may not be personally involved in the project.

The steering group should be immediately engaged in a mobilisation workshop of some sort to help complete the project charter and the governance documents, which we discuss later. If the team has been selected, then they too should be included in the mobilisation – at least those that have already been identified as part of group 1.

Group 3, the stakeholder representatives, will also need to be engaged as soon as possible, and you should consider how they (or you) are going to keep the other stakeholders up to date.

1.1.1 Immediate stakeholder mapping and engagement process

Your general project management approach should give you the tools to undertake this work, but the typical steps we undertake include:

- Building a list of stakeholder groups, and the leads for each of them, and a list of individual stakeholders. Identify which of the four groups they fit into.

- Developing and communicating a standard set of explanation slides and document to set out what the project is, why it needs doing etc.

- Developing a communication plan for each group prior to mobilisation

- Booking and holding an early mobilisation/initial meeting or workshop to discuss the issues, agree the project, and start the information gathering.

1.1.2 Communication planning

When undertaking cost management work, communication is critical.

- We want to secure commitment and active participation from all levels of the organisation, from the boardroom to the front lines (and please don't say 'from the top' or 'bottom up'). We need to develop a comprehensive communication plan that not only informs but also actively engages stakeholders in a dialogue about the cost reduction program's goals, benefits, and expected outcomes. Transparency and inclusivity are key to building trust and fostering a sense of shared ownership over the programme's success.

- We want to identify potential sources of resistance early and develop targeted strategies to address concerns. This might involve tailored messaging, one-on-one meetings, and small group discussions to ensure that all voices are heard and considered as part of the programme's development and implementation.

- We want to start embedding a culture of continuous improvement by highlighting early wins and ongoing progress to maintain momentum and demonstrate the programme's value. This includes establishing mechanisms for regular feedback and adaptation, ensuring that the cost reduction program remains responsive to new insights and challenges as they arise.

- Cost management sometimes means cost reduction, which sometimes means peoples jobs change or are lost. No matter what, it will involve change - so we need to communicate to minimise personal and organisational impact. This is a balancing act, as we can do as much harm with over-communication (and scaring people unduly) as we can with under-communication

To aid in our communication planning, we tend to split communications into three groups:

- **Initial communications** – a set of information that is agreed with the project owner and/or steering group as soon as the work starts, setting out why we are doing the work, what the work is, the plan, when they can be expected to be communicated with and who is doing the work.

- **Ongoing communications** – a mindful set of communications built on a communications plan, which we will consider in a moment.

Focus Area: Who needs to be involved?

You should think about:

- What stakeholders are needed for a steering group in order to ensure buy-in?

- Who is the chair of the steering group?

- Who are the right representatives to get things done?

- Who are the experts who know what else is going on, and help avoid duplication pr the production of a different view?

- Who do I need to involve in the redesign of governance? Of operational and financial grip processes?

- Who do I need to involve in the redesign of processes, technology, organisation and facilities for the future?

- Am I representing the diversity of my workforce in my stakeholders?

- What suppliers or providers should I involve?

- What commissioners should I involve?

- What staff-side groups should I involve?

- What service-users should I involve?

- What specialist contacts do I need from the organisation – Information governance? Data teams? Estates? Human Resources?

- Who is going to lead the programme on a day to day basis?

- Who else do we need to deliver a programme? Programme Manager? Data Analyst? Facilitators? Communication teams? Modellers? Writers? People to lead programme streams?

- What regulators or other bodies should I involve?

- **Final communication of plan** – the steps that we will take to communicate the findings. Please note that this does not mean that this is done right at the end – we will need to set the communications based on the requirements of the steering committee, but this may also need to be balanced with formal consultation co-ordinated with HR or staff-side representatives.

We mentioned communications planning above. To develop such a plan, you first need to work out who most needs to be communicated with. So, list all your stakeholder groups or individuals and grade them based on how much influence they have and how interested they are,

People that are interested and influential need to be managed closely, with two-way engagement so that you can quickly react to their information and engagement needs. If they are influential but not interested, you need to ensure that you are keeping them satisfied, so regular checks are needed, but you aren't going to shadow them throughout. Interested people need to be kept informed, and the disinterested still need to be monitored, because they have some influence and some interest, so should not be ignored.

To address this, we build it into a communication plan, which sets out the who, why, when and what of communication with various groups.

Who: Split the mass of stakeholders into groups (and individuals if they have high interest or high influence).

Why: What is the point of communication (ensuring they are informed? Getting their views? Getting their help? All of the above?).

How: Determine how you are going to communicate:

- Broadcast - e.g. regular email updated.

- Meetings - engage through a discussion at an existing or new forum.

- One-to-one contact.

- Others as required.

What: What are you going to communicate?

When: How often are you planning to communicate?

From there, all you need to do is put that into a table and keep a log of communication so that you can see that it is being done, and make sure that you aren't under doing it. If you want, you can also keep a record of who you consider to be helpful or unhelpful / who are "blockers" etc - but we don't like doing that as it is subjective, and if people see it they might not be at all happy…

1.2 Assemble the team

At this point you should start to build a team around you. You may not actually have the permission or support to consider building a team – but without one, even an informal one, you are likely fighting a losing (and lonely) battle. Assuming the organisation recognises the importance of a team-based approach, here are some pointers.

Implementing a successful cost reduction program in health and care requires a multidisciplinary team with a blend of skills, experiences, and perspectives. Here's how to identify and assemble the right team to navigate the program from inception to completion effectively.

1.2.1 Identify Key Roles and Expertise

Key roles and expertise you might need in the core teams (groups 1 and 2 from above), include:

- **Strategic Leadership**: Include senior leaders who can provide direction, allocate resources, and champion the program across the organisation.

- **Financial Analysts**: Experts in health and care finance are crucial for identifying savings opportunities and evaluating the financial impact of proposed initiatives.

- **Operational Managers**: Individuals with a deep understanding of day-to-day operations can identify inefficiencies and suggest practical improvements.

- **Clinical Champions**: Engage clinicians who can ensure that cost reduction efforts align with patient care standards and can advocate for changes within their departments.

- **Project Managers**: Professionals skilled in managing projects can oversee the program, ensuring it stays on track, within budget, and achieves its objectives.

- **Change Management Specialists**: Experts in organisational change can help navigate the cultural shifts necessary for implementing new processes or technologies.

1.2.2 Assemble the Team

This is where you get to pull the team together. We should probably put some sort of "Avengers Assemble" quip in here to prove that we're down with the kids and have watched films from (just about) the last decade, but we can't think of any.

Luckily there are lots of options as to where you can get your team from:

- **Leverage Internal Talent**: Start by identifying internal candidates who possess the desired expertise and demonstrate a commitment to the organisation's goals.

- **Engage External Consultants**: For specialised skills or to supplement internal capabilities, consider hiring external consultants with a proven track record in health and care cost reduction.

- **Foster Interdisciplinary Collaboration**: Encourage open communication and collaboration among team members to leverage diverse perspectives and expertise.

- **System Resources**: If you work within a collaborative system, consider reaching out for form or informal secondments. The diversity of perspectives, as well as the extra bodies, could prove to be valuable.

By carefully selecting a team with the right mix of skills, fostering a collaborative environment, and effectively navigating challenges, health and care managers can lead their organisations through successful cost reduction programs, achieving financial sustainability while maintaining high-quality services.

When presenting the methodology, as part of a competitive management consulting pitch, to the Board of a very large and well respected teaching hospital, one of the authors was tested on the clinical capability of the proposed consulting team. The Director of Nursing asked a very clear question - "How many nurses do you have on your team?". "None", was the true but perhaps somewhat risky response. "We heard that you already employ 7,500 nurses so we thought that was plenty." I don't think he won that one, but the point was still a good one: There is little point in bringing in external resources (often at great expense) if the organisation already has them in abundance (and ones with the added advantage that they often have a deep understanding of what does and doesn't work locally). Bring in the missing expertise that you need, not the expertise that you already have…

1.3   Understand the challenge

We always like to have a good look round before we start. Chat to people, sometimes informally and sometimes in a more formal, structured way. Read things. Understand what is going on before we leap into action. So, we start by trying to understand the challenge in two ways.

1.3.1 Stakeholder insights

First things first, let's find out what people already know. The approach to this is:

- Build a list of stakeholders for discussion regarding their insights – who are the key people we need to speak to? We should engage with a broad range of stakeholder to gather insights.

- Develop a standard agenda to ensure that you cover all the questions you need to ask – see below for a list of potential topics.

- Book and hold meetings – obviously…

- Document meetings - we've always found it useful to make sure that you have a record of where all the information came from, so you can reference it later - you may also want to agree this record of the meeting with the stakeholder and agree if their names can be used for any information provided.

- Follow up on agreed actions – if you've promised to send them something afterwards, do it.

- Develop report setting out what we have learned, so we can update the steering committee.

These discussions could cover:

- Why is the organisation in the position it is?

- Do you think we need to reduce costs? Why?

- What documents should we be reviewing?

- How do things get done around here?

- Where are the obvious places to start?

1.3.2 Comprehensive financial analysis

Let's get into a deep dive into your organisation's current financial health, operational efficiencies, and areas of wasteful expenditure and maybe utilise data analytics to uncover hidden costs and inefficiencies that may not be apparent at first glance. This step is not just about identifying where the money goes but understanding the value derived from each expense.

Key elements of this include:

- **Macro budget review:** You need to review and understand where all income comes from and where all expenditure goes to in your organisation. Who are all and who are the main buyers/commissioners of your service. Who are all and who are the main suppliers, staff group and teams in your organisation. You are looking for high areas of income or spend that you can target. You should also look to see where the largest variances are between budget and actual expenditure, and review trends over time to see where there have been increases.

- **Team by team budget review:** Build a clear understanding of the various units in your organisation – organisations, divisions, directorates, teams etc – and for each of these understand their overall budget, how that budget breaks down, who owns the budgets and how well they have been performed against in recent years. You are looking for areas where most of the money is spent, where there is a lack of ownership and where there are variances between budget and expenditure. Where possible, ensure that you align these with activity budgets and actuals as well to see where it may be that activity being out of control is the problem (assuming you aren't being paid for it). Again, you should also consider trends over time.

- **Service by service budget review:** Working from a buyer's perspective, build a view of income versus costs across your organisation, to identify profitability.

- **Project and plan review:** Identify all ongoing projects and identify their likely cost/benefit impact financially. You can also assess these plans for deliverability etc (see sidebar on current project reviews, later). It may be that current plans are going to solve the problem (or make it worse). Also, review previous plans and the impact that they had – did they deliver what they expected to. Spoilers – the answer is probably no.

- **Document review:** Read up on available information to see what has already been raised. These can include:

    - Past audit reports.

    - Internal and external benchmarking/comparator analysis.

    - Good practice documents from regulators or industry bodies.

    - Reports from units or service lines – annual plans, monthly reports, updates, etc.

    - Board papers.

- **Cashflow review:** Look at cash instead of what the accountants record (this is a favourite of the insolvency practitioners and is one of the few useful things they bring to the party – cash rarely lies).

The reason why you should do this comprehensive analysis is to look for:

- What is the problem – how much needs to be saved, and by when?

- What is already going on that might help?

- Are there opportunities to reduce cost that immediately jump to mind? Areas of large spend, recent large budget increases, underspent budgets or problematic teams that could and should be controlled now?

1.4 Set clear, strategic objectives

We need to make sure that we know what we aim to achieve with this cost management programme or intervention.

- We need to consider the reasons for cost reduction in section 1 and consider what that means do our objectives.

- We need to consider what approach to cost management we are comfortable with, and we need to consider whether we are reducing cost ourselves or working as part of a system.

- We need to ensure that any cost reduction objectives are fully aligned with the organisation's mission, vision, and strategic priorities. This alignment ensures that cost-saving measures contribute to the broader goal of enhancing patient care and operational efficiency - considering the balance of stakeholders set out in the efficiency triangle section, earlier.

We can then set an overall objective for the work, and various sub-objectives. These should be SMART – i.e. we should develop Specific, Measurable, Achievable, Relevant, and Time-bound objectives that guide the cost reduction program.

This may be, for example:

- Ensure that we put cost control in place by December, such that we will be able to identify and address budget discrepancies within year.

- Reduce costs by $3m in six months to meet the requirements of shareholders.

- Improve efficiency so that we maintain current access and service levels for service-users but reduce costs/increase income by £24m over two years, with £8m saved/earned in year one.

When setting objectives, consider the flexibility to adapt to changing circumstances and the scalability of initiatives across different departments or services.

1.5 Agree project

So, by now you've worked out why you are doing it, and some of the main issues and background to the need for cost reduction. Now, you need a project. A project is needed, because you are going to make a change and it's going to need some resources – management focus, staff time and, quite possibly, cash.

We won't go into too much detail here, as this should be covered by your organisation's chosen approach to project management – but it should include understanding, and documenting:

- The documented question or challenge we are looking to address (from earlier).

- The SMART goals we have agreed (from earlier).

- Project scope – what is in scope, what is out of scope, where the project starts and where it ends. This will help identify if there are parts of the organisation out of scope, or whether we are working across the system or just in the organisation.

- The plan – this should be a clear view of what is going to be done, who is going to do it and when it is going to be done. This is a plan for the programme, not the implementation plan, so it will typically contain much of what we will talk about in the rest of the approach.

- Terms of reference for the ongoing monitoring and steering of the programme, including:

    - Chair (and deputy).

    - Who is on the steering committee? What makes the meeting quorate?

    - How will the steering be administered? What is provided in advance and by whom?

    - Standard agenda.

    - Who it reports to.

You can search for "Project Initiation Document" online, or get in touch for examples.

1.6 Ensure Clear Governance

There can sometimes be confusion between setting up governance for cost management and setting it up for the programme to put cost management in place. For us, there should be no confusion – we should start by managing the project and managing costs in our organisation. It is likely that we have already been managing costs to some extent, so we should start with those elements, and introduce new ones as we start taking actions to improve cost management.

This includes forming a cross-functional steering committee that embodies the diverse perspectives and expertise necessary for a holistic approach to cost reduction.

We cover cost management governance in the Sustain Success phase.

Focus: Current project reviews

When considering current projects, you may want to consider:

- **Programme management** - extent to which the project has good programme or project management in place. Is there a lead, a steering committee, a plan etc

- **Outcome focus** - is there an outcome based plan being used, with clear ownership and expected benefits?

- **Accountability** - is there senior management involvement, with evidence that issues have been escalated and addressed?

- **Completeness** - do all the plans and individual benefits add up to what the project is expecting to achieve?

- **Capacity (bandwidth)** - Is there enough resource to deliver the project? Does the Senior Responsible Officer and the lead have enough time?

- **Track record** - what evidence is there that this will achieve the benefits?

- **Performance management** - is it clear that issues are being dealt with effectively, and the difficult questions being asked?

- **Stakeholder engagement -** have the right people been involved throughout?

- **Leadership -** do the key people express belief in the project, and is this being shown to all involved in the project?

- **Expert alignment and staff engagement** - are the key delivery staff (clinicians, social workers, managers, support staff, etc) involved in the project?

You can assess all projects against the above, scoring them on a scale of 1 for good performance and 5 for very bad) on each criteria to give you a view on the relative likelihood of delivery. Whilst a scoring system can give you a view, you are more likely to get a "gut-feel" for these projects following discussions with leads.

4.3

Phase Two – Generate Ideas

So, we've set our project up to succeed, but we've also already started improving our cost management through improved governance, and we've got a view on how we got into difficulty in the first place. Now it is time to get much more information on how we are going to solve our cost management issues. This phase is all about collecting as much quantitative and qualitative data as is practical.

Focus: The minimum case for change

Sometimes, we can get a bit hung up on collecting so much data that we don't actually ever get anything done. This can be called "paralysis by analysis". When we used to do this sort of work a lot, we tended to talk about the "minimum case for change". All this meant was, when collecting data, just collect enough to prove to yourself and your stakeholders that something is worth doing. Don't overdo it – but if your stakeholders need more information than you do, well you need to collect enough to convince them.

2.1 Engage stakeholders

It was the first thing we did in the last phase, and it's the first thing we are going to do in this one. If we did our job properly in phase 1, then we should have a comprehensive list of stakeholders, and now we must work out which ones we are going to engage in the idea generation phase.

We need to engage the steering group and the project team, obviously, and add all those that can help you identify ideas and provide supporting data. This can include almost everybody on our stakeholder list – staff, service-users, suppliers, regulators, the whole lot. That's because almost everyone will have some idea as to where you are inefficient. You don't have to include everyone though – a lot will depend on how important the issue is, and how much time you have. If you have a small issue and only a short time to solve it, you may well just sit down with a small inner circle to work out what you should do – or even do it on your own. You may also decide to start with this approach to get the ball rolling, and then go out to the organisation for ideas. The choice is yours.

We're going to assume a large-scale engagement approach in the rest of this section, but the core is the same no matter how big, or small, you begin.

The actual engagement actions are included in the following steps.

2.2 Collate, Collect, Create

In the journey of cost reduction within health and care organisations, this is as a pivotal stage where the Collation, Collection and Creation (who doesn't like a little bit of alliteration?) of ideas emerge and converge into a wide funnel, setting the groundwork for transformative savings and efficiency improvements in the next phase.

At its best, this step is designed to harness the collective creativity and expertise within the organisation, past (as Bob the Builder says, "Reduce, Re-use and Recycle") and present, encouraging a culture of innovation that transcends traditional boundaries. The aim is to develop a comprehensive set of things we can do to reduce or manage cost in the organisation. It is, quite simply, our favourite bit.

So, our aim is to collate, collect and create as many ideas as are possible. And, unsurprisingly, there are lots of different ways to do this – and you get to pick whether you do them all or only one, and which ones you focus on.

When you collect ideas, you want to record them in a meaningful way. So start to develop a spreadsheet here with a list of the ideas, and where you found them (possibly recording multiple sources). Later on, you can start to add columns for priority, potential savings, ease of implementation, impact on other areas, for grouping ideas etc – but for now, we need to go about our work in a methodical way, so start keeping a record.

We split these approaches into the three categories of collation, collection and creation. Let's have a look at the options:

2.2.1 Collation

Collation serves as the mainly 'desk-top' process of gathering all existing ideas, ensuring a wide array of suggestions are considered, from incremental changes to ground-breaking innovations. An irritating management phrase you may have learned is 'low hanging fruit' – which refers to those things that are apparently both easiest to do and worth doing? Well, collation is the stage before that – it is the process of picking up windfall fruit from the floor.

There is really only one approach here: - the document review

Remember in the last phase when we talked about asking stakeholders what documents were available? Here, we pick out the cost improvement ideas. You should review:

- **Current cost improvement plans** - just because they exist in a list somewhere doesn't mean they aren't still available to be used.

- **Previous cost reduction plans** - just because an effort has failed before doesn't mean they will fail now. Things change. So have a look at previous plans and find out which ones did not get implemented.

- **Business cases** - these can be a valuable and untapped resource for cost reduction. Whilst they may have been formed with the intention of seeking funding, the authors often find that either that investment will pay back several-fold or that many (or sometimes all) of the benefits can be secured with little or no additional funding. Have a look at these cases to see what has already been suggested.

2.2.2 Collection

Collection is the process of bringing into the mix all those ideas that are already available but not already placed into the funnel. This book could be your primary source of these ideas – the authors have collectively already done a lot of hard work (you are welcome) and brought these all together for you. In most organisations there is also a ready source of ideas just waiting for you – ask the staff, patients and other stakeholders. This can be done in as low or high tech a way as suits your situation.

This is where you have a lot of different approaches you can call on:

2.2.2.1 The open question to your staff

One way to collect ideas, break-down barriers and build relationships is to go to where the people are and ask for their ideas face to face. A favourite approach of one of the authors is to set up an ideas station (otherwise known as a table with a poster on it) in the staff canteen. Showing your face and being willing to answer questions as well as collect ideas can be very well received by colleagues whose main point of contact with management and management consultants is often by email. Humanising the process and putting yourself out there can give you access to ideas that wouldn't otherwise be available. Just remember to bring a thick skin and smile with you!

You can implement a digital platform to collect ideas (or just set up an email address) or make a cardboard suggestion box that allows staff at all levels to contribute ideas continuously. If nothing else, an open access cardboard suggestion box is a chance to read abusive emails - one of the authors did even try to put his head where it was suggested, but flexibility proved to be a barrier - but you do get some interesting ideas as well. You could offer incentives for actionable new ideas (and follow up with reward and recognition).

However you choose to do this, the open question to your staff to generate a list of cost improvement ideas is one that we have seen used on several occasions, and it does provide a wealth of ideas. Key steps are:

- Work out the communication and how you are going to go out to collect ideas.

- Communicate and collect ideas.

- Record the ideas.

- Sort / analyse the ideas – identifying common themes, number of times things are mentioned etc.

- Provide feedback to staff on how many ideas were suggested, what was suggested, and what the next steps are.

2.2.2.2 The open question to your other stakeholders

It isn't just your staff who have good ideas. You can also go out to your:

- **Suppliers** - what do they notice about working with you, which might suggest efficiencies for you? If there are ways of working that can create efficiencies for them (and you can then get a reduced price) then they are also worth recording.

Another thing you can do with suppliers, is to go out and ask them what is new – what do they have that might improve efficiency. And don't just go out to your suppliers – get a view on new stuff from other potential suppliers. This overlaps a bit with the creation area, so we'll look at that in more detail there.

- **Service-users & commissioners** - what do your clients notice about working with you that might suggest ways you can save money? Widespread service-user engagement might not be the way you want to go when looking at cost management (although it might, if you get the communications right) but engaging user groups and commissioners in your challenge and in highlighting solutions could be a useful step.

- **Regulators, etc** - what do these people think you could do? Is there a standard set of cost management ideas to focus on, either as an organisation or in elements of your operation?

2.2.2.3 Using the set list of ideas in this book

This way of doing this is a favourite for us. Of course it is, that's why we've spent years gathering lists of ideas. Whenever anyone calls management consultants in to help, they always ask if they have a list of ideas, as if that is the most important thing. It isn't – for us, the most important thing is building a culture where staff want to, and can, manage costs themselves – but a list of ideas does help people get started when looking at what they want to do to manage cost.

There are lots of ways to use a standard list:

- **Go and ask those responsible** - the old way of doing things, and still a viable option, is to take each part of the list to the person or team responsible and ask them whether they are already doing it. Thus, you might go to procurement with the "Procurement" list and see which ones of those they are already doing, and which ones they think are a good idea. Colin used to do this, but he got fed up of doing it because it felt a bit like an attack on the person you were talking to, so they often just said that they were already doing it, or they had tried it and it didn't work. The barriers can come up. Plus, it's a lot of work – you have to arrange meetings for each one, go and see them for an hour, write it all up – and quite often then get the responses agreed, which can then lead to a whole range of challenges and new meetings to sort out. Colin doesn't do this anymore.

- **"Poster tool" workshops etc** - his is what Colin does now. Print off all the ideas with a scale of 1-5 and put them up around the room. Give people two sets of different coloured stickers and ask people to score each idea on which they have an opinion as to whether we are doing the idea now and whether we should be doing it. Big gaps between the coloured dots for where we are and where we should be, highlight areas that we should focus on. Small gaps, less so. It gets a lot of people looking at, and assessing, the ideas very quickly. Get in touch for examples, and see the diagram at the bottom of the page.

- **Review them yourselves** - you can create a process for you to review and assess lists of ideas yourselves. Take each idea, and analyse whether it is being done already, align it with the data (see next phase) and consider whether it should be taken forward. It's a lot of work, but it is more objective and can allow you to get this done without a lot of engagement. You can get people to do this in a cave at head office.... It's not a bad idea if you want to do more work yourself first - you can reverse the steps here, looking at the data first and then working out which of these ideas might help drive that improvement the data shows is possible. You could then go out to the staff and experts and see what they think.

Key actions to take include:

- Develop your standard list - you can choose from the ones in this book that relate to you and augment them with others if you have other sources. Possible other sources include other organisation plans and the lists provided by anyone helping you with this process.

- Develop your approach to using the list (perhaps from the options above) and arrange the process.

- As always, document your findings, noting the ideas that are selected, ideas that have not been selected, and any information on who and why these decisions were made.

No	Theme	1	2	3	4	5
11	**Process designed around user journey:** Make sure that user-journey mapping is used to build the right process for all service-users. This can eliminate low value-added steps, improve the customer experience and drive efficiency.	●				○
12	**Staff only used when needed:** Optimise when you need to involve staff to reduce cost and free people up for other tasks.					
13	**Process agreed with staff:** Preferably redesign processes with staff so that they are involved from the staff - but when they have been in place for a time, make sure that all staff understand the process and agree that it makes sense, to improve buy-in to quality delivery.					
14	**User cancellations minimised:** Last minute cancellations and no-shows can reduce efficiency. Put in place controls to prevent them and review their levels to learn lessons and reduce further incidences.					
15	**Checklist based delivery:** Checklists are a great way to ensure standard processes are followed, and that staff know what they are doing. Build as many as you can to drive efficiency.					
16	**Known improvements made:** You may well find that there is good practice, or that processes have been reviewed before. Find these previous studies and reports and make sure that they have been implemented (or you may re-implement them if things have slipped).					
17	**Users used within process:** Where possible, get service-users to do the work themselves to reduce the need for staff to do the work - and get more buy-in from your service-users.					
18	**Eliminate rework/mistakes:** Identify where mistakes are being made or re-work is necessary, learn lessons and improve the process to remove these. Looking at service-user complaints can also help identify these issues, and possible solutions.					
19	**Eliminate fines for work not done properly:** Try to prevent them, but when you get them make sure that they are valid, and then put in controls to prevent them in future.					
20	**Value stream mapping:** Applying value stream mapping to identify and eliminate non-value-adding steps should be done regularly as new steps often sneak into processes to deal with issues, that may no longer actually be a problem.					

Figure 5: Example poster tool

- Report back to groups on what has been selected.

2.2.2.4 Good practice review

It is unlikely that you are the only health and care organisation doing what you do. So, it is likely that there is a wealth of case studies or ideas out there that you can call upon. Undertaking a document review to identify this good practice is a useful step to identify lots of ideas.

When doing this, as always keep a list of what documents you have review and what ideas have come from that review. In itself, this might be useful in later years to stop people having to do the work again – and it provides a clear audit trail when you look later at what ideas you are actually going to put into practice.

2.2.2.5 Use your eyes

You might want to have a good look around areas, either on your own, or with an expert. Colin used to do this in retailers – he took an expert with him who could immediately point out good practice, poor practice and opportunities to improve income or reduce costs.

Even if you aren't an expert, some things ca easily be spotted – and sometimes it is the only way to find things. So, get out there and find what the issues and opportunities are.

2.2.3 Creation

Creation is the proactive step of generating new ideas through brainstorming sessions, workshops, and other creative endeavours. It challenges stakeholders to think beyond the status quo, fostering an environment where novel solutions are not just welcomed but actively sought after. It emphasises the importance of not dismissing any suggestion at the outset, recognising the potential value in diverse inputs. Specific elements include:

2.2.3.1 The ideas generation workshop

An ideas generation workshop is a contained method for gathering ideas. You get experts in the room and set out the problem and get them to come up with the solution. This can be in the form of a Lean Rapid Improvement Event, where the participants work over 3-5 days to solve the problem, or it can be just a simple meeting with the right people to come up with a plan. Typically, these meetings will require information, so you can start with an event to set out the problem and start working on it, and pause while people go off and collect data, look at good practice - and then reconvene when the data is available.

2.2.3.2 The innovation event or festival

We've used this approach a few times, and it can be really effective. There are companies that do this really well - Yorkshire Water's events are worth looking up on-line. Basically, these are planned events, operating over a day or multiple days, where lots of people come together to understand the issue, look at different viewpoints on issues and solutions and work in creative ways to develop solutions. They can include all sorts of suppliers and experts bringing ideas and examples from other industries, as well as local organisations that have different viewpoints and strategies. It is a great way to build creativity across a diverse group of people that represent the stakeholders of modern health and care organisations. These work really well when looking at cost from the viewpoint of a system - either for the whole system or for a pathway.

2.2.3.3 Service Line Management Strategy development process

The Service Line Management approach developed by NHS England (in an earlier incarnation) was mentioned back in the approaches section. As we noted there, it is itself a great approach to managing cost alongside the requirements to manage activity, quality and staff needs. It includes an approach to gathering data and reviewing it as a team to develop responses to challenges – including budget challenges. We love it as an approach, because it gets the team looking at how to solve the issues and thus fosters a culture of doing it ourselves. It is tough to convince people of the need to introduce cost savings if they don't buy into the problem – and in public health and care companies especially, it can be difficult to build that buy in. Service Line Management, if implemented properly, can really help that.

This approach could be used by each team, and the results combined into directorates, divisions and organisations (whatever your hierarchy) to develop solutions to the issues from teams on the front-line.

2.3 Data analysis – request, collect and analyse

So far, we've done a lot, or a little bit, of work to develop a list of ideas. These are generally what we refer to as a "Qualitative" list, although we're almost certainly using the wrong word. What we mean is that we have a list of ideas with no data attached. People might say "ooh, this is a big opportunity", but we don't know how big. Or why they said "ooh" at the start.

To work out how big, we can use data. But we can also find ideas in the data. Just because no-one has come up with any non-pay ideas, does not mean that there is no opportunity in procurement. So, data can be used to both identify new opportunities, and to quantify those that people have found. When we come to theme and assess ideas in the next step, we might pay more attention to those areas where the qualitative and quantitative pictures come together – but we ignore either area at our peril.

So, data analysis is typically done at the same time as the collate, collect and create step – this phase should just be one big hunt for the right things to focus on, so let's not keep things separate while we do it.

As discussed at the start, we're trying to keep this book generic for health and care, which makes it difficult to include a lot of specific data you should be asking for. I might give you a list that includes length of stay – but you don't have beds, so you aren't interested. Instead, we'll just say that you need to look at the data that you think is relevant to the area, look at the relevant ideas (in the next section) that are right for you and work out what data would be useful, or send the authors an email and we'll send you links to standard lists for different types of organisation.

You are, in each case, looking for anything that identifies that there is an opportunity to get more efficient, bring in more income and/or directly reduce spend – depending on your objectives for this programme.

The data analysis step includes three main tasks:

2.3.1 Request data

Ah yes, data requests. Have you ever received a data request from someone? If you have, then all you need to do is remember how that felt and learn from it. In our experience, most data requests fall into the "Fill this 10-page spreadsheet in". Which may result in a "no", swearing, or it being ignored. It can be a little better if you:

- Ask nicely.

- Keep the request a reasonable size.

- Explain why you need it.

- Explain how it could help them.

- Speak to them in person, and explore whether there are quicker and easier ways of getting almost the right data. Data people know data, so they may also want to ask lots of questions that you might find annoying - but are aimed at making sure you get what you want. Take biscuits.

- Contract with them as to when it will be available.

So, this step is all about asking for the data in a mindful and reasonable way. And the reason that this is a step on its own is that data requests are done so badly normally, that we wanted a whole step to ask you nicely to do it properly.

2.3.2 Collect data

Now, you can just request data, but it's likely that some of it won't be available. You may then need to collect it on the ground. You can do this immediately in order to see if you can find opportunities for cost management, but you are probably better off only doing this when you need to evaluate an idea that someone has told you. If someone has said that cancellations are a problem, but there is no data on cancellations, you'll probably need to go off and collect that data.

Collecting data can be a lot more fun than just requesting it. You get to go out into the real world and see stuff – and when you do, you can often find opportunities (see earlier).

Options for collecting data out in the field (what a phrase that is – it makes us sound like we're heading into the jungle looking for a rare frog, rather than talking to someone putting numbers in a spreadsheet in an office) include:

- **Interviews** - collect information by talking to people – if x out of y people raise an issue, that is quantitative data. If you say, "how much spend is off contract" and they tell you – that is quantitative data. You might want to corroborate it more than something a machine has told you, but it may well be just as, or more, accurate.

- **Time and motion studies** - you can study and time a process. Colin practically grew up doing these things, and they are surprisingly easy. Basically, you follow people around, building up a picture of the tasks they do and the time it takes to do them. Which you can do with a stopwatch and a clipboard if you want to look really professional…

- **Process review** - you can do a full review of a process to look for efficiency opportunities. Use Lean, or any other approach to do this.

- **Diaries** - some people will keep diaries for you to help you see how often things happen etc.

- **Workshop** - get people together to answer your questions and provide quantitative data.

- **Survey** - as noted above, qualitative information becomes quantitative if you have a standard set of questions. "8 out of 10 people think procurement spend controls are weak", etc.

2.3.3 Analyse data

No-one needs to see every bit of data that you have found. You should be able to usefully draw conclusions from it and present it as information. That doesn't mean you leap straight to the answer though – it is important that your teams and leadership understand where the conclusions have come from. And they can help you check errors. The extent of analysis in this phase is really just enough to be able to identify if there is an issue, and roughly what the potential size of the saving might be. Later on, you'll need to do more analysis – so if you overdo it in this phase don't worry – it probably won't be wasted!

Helpful analysis includes:

Demand analysis: Building an interactive view of demand or activity. This can help you see where demand is coming from and how it is turning into activity. You can see variations in demand vs activity (showing queues and/or access issues etc) and variations in use of your services (or your money if you are a commissioner). You may also be able to see activity that shouldn't be activity, e.g. where it breaches expectations for number of outpatient clinics per patient), where it has increased recently etc. It's a great place to start, and you can combine it with others.

Capacity analysis: Building a linked (with the above) view of capacity. This can help you see where you have under and over capacity compared to other areas or standards, where additional payments have been used etc. Between the demand and capacity analysis, you can also put a:

Resource analysis: Showing how activity should be, and is, translated into the need for resources such as clinics, theatres, beds, rooms, buildings or whatever is important for your staff to deliver, and then into how many staff you need to show the impact of cancellations, lower utilisation etc.

In addition, you can create:

- Sankey diagrams showing service-user activity through your organisations resources and staff to identify where the main flows are and stop the leakage into other flows if needed.

- Process maps - showing how staff and resources align to the steps in the pathway or process your service users follow.

- Organisation charts - showing where your big staff groups are in the structure.

- Location maps - showing where all your resources and staff are.

- Service-user locations - showing where your service users are (and whether you could get more income by moving your resources nearer).

- Budget analysis – showing the big areas of spend, where there are big over and underspends and changes over time.

- Charts showing anywhere where plans vary from reality.

- Expenditure maps and charts.

- Profitability analysis.

You can have a lot of fun with this. But remember to:

- Check what you find with experts before you say something bold and stupid to people. When Colin worked at Sheffield, there was always someone he'd show all the analysis to, and only show it to the executive if she agreed that he hadn't made a complete howler somewhere.

- Align it with the challenge - are we finding enough potential to solve the problem? Do we need to extend the search? Is it solving the problem – e.g. if we need to save money and we are only finding new income routes, is that okay?

2.4 Theme and assess

Now we have a lot of qualitative and quantitative data, and we are ready to bring it all together. Our job now is to create a meaningful set of opportunities from the combined inputs, and prioritise them for attention. The key steps are

2.4.1 Idea Categorisation and Assessment

We first need to put our ideas into groups. This step involves systematically organising these ideas into a manageable framework, enabling a structured analysis and evaluation process. It ensures that every idea is accounted for and appropriately categorised, facilitating easier access and assessment. Once ideas are generated, group them into themes based on similarity or related departmental functions or any other grouping that helps you work with them and communicate them to others. This helps in identifying overlapping ideas and consolidating similar suggestions for more significant impact. If you've done all of the approaches we have highlighted above (and don't forget, you don't have to) you will have hundreds of overlaps and duplications.

Once we've done that, we can do a quick feasibility and Impact Assessment. To do this, we can use a quick scoring system to assess each idea based on criteria such as potential savings, implementation complexity, and impact on patient care. Tools like decision matrices or cost-benefit analysis can aid in this evaluation. We typically then put these on a graph that shows impact versus difficulty or similar on it.

2.4.2 Initial prioritisation

Once we've done that, we get the gang back together again – by which we mean we generally arrange another workshop with the steering group, wider stakeholders or the team, and do some prioritisation.

We can use the prioritisation matrix to rank ideas based on their assessed criteria, focusing on those that offer high impact and ease as a group, and work out what we believe should be the main priorities. When we are doing this, we need to consider both short-term wins and long-term transformational changes at the same time - as we should just be getting on with obvious things while we plan longer term things.

2.4.3 Continuous Feedback Loop

Finally, we should create mechanisms for ongoing feedback throughout the idea generation and selection phase – and even into delivery. This ensures that the process remains dynamic and responsive to new information or changing organisational priorities. Don't close the door on new and good ideas – even if you can't do them now, they can be kept in reserve for when they are needed.

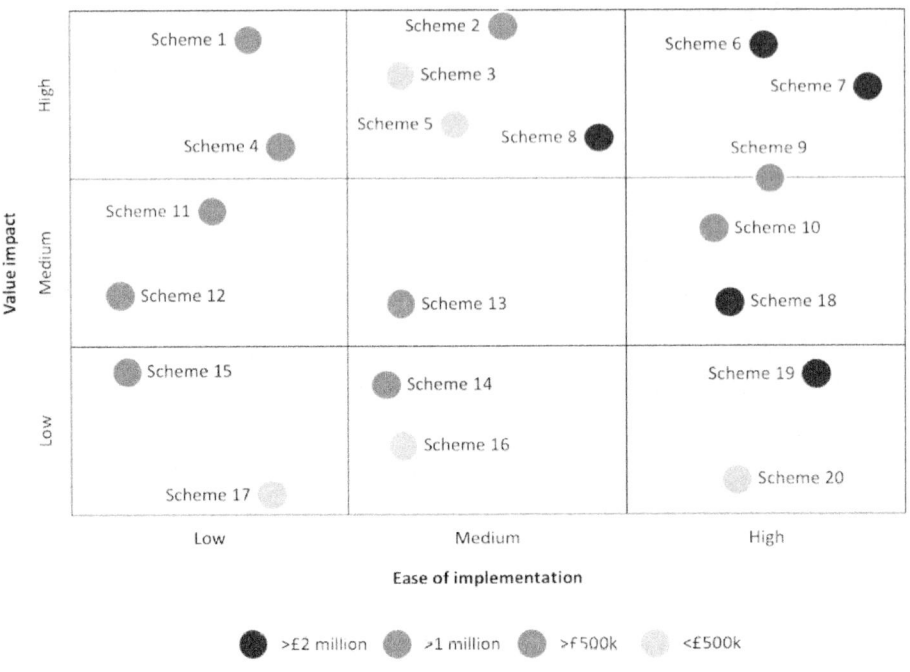

Figure 6: Prioritisation matrix

So now we have a prioritised list of ideas, with an indication of their likely impact and difficulty. Onto working out what we are actually going to do

Focus: What data?

The sort of data that is generally useful, includes:

Staff information

- Staffing information, including grade.
- Turnover information – numbers and reasons.
- Variation between establishment and actual staff levels.
- Details of any additional payments to staff – overtime, locum, agency spend etc.
- Staff satisfaction information.
- Sickness and absence amounts.
- Job plans.
- Rostering information and variance to rosters.
- Breakdown of time spent delivering, versus other time – planned and actual.
- Case load expectation and actual.
- Information on staff working on areas that are not in their job description.

Activity and standards

- Activity.
- Any activity per person information and/or expectations including staff: service user ratios and performance against them.
- Queue lengths (normal and "waiting list").
- Standards on use of resources per person (e.g. expected length of stay, number of outpatient visits and actuals.

Commissioning

- Commissioned service information.
- Information on activity vs contract, including who requested the work. For commissioners this would include working out referral patterns.
- Complete set of contracts.
- Most recent contract review information/anything that shows that you have got what you have contracted for.

Income & profitability

- Breakdown of expected income.
- Actual income.
- Car parking income.
- Income deductions.
- Profitability information for all services provided.
- Debt costs.

Resource utilisation

- Planned usage of any resource – rooms, beds, machines.
- Actual usage of any resource.
- Details of any cancellations or lack of

use (Did Not Attends etc) service user side.

- Cancellations and rebooks caused by us.

- Details of any downtime of resource – maintenance, etc.

Finance

- Budgets per team.

- Budget performance (over/under)/ actual expenditure against each budget.

- Tax information – everything spent and why.

- Cashflow over time.

- List of liabilities.

- List of money owed to you.

Consumables information

- Detail of all expenditure (consumables, medicines, etc.).

- Standards for consumable use versus actual use

- Off contract spend.

- Invoices vs paid vs goods received vs orders information – both for contract and off contract spend.

Other non-pay information

- Complete list of assets – buildings, equipment, other resources, with age.

- Maintenance schedule vs actual for equipment.

- Planned capital expenditure.

- Training budget spend.

- IT licence spend.

- Subscription lists.

- Energy spend.

- Printing costs.

- Travel and subsistence spend.

- Insurance spend.

- Outsourced service spend.

Other

- List of projects, with signed-off costs and expected benefits information.

All of this data should:

- Include as much detail as is possible (as long as you can summarise).

- Be the same time period where possible (so you are comparing apples with apples).

- Be broken down by month or week so you can see patterns.

- Include at least summary information for previous year and years so you can see patterns.

- Be broken down by team and area (or include detailed information in any data) so that you can identify teams or areas with specific issues and benchmark between them.

Now, you might not be able to get all that, but even that might tell you something (if there is no breakdown of off-contract spend, for example.that tells you that off contract spend is probably not well controlled. What gets measured gets managed and all that...

4.4

Phase Three - Developing Future State

Once the ideas are generated, the future state needs to be developed so we know what the programme is going to include and the impacts it will have. We need to look at the operations of the business and a range of changes to improve efficiency. This phase includes engaging stakeholders (again), preparing the information to support developed ideas, developing the changes, and aligning the findings to the challenge to make sure that it is all adding up to a programme that will meet the organisational objectives. If not, it is back around the process again. This phase also includes assessing the impact of changes.

3.1 Engage stakeholders

New phase, old step – we start with the classic, "engage the stakeholders". What a surprise. This time, we are working out which groups and individuals need to be involved in setting out what we are going to do, and which groups need to agree it. In many cases, this may be the same.

The people we are going to engage will depend on the approach we are going to take from here.

We have a few options that we can consider:

- **Set of central plans:** We could build a set of programmes that are run from the centre. These are typically larger scale plans, but they can be any size. In this case, your plan might consist of a set of any number of plans – the key element being that they are all run from the centre of the organisation and the control of them is therefore more direct than others below.

- **Plans by theme**: You could get each of the areas of the organisation to develop their plans based on the ideas in their area. Thus, procurement could build a set of responses based around the procurement ideas raised in the previous phase. In this case, someone responsible for an area, but not necessarily the associated budget is running the project.

- **Individual plans for each area:** Each budget holder could develop plans to bring their budgets more back into line and to improve cost control. In this case the budget holders are the ones running the projects. These tend to be smaller plans, but it is not necessarily so.

- **A combination of all the above:** The best cost improvement plans include a bit of all of these. Some, preferably larger centrally run schemes, a set of theme plans and some, generally smaller, schemes undertaken within divisions, directorates or teams to bring their own budgets back into line.

The approach you take will depend on where the opportunity and likely savings are primarily, which you would have established in the last phase. Your job this time is to work with the right individuals and teams to build those up into a future state.

3.2 Prepare Information

The information from phase 2 has shown us where the opportunity is, and we have established how we are going to split the plans in the last step. We now need to prepare the information for each of these groups to help them identify which ones they are going to address.

In preparing the information, you should be able to:

- List the ideas that are relevant to each group that have been identified, with indications of impact and priority.

- Provide supporting data for each, to help them further develop the ideas.

- Provide good practice or industry standard information.

Thus, you may provide individual teams with their own budget information and a prioritised list of schemes that were identified by their team and others relevant to them.

3.3 Develop Changes

We've identified, prioritised, and allocated the ideas, now we need to develop these to identify exactly what we are going to do, and what the future looks like.

The aim is to develop the improvements in the way we do things to ensure that we control costs properly in future (assuming that this is needed) and that we reduce the costs or improve efficiency (in line with our objectives).

We've shown a process that moves through phases and steps, but we don't need to do everything at the same pace. There is going to be quite a difference in the speed we need to, should, and can move at. Easy to implement, low impact ideas with decent benefits can be implemented straight away, with their development and planning done at high speed. If we are in dire straits financially, we may need to focus on these to save our organisation. Large scale, high impact and risky ideas will need to be taken slower (not necessarily slowly) in order to mitigate the risk, plan and implement effectively.

3.3.1 What is a "developed change?"

At this stage we need to ensure that we have enough detail to

- Clearly understand the issue – qualitatively and quantitively.

- Set out exactly how the idea will be solved – what the process, team, systems, organisation, estates etc look like when the issue is solved.

- Any sub-projects/ideas that will add up to the solved issue.

- What is in scope – the processes, teams, systems, etc, that will be affected and what is out of scope?

- What Key Performance Indicators will be affected – what are their values now and what will their values be when solved.

- Expected benefits and when they could be released (normally year by year, but we may need to know approximately which month). This will obviously need to include how much we aim to save.

- Cost of implementation.

Typically, when undertaking a cost management programme, this is all at a reasonably high level, and can be summarised over a page or two. But there are a range of scales you can use, from a single line each in a spreadsheet (which might be appropriate for small, easily identified schemes in team cost reduction plans, to full scale business cases. Completing business cases is a skill in itself, and full cases will be overkill in many cases, but as we said earlier, all schemes are "spend to save" schemes, so you need to apply a degree of rigour to ensure that they are all worth doing.

3.3.2 How do we develop changes

We can develop changes in a range of ways:

- **Data analysis** - picking up on where we left off from our initial analysis in phase 2, we can deepen our understanding of the data. We can analyse variances between teams, use benchmarking, review past experience, undertake item by item analysis – whatever it takes to identify as much information on what the future might look like in terms of money, activity, efficiency, improved key performance indicators and the impact on staff.

- **Team and expert workshops** - sometimes, data isn't available, or on its own it just does not give you the information you need. Bringing together an expert group to look at an issue and develop a solution is a great way to consolidate everything. We talked about Lean rapid improvement events in the last phase – and they can also be used here as one example. But just running a workshop or a series of workshops to consider the solution, and estimating the impact that it will have, is a perfectly valid way to work.

- **Process reviews** - getting into the detail of a process and its attendant technology, facilities and staffing can be a strong way of showing what the future will be like and very accurately identifying the benefits (especially savings).

- **Looking for good practice** - researching how others do things, and the impact that they have had is a great way to envision the future and collect information on the potential benefits. It also gives confidence that it can be done – and they might be able to give you all sorts of useful stuff for the next phase – plans, suppliers, process maps, policies etc. Similar organisations, other industries, regulators, central support teams (e.g. ECIST for Emergency Units), can be a great source. The innovation events we talked about earlier can also be used as a way of generating a future state as well as ideas.

- ***Modelling*** – Developing detailed future state models to complement the current state versions from the previous phase can provide very detailed information on what the impacts of change will be on activity, finance, and staffing.

When undertaking the old-fashioned health turnaround work in the early 2000's, this phase – and this step – was the primary focus of a lot of the work. Generally, they would split an acute or primary care trust into different areas – wards, outpatients, procurement, theatres or prescribing, corporate services, commissioning etc - in fact any of the areas we focus on in the "ideas" section later - and work with a lead in each area to identify the opportunities and work them up into high-level schemes.

Thus, the theatres lead might develop £8m of potential benefit from schemes such as improving utilisation (through implementing a "golden patient" approach, improving booking etc), changing skill mix and standardising the use of orthopaedic implants).

This would typically be done by assigning a central (often an external) lead to each potential work stream to work alongside the organisation lead. And typically this would include the external lead trying desperately to convince the organisation lead to buy-in to as many savings as possible. While the lead tried to avoid buying in to too much, knowing that they'd be the ones left having to implement them. Which wasn't the best way to go about it, but it did at least provide some interesting interplay which tended to avoid over-stating savings by too much. These teams were often not the actual budget owners (or at least not the main budget owners) so it was generally possible to build enough potential plans to meet targets.

Typically, the leads all got together each week in what was sometimes called a "Star Chamber" (although historically this term was used for an oppressive court, so it's hardly apt – or at least shouldn't be). Each lead would set out their progress, and would be challenged by the steering group if they hadn't gone far enough and would be supported as required to develop ideas further – i.e. to find more savings.

This phase also included working with the most challenged teams to help them work out how to balance their budgets. This was often far less easy to do, as these were the actual budget holders, as well as enough of the issues being far more structural and out of the control of these teams to essentially close the door on them feeling able to save enough money.

Finally, this phase also included working with executive teams to develop improved operational grip – for more detail of which you can see the Sustain Success phase, and/or you can consider the learning within the Service Line Management approach.

3.3.3 Undeveloped changes

We should not ignore undeveloped changes. Where we do not develop ideas, there could be various reasons:

- ***We don't believe that it is an issue:*** If the data, or expert opinion, suggests that we do not actually have an issue, then we should record our thinking and evidence, so that we can feed this back to groups who raised it as a problem, and avoid going round the loop again at another time.

- ***It is an issue, but it is not worth going after:*** The data may indicate that the issue is real, but it either isn't cost effective to go after it, or it will be superseded by expected changes. This should be kept on record as a potential issue to address, along with the current thinking on its value.

- ***It is not high enough priority to go forward:*** The issue is worthwhile, but we have bigger things to go after. These ideas should be retained, alongside the supporting analysis, for use in future years, or should the chosen plans fail to meet benefit expectations.

3.4 Align Changes to Challenge

This step can be done now, but it's really the sort of thing you need to keep doing all through this phase. We are trying to meet a challenge - and if the set of schemes that comes back doesn't align with the challenge, then we have a problem. Whilst technically you might miss the point by, for example, generating income when you should be saving cost, that is unlikely. What is most likely is that you just won't save enough.

And it gets worse – at this stage, any savings that you identify are not going to get implemented. There's a hierarchy of savings opportunity, which we call the law of diminishing savings:

1. Results of data analysis.
2. Amount of savings once experts have considered the data.
3. Amount agreed with the team responsible for delivery.
4. Amount team agrees with once detailed planning and consultation has been done.
5. Amount delivered in reality.

And at the moment we are at stage 3 – which means we will get some drop off. So even if you have identified enough savings, you will need to leave a contingency in place. The level of contingency will come down to how much confidence you have in the plans – but you probably need around 50% more savings at this stage than you expect to realise. It's a fact of life that savings never actually go up the further down the process you go. In addition, implementation should be resourced properly, as we see later, so we should either be estimating costs as part of the savings (giving a net figure) or adding more to the gross target.

So, check that you have enough savings, and that the other objectives have been met - otherwise, you'll have to go back round the process. In reality, you'll go round this circle a few times probably, as delivery teams don't tend to push the envelope the first time unless they are really bought in to solving the problem.

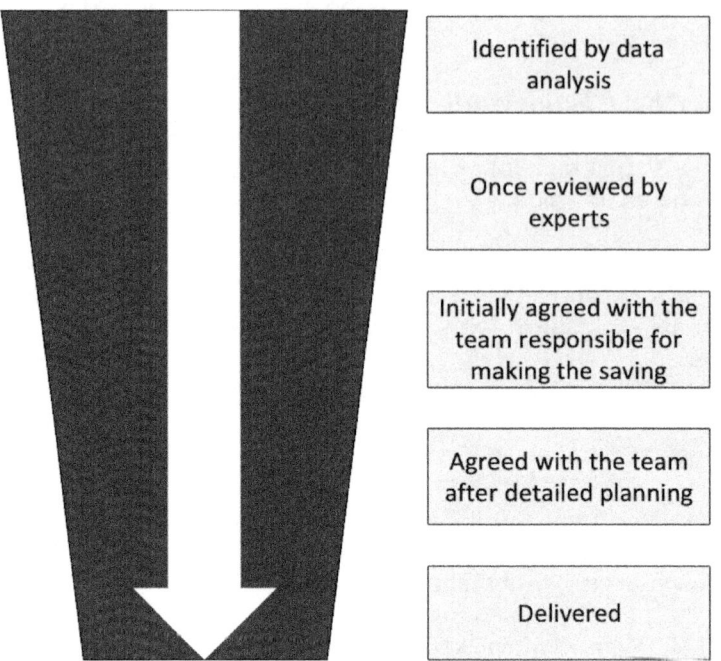

Figure 7: Law of diminishing savings

When you go back round the process, you can't just force people to come up with bigger numbers, that isn't the point of this - all you will do is to increase the likelihood that you won't deliver the numbers. In many organisations where we have worked, agreeing with plans that people know won't work is often a defence mechanism that staff use to get through a meeting, and they worry about the ramifications later.

This is another reason why the check against objectives should be happening constantly in the previous step.

3.5 Assess impacts

Once the schemes are developed (again, this step is best done alongside the previous ones) we need to assess the impact of the change. Your organisation should be able to tell you what assessments it expects – these are typically Quality Impact Assessments (QIA) and Diversity Impact Assessments (DIA). Both are important - so if your organisation doesn't have one, then you should at least consider the following:

- Will this increase the work of staff without raising staff levels, make their jobs worse or reduce their opportunities to grow? What benefits does this change bring to staff that at least offset the disbenefits?

- Will this change adversely affect any individual group, especially those covered by the Equality Act? This includes staff and patients. What does this change do to actively reduce inequalities?

- Will this change reduce the quality of services to service users? Will it reduce access to service-users?

- Will this change degrade the environment so that service-user and staff safety and experience is impacted in the future (e.g. lower standards of training)?

- How does this change align with the objectives of the Trust (where not covered above). How does it actively advance these objectives?

- How does the change impact on other areas of the organisation? Does it follow central policies (HR, IT etc)?

We want to ensure that the change to improve cost, is not adversely affecting the rest of the efficiency triangle. So if we are reducing cost, we aren't reducing access for example.

Check each proposed change against these criteria. The results of this may mean that you need to reconsider the financial impact of the change – or may raise things to consider in the next phase when you plan and implement the change. Just because something does have adverse effects doesn't necessarily mean that we don't go ahead with the change - sometimes we need to play off different parts of the efficiency triangle. But we should do that in a mindful way, rather than just plough on causing chaos regardless, and we should look for mitigations in all cases where this does not increase cost.

4.5

Phase Four - Plan & implement

4.1 Document case

It's always good to build a report, presentation pack or business case to document the project to date. It should include the reasons for doing it, the objectives, the work done, the ideas funnel, prioritisation, the plan areas and the future case for each one. This document will be the case for change, the vision for the future and the basis for planning - and is useful as a basis for all the communications to your commissioners or providers, service-users, staff, investors, regulators, etc.

So, write up where you are at this stage, and keep it up to date as you plan the detailed actions.

At this point you may also want to consider a formal review with the steering group to agree whether we can proceed to planning. But that's only if you are following some sort of weird, old-school waterfall approach to delivery – we like (as you can tell) to keep this pretty loose – you should have been planning the obvious ideas ages ago, not waiting for some dusty committee to sign off moving to planning…

4.2 Allocate and manage resources

You might be looking at these steps and thinking – "Well that's all pretty obvious" – and this reminder that you need to resource projects is probably one of those times. But this is another time when we see, time and again, that projects are given to people without the time, without the skills and without the support.

4.3 Plan detailed actions

Every good project and business case needs a good plan.

4.3.1 Develop.individual plans

For each of the changes, the project team or lead need to develop a step-by-step delivery and action plan. This should be documented in a properly annotated Gantt chart and include:

- What each step is.

- Who is doing the step.

- When the step is going to be done.

You can also consider critical paths and lots of other fun stuff – we said we were going to rely on your project management approach, and this is one place where we will just say – build a plan.

When building a plan, it is worthwhile ensuring that it stretches well into the future. Any plans should include quick actions on "just do it" changes and then a range of short and long-term plans. If you have done a comprehensive look for opportunities, then you have taken up a lot of people's time and effort (and spent money if you have brought in experts to help) so you don't want to do that every year – but you might not be able to solve everything in one year. In that case, you need a long term plan.

4.3.2 Bring the plans together

Each plan needs to be reviewed centrally to ensure that they do meet the requirements – the key element being that the delivery of benefit is occurring quickly enough to align with the overall plan. But assuming that everyone has done their job properly to this stage we also need to align the plans against each other. This means checking:

- Will delivery or support teams be overwhelmed? Are they all asking for HR help at the same time, for example?

- Are there interdependencies between projects and do these all align so that one project won't be waiting for another to get to a certain point?

Yet again, this checking can be done while the plans are being developed, so that potential issues can be flagged early. Otherwise, this review step may result in another round of re-doing plans. Which might delay projects in itself...

4.4 Implement plans

Let's face it, you lost interest in this topic once you'd developed the plans. If we had a penny for every time we'd helped clients develop a plan and then not been asked to help implement it, then we'd have more than £1. Which doesn't seem a lot, but it is more than 100 times between us.

It's probably why we also haven't got much to write here. This step is going to be one of the biggest but there isn't much we can say - all you need to do is actually implement the plans that you developed in the last step. Simple...?

4.5 Monitor, evaluate and adjust

This is the final step in the actual initial programme. And yet again, Captain Obvious comes to the rescue here by telling us that you need to continually monitor the implementation of the plan, as well as the financial situation to see whether we need to adjust what we are doing.

4.5.1 Monitoring

This includes:

- **Evaluate Performance**: Using KPIs to measure the outcomes of the initiatives against the original objectives. This analysis should include financial savings, operational efficiencies gained, benefits for staff, and any improvements in service delivery expected.

- **Gather Feedback**: Collect feedback from stakeholders involved in or affected by the initiatives. This includes employees, service-users, commissioners, providers, and external partners, providing a holistic view of the impact.

4.5.2 Evaluating

Evaluating includes assessing and documenting the lessons learned - Identify what worked well and areas for improvement. Documenting these lessons is crucial for refining future cost reduction efforts and for sharing knowledge within the organisation.

We may need to respond if:

- Plans are running behind.

- Savings aren't coming out – this will be the main one.

- We are spending more money in areas we didn't expect – sometimes cost reduction is like the game, "Whack-a-mole", as costs rise in areas that you aren't currently hammering.

- Costs are rising within projects.

4.5.3 Adjusting

This involves making necessary adjustments to existing initiatives - scaling successful projects, modifying underperforming ones, or discontinuing efforts that did not meet objectives.

In each case, the actions will depend on the source and seriousness of the issue – but good responses will always include trying to resolve the specific problem, as well as looking for more opportunity elsewhere. In some cases, you may have a plan for next year that you can bring forward.

4.6

Phase Five - Sustaining Success

Reducing cost, improving efficiency and getting a grip of your costs and operations is a long game. It's a bit like dieting – a crash diet might get you thin for a bit, but the pounds will come back slowly but surely. The secret is to change your long-term dietary and exercise habits – or in this case, to change your approach to money and efficiency. Look out for our next book – "The Book of Health & Care Manager Diet Tips" – it'll be in the shops for Christmas.

Cost management is a long game. And it's about as difficult as dieting. Believe us, we've done both.

This phase is less about a set of steps, and more a list of areas that you should address to ensure ongoing operational grip of cost and operations. It consists of six areas of focus.

5.1 Improve governance

There could be lots of reasons why costs are out of line with income, but it is more than likely that one major reason will be that, until now, the Executive as a whole has not monitored costs effectively and addressed the issues quickly.

Typically, finance will have a clear handle on the cashflow and cost and income variances, and thus so will the Finance Director – although this cannot be assumed. It is also likely that the Finance Director has told the rest of the Executive that things are not going well financially. Normally, the lack of cost control has come about because finance cannot wave a magic wand and bring things back into line – they need the help of the rest of the Executive and their operational teams. And because these operational teams may be more worried about the rest of the Efficiency Triangle elements (staff, service-user access and quality) or because they don't understand or really care about finance, things have not improved.

No matter the reason why cost management has gone wrong in the organisation, you need to check and probably enhance the cost management governance.

When the authors were engaged to help organisations reduce cost, they were normally bought in by an executive team that didn't know how to deal with it and wanted expert help. That team were thus focussed on this as an issue (we used to say that they were experiencing "pain"). That allowed us to put in place governance changes quickly and easily – but you may need to be a bit more convincing.

Good governance elements include ensuring that:

- Clear accountability and responsibility for cost management (control and bringing costs/income back into line) is set at executive level. That means:

  - Bring clear what everyone's accountability and responsibility is as a group and as individuals.

  - Identifying specifically who is responsible for the programme to bring things into line and implement greater control – sometimes called a "Turnaround Director" but, to be honest, anyone on the Executive can take this role (the difference from business as usual is that they have a team that is working on it this time).

- A weekly meeting (initially, moving to monthly as things get less desperate) is in place so that the Executive can understand where the organisation is on its journey towards cost management. This includes having a standard agenda, minuting or writing up an action plan, checking action progress, reviewing metrics and reviewing progress reports – and, very importantly, time to discuss how to deal with issues.

   When we were in full project mode, we made this meeting a bit more engaging by having the information displayed in the executive corridor and walking between information boards showing the issues. Of course, this can just be a part of normal governance meetings if you like.

- Clear progress reports need to be provided to the executive, showing whether projects are on track to deliver, and if the expected benefits are being realised. Someone needs to be checking how projects are doing, and this is often the role of a Programme Management Office. Again, this is an area of expertise that may already exist in your organisation, and there are a wealth of systems, training and experts out there to support in setting these up. There is often a challenge between bureaucracy and control to be overcome – but the key thing is that the executive should know where things are going well and where they are not, so that they can plan to address them.

- Clear metrics are reported to the executive. The exact metrics depend on what you are trying to address (see later). Someone needs the responsibility for developing these, and presenting them in a way that allows the executive to quickly see the issues. The metrics should not just be "lagging" - they shouldn't just show what has happened. They should also include "leading" indicators that help identify when things may start going wrong (an example of a "lagging" indicator could be the amount of staff turnover, whereas a "leading" indicator for this could be staff morale, or the number of appraisals completed). This is a whole area of expertise in itself, which your data teams may already have.

- The objectives of the business include the management of cost – although this is one that can take a bit longer to put in place, and one not all people agree with.

5.2 Monitor cost

We call this "monitor cost" but it could also be "grip your operations". A key part of ongoing cost management is, well, managing your costs. You need to ensure that you have a clear approach and the right skills to manage costs across your organisation – and in doing so, monitor such linked things as the state of your workforce and the activity and service levels you are delivering. This can include:

- Ensuring that you maintain the good practice control elements that you put in place as part of the work, including:

    - Demand and capacity modelling, maintaining a clear view on how much activity has been commissioned or expected versus the amount that has been delivered.

- Workforce modelling, maintaining a linked view to demand, showing the requirement to staffing.

- Benchmarking of performance with updated benchmarks.

- Enhancing demand and capacity modelling to include expected inefficiency metrics (cancellations, Did Not Attends (DNAs),, utilisation, etc).

- Implement strong, true budget management:

  - Clear budgets for all teams, based on an understanding of expected activity.

  - All budgets agreed with teams and the budget owner.

  - Clear cost and income information available quickly so that issues can be identified and options to reduce cost implemented quickly. The harder it is to find data, the less control you'll have over cost.

  - Training for staff on budget management and cost control.

  - Identification of variances from budget, taking into account activity differences.

- Focus on addressing key indicators of efficiency – cancellations, productivity, utilisation, DNAs, variance to budgets, variance to planned activity per staff type etc. By not allowing these indicators to get outside reasonable parameters, you can help prevent cost getting out of control.

5.3 Annual programme refresh

There tends to be annual pressure to reduce costs and improve efficiency, and programmes can start to run out of steam. In the Service Line Management approach, teams were encouraged to update their plans every year and their strategy every 3-5 years. By reviewing the current plan with the teams, adding new plans, stopping programmes that are no longer bringing enough benefits, re-assigning leads and generally giving everything a new feel for the next year, we can reinvigorate the programmes – and reconnect teams to the reasons why they are doing them.

5.4 Build capacity and capability in management teams

You should also focus on the skills of your people. Let's face it, many health and care companies have not focused on the skills of their managers. There actually aren't enough managers in the English NHS, for example, despite the national press' weird obsession with how much is being spent on managers. And the Agenda for Change contracts drive managers to constantly look for promotion in order to be able to earn more money - and that drives a lot of churn.

We need to ensure that we have a stable, valued set of managers that have the right skills to do the job – and the time to manage. This requires a proper development programme, with required skills for different jobs, skill needs assessments and funded development programmes.

5.5 Develop culture

As we quoted before, "Culture east strategy for breakfast". The best approaches to cost management are about improving the culture. Ensuring people care about meeting updates, that they have the tools to do it, and feel free to make changes in a supportive environment - rather than holding a team to account when it doesn't care about budgets and is scared to make changes for fear of censure even if they knew what to do. Alongside this, the desire and ability to care about service-users – to want to provide fair access for everybody, and to do the right job for the people they service, while providing great service is very important. As is the desire to care for their own teams - not to drive short-term overwork at the expense of long term fulfilment and development.

All of this comes from a complex mix of current and past behaviours of senior and front-line staff, the staff that have been hired, the rewards that have been given, meetings that have been held, etc. It's a complex area and won't be put in place overnight (but can be dismantled quickly). So, a focus on developing the culture is important. It's not our main area of expertise, but we know enough to know what we don't know and to ask you to ensure that you have the best help (internal or external) and the right desire to make this journey. There's that "journey" again - we're all on journey's now…

Specific things you can do though, throughout the programme include:

- **Embedding Changes into Organisational Culture**: Integrate successful cost-saving practices into the standard operating procedures and culture of the organisation. This ensures that the benefits are maintained and that a continuous improvement mindset is fostered among all staff.

- **Promoting a Culture of Efficiency**: Recognise and reward teams and individuals who contribute significantly to the cost reduction efforts. Use these success stories to inspire ongoing commitment to efficiency and innovation across the organisation.

- **Co-planning for the Future**: Use the insights gained from this cycle of cost reduction initiatives to inform strategic planning and future projects. This includes setting new targets for cost savings and efficiency improvements working with the teams who did the work this time, rather than just top down.

- **Service Line Management:** Have a look at the resources we have flagged for Service Line Management. There is quite a lot of useful stuff in there to think about.

5.6 Set up required teams and resources

Finally, you may want to set up or bolster the teams that are needed for ongoing success. These include:

- Transformation, change or programme teams to provide expert capacity to deliver change. In themselves, these teams can become targets for cost reduction if they do not make a difference, so the focus will probably be on having relatively small teams working to have a big impact, but many organisations build large expert groups to help deliver projects.

- Training teams to ensure that there is the accountability and capacity for developing and maintaining the skills of managers in the control and reduction of cost, and the improvement of efficiency.

- Enhances support teams to ensure that there is enough finance, HR, digital and other resource available to ensure that cost control remains on track. This generally involves redirecting transactional resources to more supportive resources through the improvements in process and technical efficiency undertaken in the cost reduction programme, rather than hiring more support staff.

As noted, these areas can become inefficient and thus become targets for cost reduction in the future, so their effectiveness needs to be governed as part of business as usual cost management.

This phase closes the loop of the cost reduction program by helping ensure that benefits are lasting and contribute to the organisation's continuous improvement culture. It sets the stage for an ongoing process of evaluation, learning, and adaptation, which is essential for health and care organisations aiming to remain responsive to changing environments and service-user needs.

SECTION 5

THE IDEAS

"Alright, enough messing around – give me the list of ideas so I can save money", I hear you say. Well, if that's what you want, this is the section for you. Of course, health and social care is quite a big area. It includes everything and everyone in Integrated Care, including voluntary care, primary care, social care, secondary health care, tertiary health care. In that it includes charities, dentist practices, GP practices, hospices, care homes, community hospital providers, mental health providers, community care organisations, private and public and third sector organisations, ambulance trusts, large and small organisations, pharmacies, Primary Care Networks – and that's if you don't get into the wider Integrated Care System and start bringing in the police, education etc etc etc.

We've tried to keep these ideas as generic as possible, but there are some specific examples of each that apply to only some of these and are a little more specialised. Radiology, Theatres, Wards, Virtual Wards, Clinics etc are specific only to certain organisations, but they do have to be considered here. If there is something that isn't relevant to you, just ignore it. And if we've missed something big that is relevant to you, let us know and we will update the list for everyone.

Right, on with the list. First, the headings:

5.1

The Headings

We are going to consider our ideas under the following headings:

- **Tactical cost review.** A set of ideas based around quick actions you can do to reduce costs in your organisation. Tactical cost review is at the most short-term and tactical end of the spectrum of cost control elements – with transformation at the more fun end. It covers the things that you need to do when you are in "turnaround" and need to cut costs quickly – some of which will reduce efficiency in the long term but might be needed for organisational survival. Within tactical cost reduction there are three key themes: (a) Address known issues, (b) Review quick opportunities to reduce cost and (3) Short term cuts.

- **Grip Operations.** Operational grip is about making sure that everything is working in the organisation the way it should be. If we had the right amount of operational control in the first place, we probably wouldn't have the trouble with costs that we have. So, we should do this one no matter how transformational we are thinking of getting. This heading includes five themes: The Operational Grip process and gripping each of Demand, Staff costs, Income and non-pay costs.

- **Plan Workforce.** Circa 70% of hospital costs are staff, and I'll bet that's higher in social care. Developing a clear view on the staff that you need, and ensuring that you have the best, and most cost effective, levels and mix you can have, are all covered in this section - and we're not talking about staff cuts. Workforce planning is fundamental to cost control and cost reduction. Building on the demand planning that you do as part of operational grip, this heading focuses on translating that into the right staff at the right time, and on keeping those staff so you don't spend a fortune on recruitment and re-training. There are two parts - some general considerations for job planning, rostering, flexible working, grade and role alignment, sickness, bank & agency optimisation and staff retention, and some specific role considerations for certain staff groups.

- **Manage non-pay spend:** Whilst circa 70% of health and care costs are staff, 30% is in non-pay - and this area can be a lot less painful to realise as it does not include putting less money in staff members' hands. Optimising the spend on non-pay spend of all sorts should be a key part of any cost control plan. Managing non pay cost themes include the control of pharmacy spend, procurement, energy costs and taxes.

- **Improve Efficiency.** Improving your process, technology and facilities can help optimise the use of all your resources, including your staff. This section covers the generic ideas for improving your processes. There are also thousands of specific process improvement ideas that you could consider. This should be the absolute core of any cost control and efficiency programme. So much cost is based on inefficient processes, demand in the wrong places and a failure to build innovations into practice. Process improvement can be targeted at efficiency, and at reducing the need (or changing the type) of staff and consumables needed. Improve efficiency as a heading is focused on: The administration, use of resources and the improvement of process, estates & digital. There is also a section which is very specific to providers including theatres, bed-based services, diagnostics, and many more.

- **Align the back office.** A lot of controllable spend sits outside the direct delivery of health and care - and corporate, support and back office spend can often get out of control through a lack of alignment to the core operations of the organisation. A key part of a cost control programme should be the review of the value of these functions, their strengthening where they can help the front-line be more efficient and their removal when they are in the way. Specific themes under this heading include the consideration of spend in all main corporate areas (finance, HR, executive teams etc) as well as a focus on billing, business development, outsourcing, and compliance.

- **Transform.** The transformation heading contains the bigger ideas generally, focusing on revolution in the approach to cost control. Specific themes under this heading include: Organisational approaches to transformation, system shape change to reduce secondary care involvement, transformational changes and focusing on prevention rather than care to reduce reliance on the health and care system. Any cost control plans should include some element of the transformational to give the plan some excitement, but bold change could be at the heart of truly transformative efficiency programmes.

Within each area, we consider the main topics, and present a set of ideas.

These ideas have been included in a cost reduction plan somewhere at some point, but it is up to you what you want to put in your plan. If you don't like something, or you've already done it, then move on to the next one...

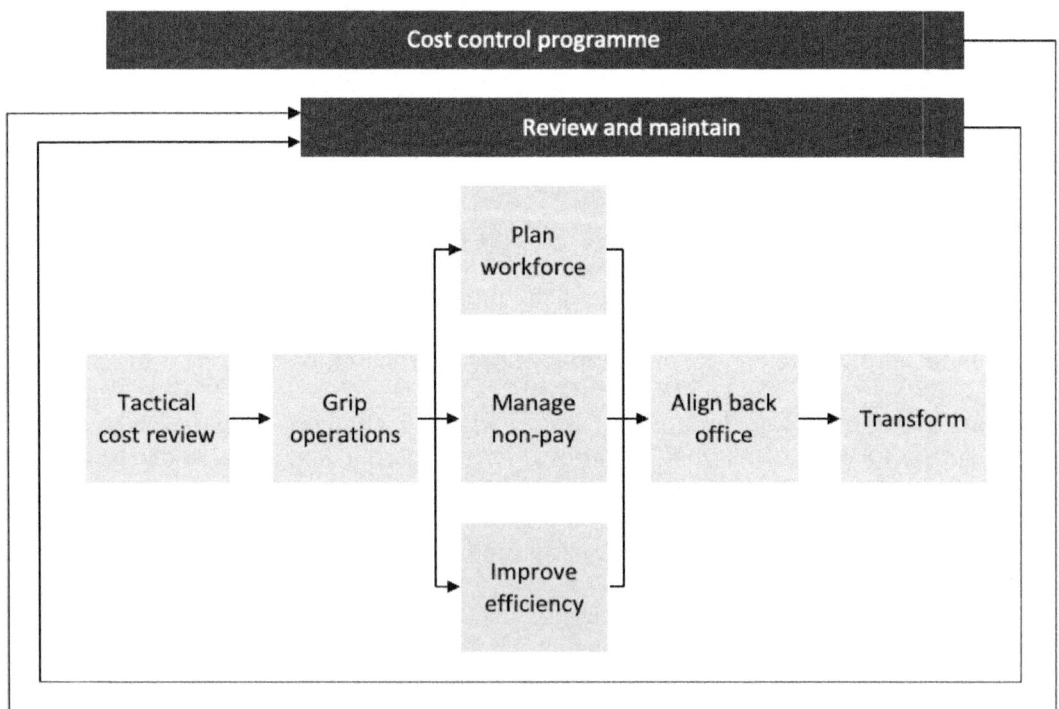

Figure 8: Cost management headings as part of the approach

Figure 9: Cost management themes

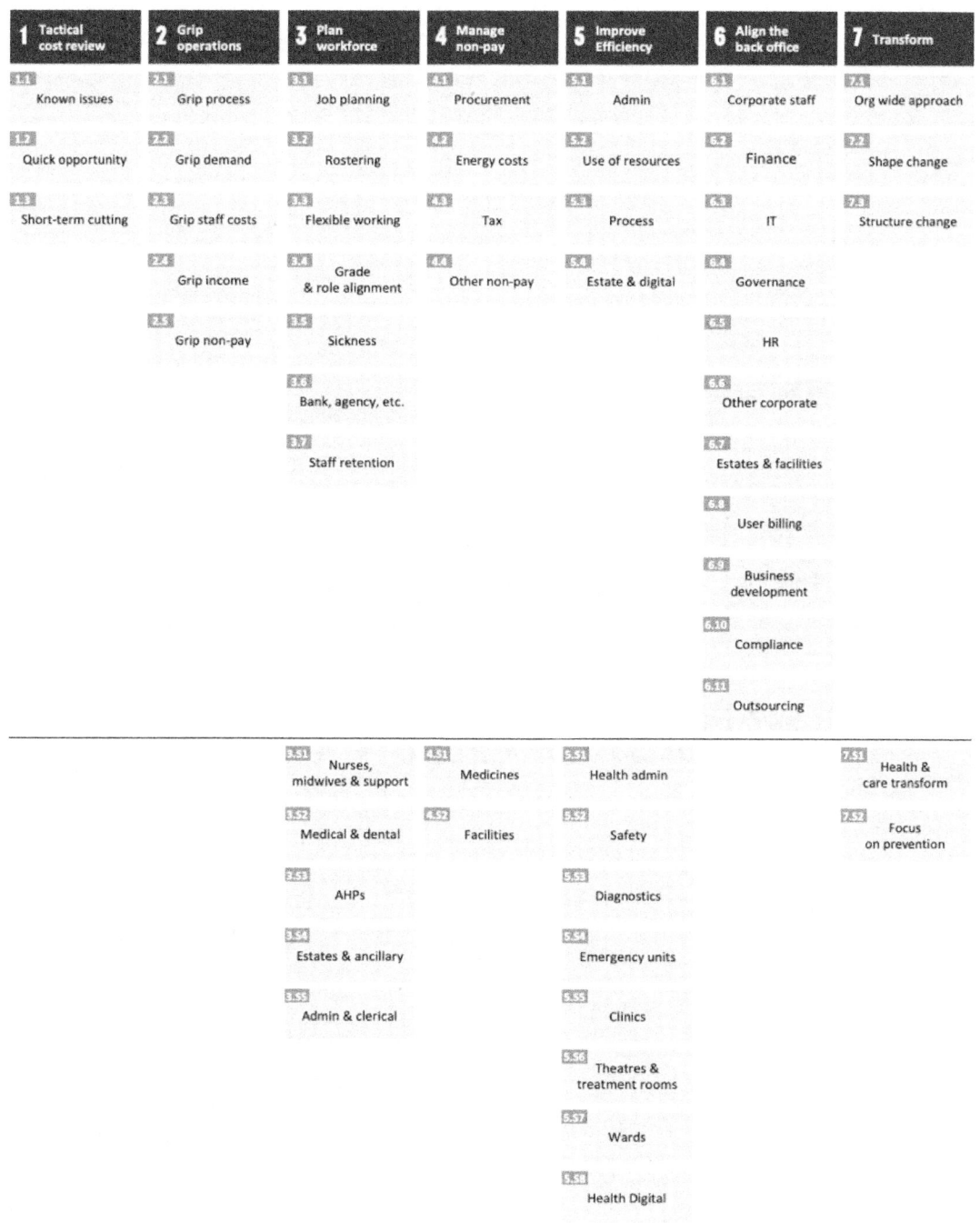

5.2 Tactical Cost Review

Within tactical cost reduction there are three key themes:

- Address known issues.

- Review quick opportunities to reduce cost.

- Short term cuts.

The whole aim of tactical cost reduction is to quickly bring down costs. This is where we get closest to the old-fashioned turnaround ideas, and include the old favourite "stop providing biscuits" and the (it could be argued) somewhat evil, "parking charges for disabled people". Now, we've included them here because they are part of the cost reduction canon, but (a) we don't tend to include them unless staff or service-users really want them (unlikely) and (b) tactical cost reduction should be about so much more than that. It should be about undoing the damage that a lack of control has thus far done. It's a chance to review and address bad deals and to sort out the things that everyone knows we should have sorted out by now.

A tactical cost review programme should include a review of opportunities, specific plans to address each one, and then an ongoing programme to deliver them. This can get tough, as deals aren't easy to change and intractable staff issues are, well, intractable – but if you don't think about the options, plan to deliver them and then take action to change them, then you'll never do them.

THEME 1.1
Address known issues

So, whilst we generally hate this section, this theme is actually a good one, and one that we like to use when we can. If you ask people for their help, then not only do you get great ideas you wouldn't otherwise know about, but people actually feel better about the change and are less likely to fight you on it. And there are always things that people know are wasteful and it annoys them that they aren't being addressed – so why not sort that out.

In one care home Colin worked in, the staff were always complaining about the heating being far too hot in the staff areas – so they had the heating on and the windows open all the time. The building supervisor had always said it was too hard to change – but when the managers focused on this, cheap changes were implemented to stop it.

Specific ideas for this theme include:

- **Ask staff for their ideas:** Introduce a scheme to ask the staff for their engagement in working out what quick ideas they have for reducing cost. This includes:

    - Start with your own list of problems that you know about.

    - Spending time to explain the problem.

    - Asking staff for help through a suggestion scheme.

- Reviewing and prioritising answers.

- Building a business case and programme of change, backed with metrics.

- Delivering the savings.

- Undertaking "you said, we did" type feedback to people who engaged.

- Executive-level review of progress and completion.

- **Ask suppliers or providers for ideas as to how to save money:** As well as engaging staff, suppliers and providers can also be engaged in helping solve the problems. Is there anything that we can do as an organisation to reduce the costs for suppliers so that they can pass savings onto us? How can we help them meet their targets for mutual benefit? Would they be willing to agree to a % reduction? Again, a proper programme to list suppliers, prioritise conversations, agree the questions and approach, recording the impacts etc is needed in order to help ensure that the benefits are realised.

THEME 1.2
Review quick opportunities to reduce cost

So, you can ask your suppliers and staff, and you can work on the things you know about. But there are areas that have come up in other people's areas that are worth thinking about. Go through this list and see what might work for you:

- **Quick sale or lease of unused buildings**: Buildings, even when empty and unused, have an impact on the finances. Unfortunately, this isn't an easy area as depending on weird financial shenanigans, the sale of buildings can actually have a negative impact on finances – but a good look at unused estate by your finance and estate teams could lead to savings.

- **Review bank and agency spend:** We will look at bank, agency and locum spend as well as overtime and additional payments of all sorts. But if you haven't done it already, getting a small group together to examine the historical use of bank and agency staffing, and looking for quick opportunities to optimise it, is certainly worthwhile. Look at the section on this for more details, but some companies will do a free (or at least a low cost) review for you, in the hope that they'll be able to sell you their solution, and we have used many of these in the past.

- **Review all contracts** to see what you should be getting and make sure you are getting it (or negotiate a reduction). Another relatively quick one (and some companies will again do a free or low-cost review) is to look at all of your contracts, especially the big PFI ones and work out a few things:

    - Have you overpaid for anything?

- Have providers over-delivered and been paid extra as a result? Have they under-delivered?

- Have you been promised things you haven't had? Can you get a refund for the past, and either a reduction for the future (if you don't need it) or at least get them to do it (and thus reduce cost if you've been doing it yourself)?

- Are there break points to get out of contracts that you might be able to source more cheaply.

Especially if the suppliers haven't been helpful when you asked them for a reduction earlier…

Obviously, this whole area of contract control is a very large one for Local Authorities or similar that deliver a lot of services via contracts.

- ***Consider all spend that you are not contracted to***: Anything that you are getting that you are not contracted to should be looked at by a working group and opportunities to reduce cost identified. If you didn't ask for it, didn't contract for, or produce a purchase order for if that is the agreed practice etc, should be considered and stopped. This can include longer term deals that may be costly now, even if they would be more cost effective in the future (assuming you are after cost reduction rather than efficiency).

- ***Review all programme spend:*** You may have lots of internal (and some external) projects going on. These cost money in terms of staff and other expenditure, but also take up headroom. Pausing or stopping programmes based on their priority can result in the freeing up of programme and project staff that will be needed for the control of costs. Again, this can be short sighted, so is best done based on a good cost/benefit analysis – but lots of companies and teams have "zombie projects" that are shambling along not producing anything (nor ever likely to). It's time to get out the stakes and garlic. Although that's for vampires. How do you kill zombies? Please write in.

- ***Review and reduce subscription costs:*** Any money being spent on membership of groups that take up time for little value, magazines that don't really get read or anything similar, computer licenses for your Commodore 64 (ask your parents), can be a drain – get a list of these, stop them if it makes sense, and try to get a rebate for whatever is left of the year (good luck with that, but hey, it's worth a try). Maybe even negotiating a payment holiday for the year – these companies do not want to lose future years' money for the sake of a short term issue. It's a bit like when you cancel your broadband package at home.

- ***Review tax costs:*** You can often get a free review by experts on your tax spend, which has to be worth a quick look. There is some fun stuff you can do with taxes, especially staff taxes, that are worth looking at depending on what the government is looking to stop or start people doing.

With all reviews and contractual matters, you need to engage legal support to make sure that you won't end up paying more through misunderstanding the legal position. So, you need to weigh that cost and risk up in any decisions. Supplier relationships should also be positive, so pickiness may have a downside - but if they have been taking advantage, no matter how accidentally, then they haven't been meeting their relationship responsibilities

- **Complete budget review:** One of the things we always do in situations where we need to actually reduce cost, is to look at budgets. If you do a complete review of budgets by theme and area you can spot where (a) they are going over budget – and thus you need to go in there, educate, investigate the issues and either get them in line or reset the budget; or (b) they are underspending – which may represent a chance to get them not to spend money this year. Resetting their budget because they are underspending is unfair and drives profligate behaviour, but if their budget is overstuffed then you can adjust it down as well for future years. But if someone is actively monitoring a budget to bring it in underspent, then that person and team deserve rewards. If we gave people half the money they saved on budgets – well, we'd have a whole new set of problems probably, but we'd definitely get savings against budgets…

- **Minimise energy spend with quick actions:** There is a whole host of things that you can do to reduce energy spend fairly quickly. These include:

    - **Turn off lights and heat in unused buildings**: A common issue is the uncontrolled use of energy. The impact of this can be complex depending on whether the organisation is responsible for this spend or not – but, assuming that they are, then identifying unused areas and physically restrict the use of utilities in those areas, or proactively monitor what is being used.

    - **Undertake an energy-efficiency scheme**: Deploying your facilities team to look for opportunities to improve efficiency and engage staff in keeping costs low is a relatively low-cost way to improve energy efficiency. We have seen this be the focus of a single, enthusiastic staff member who runs around putting up posters, analysing usage, spotting when lights are left on etc – and single-handedly changing the ethos of an organisation. And getting in trouble with infection control teams at the same time for putting posters in wards, but you can't please everyone.
    ..

    - **Get professional help to identify the opportunities to reduce spend**: Some companies offer low cost or free reviews to reduce cost – and could be engaged on a no-reduction no-fee basis to implement changes. Make sure that you've done the obvious stuff first though – don't make it easy for them…

    - **Switching to LED Lighting:** With energy costs high, anything that you can do to quickly get the bill down is well worth considering. One thing that you can do is to replace traditional bulbs with energy-efficient LED lighting throughout the organisation. Obviously, new bulbs cost money, but there may be grants available to replace old bulbs and you may be able to sell them on if they are still in some sort of decent condition.

    - **Turning Off Equipment When Not in Use:** Ensuring all non-essential medical and office equipment is turned off after hours to save energy. If infection control allows it, then stickers and notices letting people know how much energy gets used when equipment gets left on is a great one. In the nursing home that Colin's in-laws are in, they have notices saying how much it costs to leave a food heater on overnight – and this makes people think. You can also monitor energy use overnight, especially if you have local metering, which allows you to address poor behaviour.

- **Optimising Thermostat Settings:** Adjusting thermostat settings for optimal energy use, especially during off-hours or in less-used spaces. How many times are you in a roasting room with the window open at work? At the voluntary organisation where Colin's mum works, it's like a furnace in the room all the time. That can't be efficient, right? Again, monitoring is your friend here to see where the issues are.

- **Regular Filter Replacements and HVAC Maintenance:** HVAC stands for Heating, Ventilation and Air Conditioning. Routine maintenance of HVAC systems to ensure they are operating efficiently can reduce their operating costs (and improve their lifecycles and reduce maintenance costs).

- **Address printing costs:** Printing costs are another area where costs can be cut relatively painlessly (relative to reduce staff at least). There are a few things you can do in this area, including:

  - Setting printers to double-sided printing as default to reduce paper consumption.

  - Using the cheapest paper that the printers can cope with.

  - Engaging staff in the campaign to reduce the use of paper, asking them to consider what they are sending out to service-users (the amount of time we have seen someone holding a sheaf of papers they have been sent, wandering around a hospital lost because in all of the rubbish they haven't actually been told where to go for their appointment in a way that a human could understand....). And why does Colin's GP always print something out in a practice, when the physio just emails him the exercises? Answers on a postcard please...

  - Engaging people to consider how we could use email and other mechanisms to communicate with service-users and promoting the use of emails for internal communications.

Colin has been lucky enough to work with some truly inspirational leaders at lots of health organisations. At Sheffield Teaching Hospitals, one individual sparked change through a simple campaign against using fax machines – why don't we have the same thing about eliminating paper?

- **Using reusable items where safe:** Engaging with the procurement teams to identify where we are spending money on disposable items, and working out whether re-useable items might be more cost effective. This is a tough area, but we do find that many staff get frustrated with what gets thrown away (and attracts a wastage cost), when there are more robust alternatives.

- **Water-saving fixtures:** Installing low-flow taps / faucets and toilets to reduce water usage and looking at areas of high usage can bring down water costs.

THEME 1.3
Short-term cuts

We really hate this list, as it represents the worst end of cost reduction – a thing that we've already established is not really what you are trying to achieve in anything but the most specific of circumstances. But this is a book of cost management, so we have to include it. Let's get this out of the way before we get onto the actually useful ideas. Some (largely stupid) ideas include:

- **Review and reduce training costs / course fees:** Our view is - do not cancel training. Staff don't get trained enough (and Colin runs a training company, so he may be a little biased). However, training is an area that takes up time and costs money, so maybe a holiday while you get the money back on track is an option. Don't do it though.

- **Review and reduce travel and subsistence:** An old favourite, which again can do more harm than good in terms of staff relationship, is to review the use of personal expenses. The Head of Security where Colin once worked told him that everyone fiddles their expenses, and whilst this somewhat less than rose-tinted view of the world might not be completely accurate, looking at this area of spend and reducing it is always an option.

- **Car parking charges:** Not strictly a cut, but you could put the car parking (or other) prices up if you get the income from doing that (rather than it going to a third party, for example). Obviously, you should consider the impact on service-users and the potential that it will be so expensive that you lose money overall, but an assessment of this always used to be part of the plans in the old days.

- **Bottom of the barrel:** If you are channelling your pre-ghost Ebenezer Scrooge, then you won't be alone, because actual cost reduction plans have included a set of schemes that would have made him think twice. They include:

    - No tea and biscuits in meetings – and whilst health and care organisations may not want to offer fattening snacks (there is such a thing as passive eating you know, not all of us have an iron-will when faced with a Bourbon biscuit) taking refreshments away in all circumstances is quite Scrooge-like.

    - Holiday celebrations – Go full scrooge with a complete removal of Christmas (and other holiday) celebrations.

    - Make disabled badge holders pay for parking. Some places do, many don't.

  Bottom of the barrel ideas are any little thing that you can cut without affecting income.

- **Voluntary redundancy or MARS schemes:** If you don't need people, then why did you hire them in the first place? Well, a lack of control at the right time is probably the answer. But if you need to reduce ongoing staff cost quickly – and (crucially) if someone else is picking up the redundancy costs, then a VR scheme is a way to get bums off seats. But, like all ideas in the short-term cuts group, it really only makes sense in very certain circumstances. Even when you need to make redundancies due to a major change (e.g. if there was a sudden drop in demand), then voluntary redundancies seem to me to be a great way to lose your best staff…

Right, that's that horrible lot out of the way – onto something more useful - "operational grip".

5.3 Grip Operations

Operational grip is such a great phrase, because it says what it is – gripping your operations. It's not loose, it's gripped. Controlled. It could also summon up images of Darth Vader's gloved hand, which is going a bit far towards the darker side of things – this isn't some evil overlord approach, this is about making sure that everything is working.

If you don't control your operations – check that your income is on target, your costs aren't exceeding budgets, staff aren't hired when not needed and are relocated when they aren't, etc – then you end up in the mess that lots of organisations end up in at some point – a need to start "controlling costs".

Lots of people like a bit of control. If you are the sort of person who works hard and does what you are asked (maybe more), then you like to see your effort rewarded, and want to see the lazy sausages elsewhere getting prodded a bit. You don't want to overdo it, but you don't want to under do it either.

In many large NHS organisations that Colin has worked in, you have the worst of both worlds – no real control but hundreds of rules and occasional horrible "review" meetings.

There are set of individual ideas that fit in that theme:

- Operational grip process.

- Grip demand: Managing the work/activity coming into the team or organisation.

- Grip staff costs.

- Grip income.

- Grip non-pay.

Let's look at each of those:

THEME 2.1
Operational grip process

This section covers some of the high-level elements that you can put in place to control and reduce cost and improve efficiency. Individual ideas include:

- **Operational grip process:** Put in place a clear process to gain and maintain "Operational Grip" over the organisation, including having clearly agreed budgets that staff stick to, clear controls over spend and income, operational control over the processes, monitoring of benefits and variances and a process for resolving them. You can also put in place the daily review, supported by a PMO process for improvement activities that we covered in the operational grip section. Basically, this is proper operations behaviour.

- **Demand and capacity planning:** Make sure that every team, adding up to the whole organisation, has a model that shows the relationship between demand and capacity, and the variances between the expected level of both. A demand and capacity model is the best mechanism to show what work is done, and what cost is generated, to meet demand, allowing operations and finance staff to clearly agree on the specifics. This can then feed into an activity-led budget and can also be a mechanism to show the impact of proposed changes and innovations. There are no silver bullets in cost reduction, but this is the closest thing to it. Do silver bullets kill zombies...? Key elements of capacity and demand planning include:

- You should have a clear understanding of demand for the following year, which is based on what you are commissioned or budgeted to deliver, adjusted for actual expectations where this is necessary.

- This should be translated into a clear understanding of the number of key resources that you need - rooms beds, clinics, theatres, etc.

- The staffing needed for each of these key resources has been established.

- Ideally, the initial demand in each of the front-line delivery teams should then flow into the requirements for resources, staff and other resources for other teams (diagnostics, etc).

- The capacity and demand planning should flow into a rostering system that allows the changes in demand across the year to be taken into account.

THEME 2.2
Grip demand

Now here is a can of worms and a kettle of fish rolled into one if we've ever seen one. If you need to reduce costs, one clear way to do it is to stop doing stuff. There are different ways to do this – some are about efficiency, some are about control and some are about cutting, but we think that an exploration of this area is vital for any cost programme.

Where demand is infinite and money or funding is available for it, then you can fill your boots so to speak when it comes to the work that you do, because more work = more money and as long as money > than cost, you are good to go. However, in health and care, we typically face the situation where need is almost limitless in realistic terms and where demand is high - but there isn't the requisite funding to cope with it. In England, many NHS Trusts started getting into cost trouble again after the last load of turnarounds, when emergency tariffs were capped at prior year levels, despite the fact that demand was surging. And that was before austerity measures pretty much destroyed any hope of Local Authorities, health commissioners, or NHS Trusts being able to balance finances.

So, this is why we asked you earlier to consider what you are in this for. Why are you doing this? What we should be doing as a country is working out what we want to fund and how we are going to fund it - but at the moment (in England at least) it is mainly left to your organisation to do more and more work with only slightly more money. Or less money in some cases. So, in the absence of the grown-ups knowing what they are doing, the demand conundrum is down to you. Specific ideas in this area include:

- **Ration care:** You can just decide to only offer enough services, clinics, caseload slots, bed nights or whatever activity you do, as you can afford. There is that little thing called service-users, which is why we are in the business of health & care, but if money is all you want, then that's what you'll receive, to quote Princess Leia. And people need help – physically and mentally. People will literally die if we don't help – or face years of issues. So rationing care is no laughing matter – but the reality is that we are rationing care all the time because we don't have enough staff or enough money or enough equipment. So, any cost reduction project needs to pay attention to how much work we are going to do – and shutting the doors will help save money.

- **Procedures of Limited Clinical Effectiveness:** A better way than just shutting the doors when the limits are reached is managing demand for clinical reasons. It's not always best to deliver care – sometimes it may have limited impact, and in others a higher risk of negative impact than is worthwhile. NICE is the best example of this sort of demand control in the UK – they will assess drugs etc and only allow them to be used in the NHS if they are cost effective. But on the front-line, we've got ambulances bringing people into hospital when they've asked to be left at home. In the old days we had "The Croydon List" that listed a whole raft of procedures that have limited effectiveness. Getting agreement between commissioner and provider staff as to what you should and shouldn't be doing will help manage demand better. You also need to be able to build processes to deal with exceptions, identify when they are done, etc.

- **Pathways / guidance:** Demand management doesn't end once you've decided that someone is in the care-needing category, as it were. The amount of intervention that we embark upon will also make a difference (remember, demand is made up of the amount of time something takes multiplied by the number of times we have to do it). If we are in a VCFSE sector organisation and have 12 counselling sessions for each person when we are funded (or expect) 9, then we have an issue. If we are in a hospital and put everyone forward for an MRI scan when only 1 in 10 should have one, we're going to go over cost. This is about setting standards that are agreed professionally / clinically, and then robustly monitoring them, but in can also include putting in electronic systems like Map of Medicine.

- **Access conditions:** Lots of issues with care delivery are because the wrong people come in at the wrong time and in the wrong condition. If there are certain access conditions (professionally/clinically agreed), with the right information made available for referrers, and these conditions are enforced through a gateway or similar, then the right people will go to the right places.

Demand management can just delay demand at times – and if you aren't providing the care, and if that care was actually needed, then it is either going somewhere or someone is losing out.

We like to get a grip on demand, but not to overdo it in this area. But with staff stressed and with people shouting at you to meet an unrealistic budget, then demand control is a lever that you may just need to use.

THEME 2.3
Grip staff costs

Staff costs are something that do need controlling, but this is far better done generally by a thoughtful process. Staff are our greatest asset in most health & care organisations, so unnecessarily annoying them is not great for the long-term health of a business. And Colin can tell you from very painful personal experience, that things that make sense to you when trying to control costs, can look like the flailing actions of a rabid badger to your team. Pretty much nothing is going to work unless you can engage your teams in solving the problem. That said, and as I have said before, staff generally do like a bit of control – a bit of order. There are a few actions you can take in this area, one of which makes absolute sense:

- **Long standing staff issues controlled**: Some organisations have people working in them that are generally viewed as a massive problem. Staff that take up so much managerial time with their behaviour, exhaust managers' and HR's ability to deal with their behaviour and generally know all the rules. Normally things have got to this pass because their behaviour wasn't addressed in line with policies - we didn't use the induction period properly, we haven't had a review meeting etc.

  Before we get into the action, the one thing you really need to do here is to check your bias. Sometimes people are seen as a problem because they don't look or act the same as the rest of the team, and teams can be a bit unforgiving of the different. So make sure that you are applying a fair and rational head in this area.

  That said, if there are intractable and long-standing issues with staff members, it's time to put your weapons-grade experts on this to develop plans for each problem and execute them. Execute the plans, not the people – let's be very clear on that.

- **Staff recruitment controls / vacancy panels etc:** An audible sigh can be heard in English NHS Trusts at the bureaucratic nightmare that is the vacancy control panel. Poorly implemented, these are a massive waste of time for everyone concerned and just drive people towards bank and agency spend. However, there is something to be said for a mindful, but light, process for making sure that we aren't recruiting people we don't need. Setting out clear views on what new staff will be allowed and what won't, being clear on what (minimal) information we need to assess this, and a quick process to check and agree/stop recruitment makes sense. When we are struggling financially, sometimes we do need to stop people starting new projects and bringing in new staff, so a vacancy control process, which might involve a panel if we really cant think of any better way of doing it, might be needed. I hate them though.

THEME 2.4
Grip income

If you are just interested in cost, then this one won't be of interest, but in any normal world, we need to make sure that we are getting all the money due to us. And we face a choice – anything that isn't necessary we either need to get paid for, or we need to stop doing it and redeploy the staff. Some specific ideas in this area, include:

- ***Maximise core income recovery:*** This is a tough area to be specific on as income opportunities are variable depending on your business model and contracts. In the English NHS there used to be activity-flexible models, so you got paid the more that you do, whereas now more contracts are block contracts, which do not flex with activity. Some are in the middle. In some private sector organisations you'll collect the money when people come through the door. However you get your money, you need to make sure that you are getting all of it for your core operations,. and even if it doesn't make a difference to the bottom line, you need to make sure activity is accurate anyway so you can make the case for more funding. Specific ideas include:

    - Put controls in place to ensure that activity is recorded accurately for everything you do - contacts, case loads, clinics, bed nights, scans, counselling sessions, etc.

    - Check all contracts for income and ensure that you are clear on what needs to be delivered for the contract, and what can make you additional money.

    - Get your coding right – if you are paid for your activity then you need to focus on this. Every element of the bill needs to be right if you are being paid on the basis of work actually done. Some specifics include:

    - Eliminate un-coded spells (u-codes).

    - Engage clinicians/delivery teams in a rolling programme of training/discussion to make them aware of coding impact on income.

- Documents and systems should be designed to allow for the nuances of activity to be quickly recorded.

- Management information should be available on coding where it impacts on income, including KPIs on "with complication/ comorbidity" levels, complexity levels, u-codes, % coded from notes, % coding forms returned and % delivery teams that have reviewed their coding.

- Develop a management information system that allows the above information to be produced at individual, group/team and organisation level.

- Coding can be supported by automatic audit software to make sure it is being done right.

- Individuals within the coding or finance team can be aligned to each specialty, responsible for building links and dealing with issues regarding coding.

- Reports on what has been coded are reviewed by the delivery teams to make sure nothing has been missed.

- Teams take part in regular audits of coding to understand issues.

- Each individual element of coding should be provided to the billing teams via an electronic system with appropriate controls over completeness, accuracy and validity.

The coding team at Sheffield Teaching Hospitals in the late 90's and early 2000's built an amazing team ethic in their coding team, taking things further by producing an annual impact report, as well as focusing on many of the elements above.

- **Maximise other income recovery:** The specifics of this will depend on your organisation and business model, but you may be doing work outside of your core contracts that might be worth looking at. Specifics include:

    - Review and make sure that income for any of your staff working outside the organisation is received. Work for other providers for example?

    - Are any of your staff doing any delivery work that should attract funding?

    - Are any of your staff doing any project, corporate or other work that should be paid for by someone (or stopped)?

    - If we are training people, are we getting all the payment for that?

    - Review of contracts with commissioners to challenge penalty charges and highlight opportunities to maximise income take place.

    - Are we getting paid for all external use of our admin team e.g. Medical Litigation, charging for FOI request completion etc.

    - Where we have contracts for work done for other organisations, are we getting the income for these, and are they profitable enough? Could we increase contract prices through clauses in the contract? These often apply to payroll, occupational health, estates work, etc.

    - Are you recovering income from people that are using your service, but are not actually part of your service agreements? By this, I mean out of area or international users, private patients if you are a public provider (or vice versa), etc

- **Manage income deductions:** Getting a grip on income requires an understanding of what money you are losing, and what you could lose if someone was to check, based on your income contracts. If you get money direct from the service-users then credit card chargebacks might be an issue. If you are paid on a contract then you need to know what money you are losing for quality issues, people being re-admitted, not doing enough, doing the wrong things ,etc. A review of the contracts, followed by action to improve and then clear reporting of potential and actual losses may help you grip your income a little more tightly.

THEME 2.5
Grip non-pay

You've got to love a bit of non-pay grip, as it doesn't mean taking money off your staff. Generally, this is about paying less to your suppliers, mainly by not buying as much. We will look at supply-chain and procurement improvements later, but in terms of grip, you can consider the following:

- **Implement controls on non-essential purchasing:** When Colin worked in retail, he worked with some recently taken over organisations in turnaround who would not sign off purchase orders until they had been reviewed and signed off by someone who is looking to minimise spend – once that was even the person who had bought the company. This might be a bit too heavy, but understanding spend by area and type and implementing controls in the biggest areas of spend may be necessary. In some organisations, staff spend the rest of their budgets in the last few months for fear of losing the money (either in year or off their budget next year) on furniture, or to get projects delivered. This can be targeted specifically as an area if you are looking to reduce cost.

- **Tax recovery:** Where you can recover tax, it is worth ensuring that the controls are in place to ensure that people are recording and evidencing any value added tax spent on non-pay, especially personal expenses. You need to be able to identify where tax is expected but is not part of the expense claim and identify individuals that are poor at evidencing or recording it, so they can be "re-educated". We put that in speech marks to make it more menacing... We will consider taxes as part of wider cost reduction later.

- **Insurances:** Where you are paying for clinical or delivery insurances, it is worth understanding what drives their variable nature. If there are things that people are consistently doing that drive increased premiums, then you can "grip" those areas.

- **Debt financing:** Careful management of debts is critical for maintaining fiscal health in many health and care organisations, especially if you are in a turnaround situation and need to ensure that interest payments aren't what tip you over the edge. Reviewing all debts and considering how to reduce the interest payments by better deals, repayment "holidays" or potentially getting them written off, would be a good idea if this is a large spend for your organisation.

5.4 Plan Workforce

Now we're into the really good stuff. Don't get us wrong, we love a bit of operational grip at the right level, but if there is one thing that we are right at home with, it is workforce planning. If you want to learn more about this fascinating subject, then don't forget to check out The Bumper Book of Health & Care Workforce Planning, available in all good bookshops. Well, Amazon, anyway.

Workforce planning in the cost reduction context is about optimising the staff that you are spending money on to meet the demand that you are being paid for. As a subject, there are many themes that we need to consider. These are:

- Job Planning
- Rostering
- Flexible working
- Grade and role alignment
- Sickness
- Additional Payments
- Bank, agency and locum spend
- Outsourcing
- Salary sacrifice

For health & care organisations, we can also consider individual groups that have their own nuances when it comes to workforce planning (normally centred around the above ideas). We have included a few in this book - nurses, medics etc.

A workforce planning programme doesn't need to be about cost reduction, but it is about making sure that you have the right people with the right skills in the right place at the right time. And that means making sure that staffing is right – that should mean the right cost (the cheapest overall to meet the needs). But that doesn't mean that you cut costs everywhere. You need to make sure that turnover is not too high, that staff are continually trained, that there is time for improvement activity etc – and you must not have fewer staff than you need to meet the agreed activity.

Right, onto the ideas.

THEME 3.1
Job planning/clinical and delivery productivity

This is a tough area not to make staff or even country specific, as each has its own considerations. When controlling and looking to reduce cost, it is worth considering each type of staff in its own right, as there are nuances for each: In England, medical consultants have formal job plans in most cases, junior doctors work in multiple teams (and across multiple organisations), nurse establishments are set by standards etc. We will consider individual roles later.

This section is about setting and getting what you expect in terms of delivery. If you have built a capacity and demand model, that will tell you how many people you need – but if that does not translate on the ground into actual work done, then you are going to be inefficient.

This theme is all about making sure that you get the amount of work you expect out of staff.

Specific ideas within this theme include:

- **Set delivery / non-delivery split:** Staff cannot generally deliver services for their entire time at work. At the very least, people need breaks and holidays – and in almost all cases, people should have training, may be ill on occasion, etc. Any demand and capacity model will need to consider how much time is spent not delivering.

  - **Annual:** On an annual basis, there should be time set aside for annual leave, bank holidays, training/development, improvement activities, conference attendance, sickness, parental leave and special leave. Each of these should be set based on expected levels, which will then have to be adjusted for the real level (parental leave is particularly tough to guess at the start of the year).

-

  - **Weekly:** On a weekly basis, not all the time will be spent delivering even in a "delivery" week (e.g. one when not on holiday). Breaks, admin time, time to deal with the unknown etc can be built into delivery hours (e.g. you take those into account when working out how many people can be seen per hour) or they can be separated out as "downtime". Some roles, however, have set time for development and training - medical consultants have Supporting Programmed Activities (SPAs), staff in English GP Practices may have Wednesday afternoons for development etc.

- **Set delivery expectations:** When you have established how much delivery time staff have, you should set expectations for how much activity they do. There are many different examples of what this should look like depending on the staff. For medical consultants, their job plans can be broken down into clinic, theatre, and ward time for example – and expectations for the work done on each of these would need to be set. Some staff may just do one thing. Social workers may have a case load, whilst counsellors have a number of 1:1 sessions to run. Whatever the activity that people do, we need to understand how much of that activity we expect in a week, day or session.

- **Activity monitoring:** Setting activity levels that are built into the capacity and demand plans is a first step, but it must also translate on the ground. The next step is to check that activity is being delivered. You should gain agreement from teams that they will deliver a certain amount of activity, then undertake regular checking so that you can identify if you are below or above expected delivery levels. Typically this includes checking that there are the right number of sessions, and that there is the right amount of activity within each session. This might also be a caseload, or the right number of people discharged, depending on the role. Checking activity levels also allows you to spot where process issues are causing problems for the staff, and thus to solve them quickly. You can also identify if staff are regularly having to stay late, or are finishing early, and thus where the model may be wrong.

- **Non-activity monitoring:** A good chunk of staff time should be spent away from direct service-user care where possible. Training, research, administration, management responsibilities, redesign work etc can all be done outside of the time which is allocated to service user delivery in your model. The use and impact of this time should also be monitored to ensure that staff are getting the most from it, and that it is optimised for the good of the organisation.

THEME 3.2
Staff rostering

Staff rostering is a core part of good cost control, as well as being beneficial for staff and for service-users. It is typically something that is considered for nurses but is needed for everyone. There are two levels of rostering:

1. Across the year – ensuring that you have the right number (and type) of staff available each week.

2. Across the week – making sure that you have the right staff available across the week

When you look at it like that, you can see that it is for everyone – equally needed for care home staff, volunteers, doctors, nurses, Allied Health Professionals. Everyone.

- **Staff Rostering:** We may already have made the point that all staff should be rostered - even executive team members should be scheduled across the year, making sure that the required executive tasks are covered, and the same is true for support staff. Then for all staff that work with the service-user. Once you get to the stage where we need to roster them across the week (or fortnight, as is more common with nurses) all staff should be rostered across the week, ensuring that: (a) the contracted hours of all staff are all used; and (b) there is exactly the right number of people working as is needed to meet demand across the week. Of course, those are harder to make happen than they sound, as variable demand and the need to create reasonable rotas can make it difficult.

- **Electronic system:** Rostering doesn't need an electronic system, but it makes the whole process a lot easier. An electronic rostering system, of which there are many to choose from, should make the process more efficient, fairer, and more likely to achieve the goal of ensuring that all staff are used for all their hours, and that it meets demand. Critically, an electronic system allows for communication and analysis.

- **Rosters reviewed in advance:** Rostering can be difficult, bias can be a problem, and like any task in health & care, you need to manage it if you expect it to be done consistently and well. All schedules and rosters should be reviewed in advance, with a focus on:

- Have all contractual hours been used?
- Has predicted demand been met?
- Have staff rostering rules been broken?
- Use of bank and agency
- Are staff below minimum levels?

Typically, a roster will be reviewed by a manager who will review the rosters from several teams, and then there will be a second level of review by a senior responsible person. Obviously, the level of review reduces the further up the hierarchy you go, but the general aim is to (a) ensure that rosters have been done (b) ensure that they are as efficient as possible and (c) as a mechanism to feedback on required changes. They should be part check and part help, ensuring that those doing the rostering know that it is important, and are taught to do it properly.

Rostering review should be done to a timetable, with rosters being completed by the team leader with (for example) 6 weeks to go before the shift, and the reviews taking place 4 and 2 weeks before the shifts to allow for amendments.

- **Roster metrics reviewed:** As well as reviewing in advance, metrics on the effectiveness of rotas should be analysed after the event. The metrics that should be considered are:

  - Contracted hours not used.
  - Bank and agency use in rotas.
  - Additional duties used.
  - Staff below minimum levels.
  - Number of rosters done 6 weeks in advance.
  - Roster approvals done on time.

And if you are feeling particularly keen you can also consider the following good practice metrics:

- Service-user satisfaction.
- Queue lengths.
- Staff rostering rules broken.
- Auto-roster percentage.

- Staff satisfaction.

- Missing skills/leadership.

The review of metrics should be considered at a senior operational level, and should be costed where possible to show the impact of good, and bad, rostering and scheduling.

THEME 3.3
Flexible working

In this case, flexible working means ensuring that staff work in a manner which allows for staffing to be more easily optimised. Silo-working creates inefficiency as one team or person can be too busy whilst another is too quiet – leading to increased use of staff and bank/agency staff.

Of course, with great power comes great responsibility and all that – so if you are asking staff to be flexible there needs to be some quid pro quo. Asking staff to be flexible requires some flexibility from you as an employer or manager and should never be assumed. Specific ideas in this theme include:

- ***Shared lists/caseloads:*** One of the areas where flexibility can help efficiency is if lists can be shared. If a consultant can operate on any and all patients in their specialty, if a social worker can manage any part of any caseload or if a councillor can undertake one session in a series being managed by another councillor – then if one is ill, then it is easier to get someone to cover. Obviously, this isn't possible in all cases, but where staff can cover one another's workload in a flexible manner this will help maintain the capacity planned to meet demand.

- ***Professional or medical staff annual flexibility:*** If staff agree to work flexibly across the year to cover their total workload, so that if they miss one clinic or session, then they catch up across the rest of the year with extra sessions or through covering others' absences, then the delivery of the capacity plan is more likely and therefore more efficient.

- ***Bed-based (virtual or physical) staff flexibility:*** Rostering can be very difficult if staff have very restrictive times when they can and can't work. Some of these restrictions may be based on old life patterns, or possibly due to promises being made during recruitment when there were few candidates for roles. If ward staff are very flexible in their working hours, including working to annualised hours, rather than a set number of hours per week, then rostering is easier and there will be fewer unused hours in rotas.

- ***Location Flexibility:*** It is more efficient when staff are able to work across all locations, rather than having a set location. This can be between sites, between resources, between community and acute locations, etc. This sort of flexibility improves efficiency by ensuring that staff in unexpectedly quiet areas can work in areas that are unexpectedly busy, or to cover absence.

- **Flexible working across the week**: Flexibility is almost always challenging for staff (remember, you need to provide something to staff for all this flexibility) but this one is probably the least likely or popular. If you are able to negotiate flexible working across the entire week so that people will work any hour of any day of the week, then you really do have flexibility.

- **Minimise out of hours costs:** Sometimes out of hours payments have got a little bit out of control, so it is worth revisiting all out of hours costs across the organisation and make sure that they are reasonable.

- **Optimise part-time staff:** The use of agency staff is generally bad, as it is expensive, and new staff don't always know how the team or the area works. Overtime use is better, but it is generally paid at a premium - but use of staff from a bank, or using more hours from part time staff is the same cost, and you are using people that know the area and the team in most cases, so is the same as using staff being paid within their normal contract. In most cases, there is some variability to the demand for staff, and some in its supply (due to absence etc), so it is important to have a flexible team that can be increased as needed at no additional cost. This is where having a team of flexible staff can really help – part-time staff that are happy to work additional hours when needed, and staff on the "bank" (which is essentially the same, just generally more formalised). If these people can work across multiple areas as well, then that's even better. The flexibility that these can offer is one reason for the rise in "zero-hours" contracts in much of industry – where people are not contracted for any hours, but are willing to work completely flexibly. We don't recommend this as a standard, as it provides very little security for the staff member, but it is the extreme end of what we are talking about here.

   There is more technical detail than this, but the trick is to set your permanent staff at (or just above) your minimum requirement for staff every day, and have the rest made up by flexible additional hours. This reduces unused hours, and ensures that demand is matched by staff capacity.

   Examples of this approach are Japan's use of part-time nurses, and the UK's nursing banks.

- **Staff cross trained for flexibility:** There has been a tendency for specialisation at times, but this creates an issue for teams when a need for staff in one area cannot be covered by overstaffing in another. Such silos are inherently inefficient (although such specialisation may improve outcomes etc) so finding ways to ensure that these silos are minimised is the best result for efficiency in most cases. Identifying teams that constantly have over- or under- staffing that cannot be used elsewhere, identifying the roles within that that do not NEED to be specialised and cross-training them so as to be able to work in multiple areas can really work. And no more so than in community roles where multiple visits from multiple roles can be reduced significantly. In Singapore, cross-training health and care workers for multiple roles has been shown to enhance workforce flexibility and reduce staffing costs.

THEME 3.4
Grade and role alignment

Grade and role alignment, or workforce redesign as we call it in workforce planning circles is an area that is often talked about, but rarely done well on the ground. The effort needed to identify a need, redesign the way you work and engage teams in making sure that the change sticks is considerable. Across many systems, new roles are introduced into teams without consistent change management, and the result is misery for staff parachuted into teams that neither want them or know what to do with them.

Yet ensuring that you have the most efficient set up in your staffing model is vital for teams for financial reasons, and because there just aren't enough of the traditional staff globally to meet demand. It should also be good for staff, as they can do the interesting stuff that they are good at, whilst others do the stuff that they find easier or possibly boring. This book is not about workforce planning (we have another book on that - see links, later) so we won't go into all the detail on how to do this and make it stick – but if this is an area you decide to go for, there are many resources to help you.

Specific ideas in this theme are:

- **Top of grade:** Sometimes called "operating at top of licence", this idea is about making sure that all staff spend their time doing things that only that role can do. Any admin work is done by administrators (and the right level of administration). Any preparation work is done by others, and service-users are streamed so that only the right people cross the threshold, completely prepared so that the most qualified (and expensive) staff only see what they need to see. You might not get this to work completely, but steps towards it should be possible. There are lots of approaches to this – but the most important ones are getting engagement from the team in the redesign, modelling the changes in your capacity and demand model, and actively monitoring and adjusting the impacts in real life.

   This can have repercussions. Sometimes it is less efficient, as handovers can take time (and cause issues), and you may create a load of silos. It can also be bad for staff – we have found this when doing this with radiographers – they needed the time spent talking to patients to recover from the heavy lifting (sometimes literally) of scanning people. It can also be bad for service-users at times – the point is that what is sometimes good for efficiency is not always good for efficiency, and that a balance between the needs of the money, the staff and the service-users is always needed. But this is definitely an area you should always be looking at - and all roles should be reviewed to ensure that they are not doing work that could be done as or more effectively by a different member of staff.

- **Design and build new roles:** Swapping staff between your existing roles is good, but you may need to create new roles to take on duties – and these roles may be bespoke to you. Again, workforce redesign approaches will help you to work through how to do this.

   You generally want to avoid a proliferation of lots of new roles (trust us on that, it can get messy) so your best bet is to adjust existing roles so that their training and their governance base fits within existing structures. Training and using lower-cost staff for specific tasks, a strategy employed in Brazil's Family Health Strategy, optimises the availability of workforce and reduces costs.

- **Benchmark skill mix:** You don't know what you don't know, and you don't always know what impact your changes will have until you've done it. In the global world of health and care, someone else will have done it somewhere, so you should benchmark your skill mix against other people to see if you are missing a trick. Now, as you may know, all benchmarking is evil – a phrase we use all the time to remind us that this is a tool that is misused by people as a stick to beat operational teams with – but if you use it yourself in a considered way, it can bring real benefits. You can benchmark yourself against similar organisations (any dissimilar ones if you want a challenge) to help you consider how you might do things differently. And when you find a good example, you can visit them to check that their situation is similar to yours and see how they did it.

- **Implement known new roles:** Recent workforce challenges have turbo-charged the development of new roles that can be used when redesigning your workforce. The benefit of using these roles is that they have had all the work done for you, including job descriptions and competency guides and have often been integrated into training processes (universities are aware of them, and have available courses etc). Because these roles exist, then there examples nationally and globally, and a stream of expertise that people can dip into for knowledge and expertise. An example of the type are Advanced Practice Professionals, which have been used in the UK and Canada to good effect. In the UK, looking at the old Health Education England's STAR tool can give you a whole host of these roles to consider.

- **Effectiveness of new roles identified:** Introduction of new roles is not enough – a lot of money has been spent on introducing them, but they haven't always been successful. This is often just due to poor change management and the fact that sometimes people need time to get to get used to things. So a project to identify your existing new roles, analysing their successes and where things haven't worked, and then reintroducing them, having solved your previous mistakes, could yield better results than starting from scratch somewhere else.

- **Use of apprenticeships:** Traditionally, formal education routes have been the exclusively routes for training of new staff, but one way for countries, if not organisations, to be more cost effective is to get more people into these roles through less academic routes. This can increase the pool, thus reducing pressure on salaries, and can increase the amount of work done while training.

THEME 3.5
Managing sickness absence

When you build your capacity model, you should assume a certain amount of sickness – normally something like 5 days per year for full time staff, or 3-3.5%. In model world you have two jobs – first to get that number as small as is possible (as that means you are more efficient in theory) and then to get reality to match that number so that you don't end up failing to deliver your activity targets.

In the real world, sickness absence is a complicated thing. You want your staff to come into work as much as possible, but you definitely don't want them coming to work if they have infectious diseases. You don't want your staff to come in when they are really poorly and can't do what they are scheduled to do, but you don't want staff to take a day off because they were feeling a little bit under the weather at the start of the day but were fine by 10am. You certainly don't want staff to take a day off when they are well. But then illness is so complicated and much illness is invisible. Should someone take a day off because they are feeling a little stressed, and a day might help them get back on track?

You can also throw normal manager and staff bias into this and mix in a bit of general racism, sexism and various other isms to further complicate the story - because sickness can drive, and be driven by, team dynamics, and all the human behaviour included. Finally, team managers can sometimes not actually be trained to handle sickness, so don't feel able to challenge.

So, you want all your team members to use work absence properly, which we think needs to include a lot of trust in your team, with a bit of monitoring and intervention to keep things fair. There are a range of different ideas that you can consider:

- **Robust absence recording:** As a basic minimum, there must be processes in place to record absence monitored by thorough and up to date record keeping of sickness. This should apply to all staff including medical consultants and corporate staff, who don't always have the most accurate sickness figures.

- **Sickness recording system:** The organisation should have an electronic mechanism for the recording of sickness absence, and automatic flagging of concerns (based on Bradford Index calculations etc) as well as automatic creation of management information for all levels of the organisation, and automatic identification of staff that should now trigger statutory health pay, etc.

- **Independent system:** Staff could have to call in either to an independent number within the organisation or to a third-party provider to register their illness. This may put off people from ringing in unless they are actually ill (the word "may" doing some heavy lifting there) and does allow for trained staff to answer the call and run through the correct process.

- **Organisational focus on sickness and staff wellbeing:** Leaders of staff groups, business group management and responsible departments in the organisation responsible for the wellbeing of staff in their area, including monitoring the level of short and long term sickness in their areas of control, with robust information provided on performance against other parts of the organisation. Common themes for sickness are investigated through projects and remedial measures put in place (e.g. stress under certain managers and repetitive strain injury in theatres)

- **Sickness absence policies:** There should be a robust and up to date policy in place within the organisation, setting out the commitment to supporting staff, but minimising absence from work, developed with staff groups and organisational leadership to get the balance right. The policy must be rigorously followed.

- **Individual plans for short-term absence:** Staff with high levels of short-term absence could be subject to review of sickness patterns, to specific case review, and get assistance if necessary to get well enough to work consistently. The emphasis should be on supporting people with their health in the first place, but if it is identified as a performance problem then a robust plan should be followed to improve or remove the person.

- **Individual plans for long-term absence:** Long-term sickness can be controlled and reduced by having specific plans in place for all individuals with long term sickness. In these cases, this is normally about identifying how we can help these people back to work when possible by changing the environment or changing the role. It is also about identifying quickly when a return to work will not be possible.

- **Financial checks:** The organisation should ensure that there is a clear understanding of when state help is available for staff that are unwell and should understand when it is no longer liable (or when policies state that they will no longer support people) for paying staff. There should be appropriate checks to ensure that people are supported to move to state help at the right time.

- **Go full good on sickness:** Sickness absence can be managed through a grown-up relationship with empowered and keen staff. They can be asked to manage their own sickness - some organisations provide all staff with 5 or more flexible days which they can use for sick days, or just for a day off (so-called "duvet days"). Others provide monthly funding for fitness and wellbeing purposes and put in place Wellbeing Co-ordinators and groups. You can focus on reducing sickness by helping your teams stay fit and well, and allowing them to manage it themselves.

- **Go full evil on sickness:** Sickness absence can be managed like you ran a workhouse in Victorian England. You can do everything you can to get people into work, including demanding sick notes from doctors if people want to be paid for any sickness however short. You can set policies to say that people don't get paid for the first day they have sick, to try to stop people taking single days off. This approach is about trying to avoid paying for any sickness however you can. We just wouldn't recommend this…

THEME 3.6
Agency, locum and overtime spend

Generally, you want to spend money on staff at the optimum level if you are managing for efficiency, so that means paying them the right amount to ensure that people work hard and don't leave and no more. That's a pretty miserable way of looking at it, but it will be efficient. You could argue that this is the best way to set salaries, and then if you want to share more with your staff do it through bonuses or share ownership or similar, but for basic efficiency, pay them what is needed for efficient working.

Paying people to do more work than they are salaried for isn't a problem for efficiency if it is for dealing with variable demand or supply, as we considered under the flexibility theme earlier. But paying people more per hour can be a problem. It is inefficient, and can lead to poor behaviour, like deliberately building up waiting lists (or at least the perception that this is what has caused waiting lists).

Of course, people like overtime, and they especially like getting more per hour so you need to consider the impact on your own staff of controlling this – by focusing on the outside staff first.

This theme considers ideas to keep this spend minimised:

- **Minimise waiting list initiatives:** Waiting list initiatives is a term that can be used for premium payments made to staff to clear backlogs. They should only be used as part of a well thought through response to unexpected capacity requirements, and not to deal with lower productivity or known long term requirements. If we have a long term need for greater capacity, then we should staff at the right salary. If people are not meeting productivity levels, and thus building up waiting lists, we should address that head on.

- **Overtime minimised:** Any overtime that is paid at above normal pay per hour rates should only be used to clear unexpected demand levels and not to pay for lower team productivity or if there is a long-term problem. Overtime in roles should be discouraged, should only be allowed if approved in advance by senior management, and should be rigorously reported on.

- **Optimise additional payments:** Any additional payments to staff above their normal salaries should be reviewed to check that they make sense and are fair, and a plan put in place to address any issues. The use of additional payments should be transparent across the organisation and clearly reported on.

- **Negotiated rates:** Agency and locum rates must be negotiated in advance to minimise cost for the required level of quality. Prices should be clear and constantly renegotiated where possible.

- **Recording:** All agency and locum requests should be recorded together with the reason. These requests should be regularly reviewed for patterns to allow for lessons to be learned.

- **Sign off:** All requests for agency and locum spend should be signed off at an appropriate senior level to dissuade people from using this as a default method and to ensure that someone senior can look for ways to solve the problem without using agency staff. They can also make sure that the right processes are being used to bring them in, and can take steps to reduce the need in the future.

- **Agency and locum invoice control:** All invoices for locum and agency should be checked against requests and the price checked against expected rates to ensure that fraudulent or mistaken invoices are not paid.

- **Electronic Agency Spend:** The organisation should use an electronic system to streamline its agency and locum processes, introduce better systems and controls and to ensure adherence to policies.

- **Agency and locum outsourcing:** The organisation could outsource the running of agency and locum provision to a single provider to reduce costs and improve quality. Such a provider would be competitively chosen, and there should be controls to ensure that the provider does not act against the requirements of the organisation (which would be to minimise the cost of agency staff).

- **Agency and locum reduction planning:** Where there is high-cost locum spend, or constant agency spend for any area, then a plan to end these situations should be put in place and managed, with oversight at executive level on progress.

- **Medical locum spend controlled:** The use of medical or professional locums should again only really be used for short-term capacity problems or demand rises. Given that there is likely already a lot of locum spend in an organisation, there needs to be clear reporting on levels, and a management plan put in place to bring each of these down, by ensuring that someone is recruited to cover it as soon as possible, that demand is reduced (if that doesn't reduce income), that other staff can cover it through workforce redesign, or that some automation is put in place. The culture of using medical locums for anything other than short term issues could be quashed.

- **Agency spend controlled:** The use of agency staff should again only really be used for short term capacity problems or demand rises. Given that there is likely already a lot of agency spend in an organisation, there needs to be clear reporting on levels, and a management plan put in place to bring each of these down, by ensuring that someone is recruited to cover it as soon as possible, that demand is reduced (if that doesn't reduce income), that other staff can cover it through workforce redesign or that some automation is put in place. The culture of using agency staff for anything other than short term issues should be discouraged.

THEME 3.7
Improving retention rates

High staff turnover is a huge hidden problem for staff cost. Every time someone leaves, you need to recruit someone else, probably use agency staff in the interim, train the staff and wait for their effectiveness to get to the current staff's levels. It is difficult to quantify, but it will be big. Of course, some turnover is healthy, but you need to reduce it if it is too high. This theme includes more than thirty ideas that you can implement to increase retention.

- **Conduct appraisals regularly and properly:** As appraisal completion metrics are quite common, sometimes we can end up in a "chase the numbers" appraisal system, where people just focus on how many they have done. Appraisals are your chance to assess and communicate performance, building up your team, addressing real issues and ensuring that they have a development plan. It never ceases to amaze us how often these meetings become a nightmare for all concerned, so you need a proper appraisal approach. A "proper" appraisal system includes:

- Training on how to conduct appraisals.

- Spot-reviews of appraisals to drive improvement.

- Recording of appraisals, and follow ups where not complete.

- Feedback from staff on regularity and quality of appraisal conversation.

- Appraisals conducted to a set timescale – annually, bi-annually or monthly (with a mix of informal/formal discussions).

- **Focus on the staff experience:** Working with people is about focusing on the staff experience as a core part of the organisation's culture. Your staff are the single most important element of delivering care, yet organisation after organisation fails to see staff as precious. Of course, most have "staff are important" messages in their priorities - but, as one of the team says in the office, "You should tell your face that". It includes:

  - Staff experience part of the core priorities.

  - Monitoring of quantitative measures of staff experience.

  - Focus groups and interviews on staff experience.

- **Independent leaver interviews:** Colin's last leaver interview was done by his boss – good luck on getting quality feedback from him. Better leaver interview programmes include:

  - Training for staff who conduct leaver interviews.

  - Leaver interviews done quickly after someone resigns.

  - Independent person available.

  - No-blame (where possible) approach to resolving issues identified.

  - ESR or relevant system updated for quantitative analysis.

  - Themes gathered for qualitative analysis and issues addressed.

- **Portfolio careers:** One of the reasons by retention improves when people have worked on the CLEAR programme in the UK is that people are doing something different for a bit of their week - they are redesigning their systems and workforce. This sort of variation provides a break from what can seem like a never ending process of delivering the same thing. It's not for everyone, but portfolio type careers can work in all sorts of guises. Portfolio careers can include:

  - Introducing secondments to other teams for a number of months / years.

  - Increasing the variety of a role by working in similar but different teams (e.g. a community nurse working in primary care, or an OT working across Local Authorities and health trusts.

- Undertaking a different role part-time, for example by leading a change and being part of a project team.

- Taking on wider duties as part of a role to introduce variety (e.g. teaching).

- **1:1 Planning with retirees:** Retirement is a very specific element of turnover. Whilst there are often no set dates for retirement, there are a huge variety of potential external triggers, including reaching state pension age and topping out pension limits. There are also internal triggers such as burnout, ill-health and family changes. When someone announces they are going to retire, or mentions it as part of ongoing discussions, understanding the reasons for it, and using the event as an opportunity to discuss what can be done to keep the person in employment, perhaps in a different role or a portfolio role, can help us to retain the individual's skills and experience.

- **Build development time into roles:** If we currently work out how many staff we need by dividing the work by the available capacity of the staff, then we are condemning people to a never-ending production line. That might be a bit strong - but there are many examples of models not even taking into account holidays, sickness, mandatory training and break times properly thus stressing the staff members. And rarely is development of redesign time included.

- **Give people access to learning:** One of the other ideas deals with people having enough time to develop (which includes training) but we also need to provide people with access to training. You can "sweat the asset" if you like, but don't be surprised when retention drops. Building in (say) ½ day a week for training, like you find in many English GP surgeries, can improve retention, provide space for redesign, improve skills and actually increase efficiency.

- **Invest in redesign:** Again, this often means reducing people's time on the direct delivery to give people the space to focus on something else. The CLEAR programme does this really well – ring fencing clinician's time to undertake redesign while learning how to do it (and it is proven to improve retention) Investing in redesign could include:

    - Backfilling time for staff to be in redesign sessions.

    - Providing set time for redesign activities (e.g. after a theatre session or a day of meetings) This goes beyond telling everyone they can use E-learning for health (even assuming you can get access if you are in the VCFSE or care sectors). We need to curate it:

        - Highlight what is useful.

        - Link it to training needs assessments for the role.

        - Highlight what is needed for different career paths.

You know, do it thoughtfully, don't just chuck it at people…

- **Clear guidelines in place to define work:** Helping people to avoid the uncertainty to improve retention can include:

  - Ensuring that job descriptions are accurate and constantly updated, including expectations.

  - Building "how-to" guides for common issues. In customer service, this can include examples of what to escalate, for example.

  - Providing access to flexible pathways and flows to reduce the number of decisions that people are forced to make with little information.

- **Engage with staff to understand turnover:** A good way to find out what people want is to ask them, preferably before they start thinking about leaving. Of course, you'll get some suggestions you can't always address, but you'll also a lot of good ideas - and it means that you shouldn't waste time on interventions that no-one wants. This can include:

  - Regular listening sessions – with the right staff providing their views.

  - Suggestion "boxes".

  - Programme of improvements to respond to requests Clear analysis for staff and executives.

  - "You said, we did" communications.

- **Involvement in decision making:** Meaningful staff engagement in senior levels of management can be difficult, but can also be well worth the trouble. Tools like Service Line Management in the 2000's helped ensure that all types of staff were involved in planning how to address the strategic priorities – see the section on this earlier. Sharing the problems, and the opportunities, with staff and giving them the chance to work out how to address them can aid retention – but also improve efficiency and gain buy-in to the redesign.

- **Recognising performance:** In reality, good performance is recognised all the time. The trouble is that it can be inconsistent due to a lack of an effective system and inbuilt culture. Building the recognition of performance requires:

  - Setting clear standards for performance.

  - Rewarding good performance with monetary and/or non-monetary methods.

  - Systematically addressing poor performance with development, and punitive measures when needed.

- **Leaders live the culture:** If the leaders of an organisation role-model the expected behaviours, then it is more likely that the rest of the organisation will follow. Consider:

- Leaders showing that staff are important through their own behaviour (rewarding success, advocating for resources, etc) .
- Challenging poor behaviour on the part of others, especially senior colleagues.

- **Proper process - plan, measures etc:** This is all about building a retention programme or focus. A "proper" process will include:
    - Senior leader responsible for retention improvements (SRO).
    - Programme of improvement with plans.
    - Adequate resources assigned to the programme and ongoing monitoring of progress.
    - Key performance indicators for retention – depending on the interventions in the plan.

- **Advocate for resources:** Leaders must ensure that they advocate for staff experience improvement – and for the resources that support it. This can include:
    - Time for development, to get involved in decision making and engage in redesign activities.
    - Enough staff to meet demand.
    - Appropriate reward. Ensuring that the balance between competing priorities does not always lead to the default position (the staff lose) takes constant effort in the face of pressure from outside and inside leadership teams.

- **Embedded leadership training:** Leadership training includes specific leadership skills alongside the rules, procedures and expectations. The embedding of leadership training involves:
    - Training needs assessments – linked to expectations of skills at each level.
    - Making training available.
    - Assigning time for training.
    - Providing clinics for addressing issues.
    - Monitoring and rewarding progress.
    - Assessing quality and impact.

- **Introduction for new roles:** The proper introduction of new roles includes:

- Involvement of current staff, and new roles, in redesign:

  - Agreement of roles and responsibilities for each staff group when new roles introduced.

  - Review of whether roles and responsibilities are working.

  - Team building.

  - Appropriate time for discussion and problem solving for new arrangements.

- **International recruitment retention:** Any recruits need help to join a team, but that goes double for international recruits. In one Integrated Care Board (ICB) we worked with, we saw the best and the worst of this - the worst we've seen was a loss of an entire cohort of international recruits due to poor behaviour, the best was a planned programme for six months of making sure that everyone was settled and happy, with 1:1 support and an emergency helpline – all led by someone that really cared. Interventions that can be considered here, include:

  - Appropriate training for existing staff.

  - Team building with individuals.

  - Buddies and mentors.

  - Team responsible for ensuring international recruits are properly embedded in teams.

  - Appropriate supervision and training.

  - Language and cultural development.

  - Assistance with the practicalities of life in a foreign country.

  - Specific monitoring of international recruit turnover.

- **Diversity focus:** Solving racism, sexism, ableism, homophobia and transphobia might be a bit more than a workforce planning project can solve, but it can significantly help by specifically focusing on the needs of minorities within teams:

  - Bias training and ally programmes, and training managers to understand the issue and how to address it.

  - Name the problem by issuing statements from the Executive and assuring people of support.

  - Talk to the people affected, and act on their concerns.

- Provide safe routes for individuals to raise concerns.

- Set goals for improvement, especially in retention, monitor them and adjust accordingly.

- **Talent management:** Undertaking talent management to retain staff includes some or all of the following:

  - Developing the strategy for talent management, including how to make it "real" in the organisation.

  - Attracting the best talent.

  - Effectively onboarding talent.

  - Focusing on rewarding talent.

  - Succession planning.

  Talent management includes many of the other ideas on these cards in a holistic approach to building the most talented team possible.

- **Chance to try out learning:** Giving people the chance to try out their learning in real life covers a couple of areas – including giving people the chance to undertake redesigns etc. However the core of this idea is allowing people to operate at the level their training lets them, giving them a chance to operate at a higher grade if that is where the training is focused. It may mean taking them out of the delivery team for what they were doing and including them in the delivery for the new work, with appropriate supervision. And not just once – to try it a few times. Linked to this, is the chance to increase grades if they are good enough.

- **Lots of career options:** This intervention includes:

  - Development of options and communication materials.

  - Effective communication of options, available to staff - and to managers for them to include in career conversations.

  - Clear routes between options, including training requirements.

  - Monitoring of uptake of movements.

- **Review of programmes:** A review of effectiveness can be undertaken on a regular basis. It can include:

  - Understanding what the objectives and expected benefits were of the approach.

  - Assessing its performance quantitatively against expectations.

- Seeking feedback from staff on which elements are perceived as important.

- ***360-degree feedback:*** 360-degree feedback needs to be managed carefully, because it involves two-way feedback horizontally and vertically. With people giving feedback on each other it can get a bit messy. However, when done well it can be very powerful, as not only does having a voice on your colleagues' and manager's performance help retention, the individual can learn a lot by collecting the feedback. The good and the constructive can both be very empowering – and help you spot where your behaviours is adversely affecting others' experience.

- ***Properly talked about reward:*** Providing regular (at least annual) benefits statements to staff can help provide a view on:

    - Total reward - which may be higher than people knew when pensions are taken into account.

    - Comparative reward - showing how it compares against average wages.

    - Potential reward - showing the potential future opportunity for reward if you stay in the organisation.

    - Hidden rewards - discounts and offers that are available to the staff that they may not even be aware of.

- ***Staff awards:*** Staff awards can be a great reward for staff. We've been lucky enough to be involved in quite a few over the years (you can get income through sponsorship) including some great ones across the Manchester Health & Care system in England. They can include:

    - A range of categories that give everyone a chance.

    - A chance to show-off strong performers, and for people to see that it is rewarded.

    - Meaningful rewards for staff, including financial rewards, where possible. They can be funded by partners.

    - Awards ceremonies, where staff can be celebrated.

- ***Investment in staff awards:*** There are a range of different staff awards that organisations can go for, with the most common one I see being Investor in People. An award for the organisation that provides a set of standards, assesses you against the standards and awards only organisations that come up to scratch is valuable in its own right. A competitive one can drive even more improvement. These awards take resource to set up, so the organisation needs someone working on this.

- ***Job security:*** The way that the English NHS is funded for some roles can be quite temporary. This uncertainty is often passed to the staff member by the organisation. That's a nice way to treat staff isn't it? Never mind that some of these fixed contracts last so long that staff are no longer temporary, we still insist on using them for what should be permanent roles. And if not, we use secondments – with the threat that the person might have to go back to an old role they don't feel they can still do. Let's stop doing this to people. This can be a problem for VCFSE sector organisations when they do not have safe funding levels, which requires long-term funding solutions for these organisations.

- *Increase reward:* Sometimes you need to pay people more. It's often not the most important thing, but it is the easiest thing to compare with other industries and teams, so if you don't get this right, you will lose people - and thus increase costs. Increasing reward can include:

    - Increasing their salary or other benefits.

    - Moving people within a pay scale.

    - Re-banding roles (in NHS) or paying more. The same job gets different bands in different NHS orgs so don't tell me you can't re-band…

    - Giving people access to overtime or enhanced options.

- *Freedom to speak:* Openness and honesty across an organisation may be like workforce planning – a fine aim, but actually impossible to ever get completely right. But there are things you can do:

    - Ensure that there is executive responsibility for the staff voice.

    - Putting in place the forums for staff feedback and discussion.

    - Managing by wandering around.

    - Sharing stories of "you said, we did".

    - Rewarding behaviours, and not targeting heavy handed individual responses.

When building a cost reduction plan, you can consider things, as above, within themes, but you can also consider individual roles and plan cost control measures accordingly. Thus there are some role-specific considerations - not all of which will be relevant to all organisations, but they are worth including for completeness. As highlighted earlier, the "noisy" providers have often been the focus, but they also have very specific operations that are repeated across the country - which means that they get the lion's share of the ideas.

THEME 3.S1
Staff group: Nurses, midwives and support workers

Basically, anyone who works in a largely bed-based environment, even if those beds are virtual, can be considered in this group. It includes nurses, midwives, Health and care assistants, community nurses, mental health nurses, etc.

Thought needs to be given to this area. Why have costs not been controlled in this area before? Have we not empowered teams properly? Not trained people when they started to lead a ward or unit? Is there not a mechanism in place to monitor and support managers to keep costs under control? When you've worked out what you are going to do to improve things from the list below, you'll need to build a proper project around it AND ensure that the organisational support is in place to support these teams in the future.

Specific considerations for this group include:

- ***Staff:patient ratios:*** Ensuring that you set a staff:patient ratio for all types of this staff and for all types of patient, helps you to ensure safety and to convert your demand and capacity model into real staff numbers on the ground. These ratios help any manager to put the right amount of staff on the ground for every shift. In countries like Australia, legislation around nurse-patient ratios has been found to optimise staffing levels, improving efficiency and reducing costs.

  They can be a double-edged sword at times, preventing the use of innovative staffing models or new ways of working, but as staffing service levels are often the first thing to drop when money is tight, they are definitely needed.

- ***Nurse establishments reviewed***: From an understanding of demand, a process should be undertaken to ensure that the overall number of staff in each area (wards, clinics, community areas etc) is based on actual requirements. Once an initial review is done of existing levels, work should be ongoing to ensure that these levels are right.

- ***Nurse establishments built on workforce model:*** Nurse establishments in each area should be recorded in a workforce model or approach that transparently shows why nursing levels are as they are. This model should be flexed depending on expected demand.

- ***Nurse staffing based on patient acuity:*** An acuity tool should be used to influence ward staffing on an ongoing basis, amending establishment levels depending on changes to the needs of patients. This can be done through regular audits using a tool, and on an ongoing basis using a safer staffing tool. In the UK there is nurse rostering software that includes safe care elements.

- ***Handover times optimised:*** Handover times between shifts should be optimised so as to maximise patient care with the minimum of wasted time. These handover policies and processes should be documented and updated as things change.

- ***Productive Ward (or similar) implemented:*** In the UK, the Productive Series included an approach called "The Productive Ward". Whilst this was widely implemented, it needs to be regularly considered by ward leaders and staff so as to maintain its benefit. The Productive Ward, or similar review should have been properly implemented in each area – and been done so as to actually release time from administration to improving care and reducing cost.

- **Nurse skill mix and banding:** As part of setting establishments, the nursing skill mix and banding should be reviewed, and any opportunities addressed. Establishments are not based just on "who we have available" but on what is needed to optimise care and cost. There are a range of workforce redesign approaches that can be used for this – and if you are doing this at organisation level, then setting a "model ward" and checking all ward establishments against this is a good place to work out where to start.

- **Nursing uplift calculated properly:** The nursing uplift is the amount that an establishment is increased to take account of holidays, sickness, etc. This uplift should be calculated properly – by which we mean that it should be based on good practice sickness levels, actual leave allowances (based on years of service), and actual maternity levels. Too many that we see are based on median leave allowances and a standard percentage for maternity – which means that they are wrong in almost all cases and are therefore providing too many staff or too few. Both of which will be inefficient.

- **Senior Nurse Shifts optimised:** Senior nurse cover at night is usually paid for at a premium, so there needs to be a clear and well thought out approach to how senior nurse cover will be arranged so as to minimise expensive shifts.

- **IT supports optimal staffing**: Information Technology should be deployed to reduce nursing workloads where possible (e.g. decent ward systems, community midwife information systems, minimised admin, remote patient monitoring, electronic pens, nurse rostering software and enough equipment etc).

THEME 3.S2
Staff group: Medical staff

Medical staff have some specific elements that are worth considering as a group. When we talk about medics, we typically split them into "senior" and "junior", which is a bit arbitrary, but they have different requirements.

Senior doctors should all have a job plan, which sets how many clinical and supporting PA's (Programmed Activities) they do. These 4-hour units split a consultant's week into 10 (although many have many, many more than 10 PAs). This should be updated annually and should be on an electronic system so that analysis is easier than on paper forms – cost control and workforce planning is almost impossible without one.

Junior doctors are those that are training – most are delivering care of some sort, but they tend to work in lots of different organisations and many different departments. They are a very important part of delivering care, but the rolling nature of their employment means that a different set of things need to be focused on.

Specific ideas in this theme include:

- **Unit Productivity:** Each clinical Programmed Activity (PA) should have an expectation of how much quality work will be done in it. Those assigned to clinics should be clear on how many new and follow up appointments will be done, or how many outpatient procedures. For theatre sessions, it should be clear how many of each different type of operation can be done within a PA.

- **Job plans in place for all medical staff:** The requirements for all substantive medical staff should be enshrined in a job plan informed by the results of an analytical exercise that measures the productivity and outcomes of each type of Direct Clinical Care PA. This should clearly show the split between different PAs, and list out the SPAs.

- **Capacity plan:** The number of consultants and the number of Pas for each should be based on a capacity plan that sets out the actual requirement for PAs based on demand.

- **Agreed plan:** The job planning process includes either 1:1 or group discussion on performance using productivity and outcome data, which is used to drive improvements in performance in the following year.

- **SPA Optimisation:** SPAs should be agreed annually based on an agreed case for each one above the standard one for professional knowledge. The definition and requirements of each of the SPAs should be defined in a handbook, and there should be annual checks in place to see whether the organisation got the value it required from each.

- **Electronic job plans:** Job plans should all be recorded on an electronic system. To be honest, without an electronic system it is really difficult to control what senior medics are doing across an organisation…

- **Multi-disciplinary team time:** In recent years, the size, complexity and length of MDTs has increased considerably. They can be an incredibly effective way of agreeing the steps for complex cases, but they can also take up a lot of people's times. The makeup and costs of MDT sessions, and their effectiveness should be constantly reviewed. It may be possible to get as good a result with fewer people?

- **Mindful use of junior doctor time:** The use of junior doctors across the organisation or area should be fully understood. Staff making decisions about job planning for this group, and other medics, are fully aware of the numbers, value and amount of work done associated with junior doctors.

- **Junior doctors as part of the medical team:** Whilst training junior doctors can slow things down, quite often junior doctor activity is associated with consultants – and this should all be understood when calculating how much work can be done within a medical PA. The impact of junior doctors should be included when understanding how many consultant PAs are required. Where this makes sense, Junior doctors should be included in the numbers, thus reducing the requirement for consultant PAs.

- **Staff grade job plans:** "Senior" junior doctors should have job plans that are updated annually, just like consultants.

- **Quality Impact:** Junior doctors should be trained and monitored on their impact on quality and cost within the organisation so as to create an atmosphere of cost control and awareness throughout their employment at the organisation (impact on tests, follow up rates, cost of supplies, etc).

- **Junior doctor funding:** The use of Junior Doctors across the organisation should be properly planned and they should only be deployed where there is funding, or where they are adding value through delivery.

- **Night cover:** Junior doctors can be used to minimise night costs through a hospital at night approach that ensures that there is emergency cover across the organisation without needing staff in all departments.

- **Banding control:** In the UK, Junior Doctors can be paid more depending on the band they are on – and that banding is affected by how much work they do. Should one person be increased in band, then others are also re-banded – introducing a sudden additional cost. Banding should be controlled through all junior doctors being on the most cost effective rota and the use of a monitored on-line diary system to eliminate the chance of banding complaints.

THEME 3.S3
Staff group: Allied Health Professionals

Allied Health Professionals operate as one of 14 different types from radiographers to physiotherapists. And within that there are many sub-divisions as well, making this a group that is far from homogenous. Whilst this is titled as "AHPs" this applied to any staff member that operates in a similar way – typically working across multiple service lines delivering a part of the pathway.

Specific ideas in this theme include:

- **AHP requirements defined in a workforce model:** Whilst these staff operate across multiple departments, their activity, numbers and structure must be defined in a planned workload model.

- **AHP use based on patient acuity and service line needs:** Service-user acuity should be used to prioritise AHP interventions. Requirements should be based on the needs of service units and enshrined in Service Level Agreements.

- **System records workload and results:** Information systems (e.g. SystemOne) should be used to record all activity – and be used to provide a picture of workload in terms of activity and results.

- **AHP Interventions based on pathways:** The roles of AHPs should be defined to meet the needs of the organisation and the individual divisions rather than being based on history. The role of AHPs in each pathway should be clear and documented.

THEME 3.S4
Staff group: Estates staff

The supporting non-admin staff also have their own things to consider when it comes to cost control. These include:

- **Estates staff based on workforce model:** Domestics, portering, direct pharmacy, and similar workforce should be planned and scheduled using a resource model. This should be discussed with the service lines, and clearly communicated so they can identify and agree the resources they need.

- **Estates staff roles optimised:** These staff should all work to defined job descriptions, that are updated to remove extraneous or low value tasks.

- **Productivity of estates staff assessed:** The productivity of this important group should be evaluated, at a departmental or individual level where it makes sense to do so.

- **Support roles meet the needs of the front-line:** The roles of supporting staff should be defined to meet the needs of the organisation, rather than undertaking work based on historic patterns, e.g. porters' duties part of planned operational pathways (so they focus on making the pathways work) or the role of domestics been adjusted (aimed at infection control, reduced cleaning in offices etc).

THEME 3.S5
Staff group: Admin & Clerical staff

Last, but by no means least, the administration staff in the organisation also have their own workforce planning considerations. These include:

- **A&C resource model:** A&C staff need to be workforce planned and scheduled using a resource model (based on number of consultants, activity etc) which is communicated with the service lines so they can identify the resources they need. This will help ensure that we have exactly the number of staff we need, and that they can be flexed up and down depending on demand.

- **A&C job descriptions:** A&C staff should work to defined job descriptions, that are updated to remove extraneous or low value tasks. These job descriptions, in conjunction with the resource model, should be used to identify high-impact opportunities to use digital or process innovations to reduce cost.

- **A&C Productivity:** A&C staff productivity should be evaluated (e.g. typing completed, bookings made, call centre performance). This can be used to update the capacity model, but its main purpose is to allow for training and improvements to be made immediately.

- ***Medical secretary role modernised:*** As a specific example of where roles can be made more than they have been in the past, the Medical Secretary role can become a 'Medical PA', assigned to groups of clinicians and responsible mainly for the quality of administration – rather than there being one secretary per clinician who does everything including the typing. This is an area that needs really careful handling as it involves two important groups – admin and medics. Handle this badly, as one of us has done in the past (mentioning no names (Colin)), and this will go very, very wrong. This is a big change management journey and one where careful mobilisation, communication and engagement is vital.

Admin & Clerical staff ideas are only one area of dealing with this vital group. We will look later at the administration process, which provides a massive opportunity to improve efficiency as well as the staff and patient experience. If there was just one area to focus on, administration isn't a bad one.

5.5 Manage non-pay spend

Whilst circa 70% of health and care costs are staff, 30% is in non-pay - and as we have said before, this area can be a lot less painful to realise as it does not include putting less money in staff members' hands. Optimising the spend on non-pay spend of all sorts should be a key part of any cost control plan. We split this area into cost control over:

- Procurement.

- Energy.

- Tax.

- Other non-pay

As in the last section, there are also specific health & care areas that are not relevant to all organisations, so we have separated them out. These are medicines / drug spend and specific health facilities considerations.

THEME 4.1
Procurement and supply chain

This is another large theme consisting of many individual ideas to optimise spend on consumables and equipment in the organisation. It is not just for the procurement department - it is for any area delivering front-line care. Specific ideas are based around getting the cheapest price and controlling the levels used, but also include process considerations, education, electronic support, better reporting, and mechanisms to get stock returned.

- **Return and re-use of materials:** This is one of the areas that often gets raised as "health and care wastage". Obviously returned equipment may sometimes need expensive cleaning, but instituting a programme, and a culture of return and re-use for reusable equipment can help bring about a more cost-conscious approach to equipment even if it isn't always cheaper in itself.

- **Off-contract spend controlled:** Quite often, a large amount of purchasing is done without a contract being in place. This often includes a lot of one-off payments, like management consultancy or furniture etc. Some of this may just be to use up budgets or be vanity projects – so anything off-contract should be keenly monitored. Any large purchasing that is done outside of normal contracts should be reported, monitored on and investigated for value. Small off-contract spend items could be allowed to avoid bureaucracy but be restricted to small budgets only.

- **Standardise key items:** The organisation should work with clinicians / key front-line staff to standardise the use of key items. They should systematically consider the key items being used (cost and value) and develop a plan to standardise each one as much as possible. We cannot stress enough that this should be done with staff, not to staff, as otherwise it will have unforeseen consequences.

- **Wastage minimised:** The organisation should minimise stocks and wastage. Stock levels should be controlled through automatic ordering (re-order quantity and re-order level or ROQ and ROL) to minimise ordering errors and stock levels and wastage should be recorded and reported on – and measures taken to reduce issues in future. Service lines' wastage should be monitored.

- **Single integrated supply chain system:** Supply chain processes should be subject to "Lean" review and improved to maximise efficiency. Part of this should include a single integrated system from ordering to usage by the front-line staff. The ordering/ receipt of goods, and the receipt and matching of invoices should be an automated and lean process - including use of catalogues and automatic matching.

- **Protocol based stock usage:** The use of items should be monitored and compared to agreed protocols for the amount of stock to be used for key procedures etc, and combined with activity levels so that over-use can be identified. The cost of high use or high-cost equipment should be known by the users so they can consider costs when deciding what to use.

- **Automated stock cabinets:** These systems mean that all usage of stock is allocated to should be available in all areas so that usage can be logged to users and staff. By making the process more mindful it reduces unnecessary stock usage, and provides the information needed to bill accurately if required and to identify patterns in stock use by pathway, patient and teams.

- **Electronic ordering:** The ordering of stock should be automated – from identification of low stock levels through ordering, invoice matching and payment, as much of the process should be automated as possible to reduce administration.

- **Robust information systems:** Many organisations that we have worked with still use paper systems for off-contract spend, making its control almost impossible. Information on usage and spend should be available, communicated widely, and reviewed for opportunities to reduce cost.

- **Financial control of procurement:** The financial management of non-pay costs should be a shared endeavour. The procurement team should aim to reduce the price per item and control an organisational wide budget, whilst service lines look to reduce the overall non-pay volume through budgets, and should be measured on performance.

- **Procurement staff deployed in service lines:** Procurement staff should be deployed within a service line structure in which each line determines its usage, but governance remains central. These staff should have responsibility for minimising ineffective non-pay item usage and be monitored accordingly.

- **Supplier representatives:** There should be tight controls on supplier representatives engaging directly with consultants and others to sell their products directly. Supplier representation should be done in a much more organised way to introduce innovations as a group, rather than ad-hoc discussions.

- **Early payment discounts:** The majority of supplier volume should be covered by early payment discounts whereby the cost per product is reduced for prompt payment. If you are going to pay for goods anyway, you might as well do it promptly and get some sort of reward for it. Assuming cashflow or interest rates are such that this makes sense...

- **Materials management:** In this case, we define materials management as providing just enough non-pay material exactly where and when it is required, eliminating large stock rooms. Obviously, material is still needed in case of supply chain issues when you are in a health and care environment, but the days of large rooms full of ageing implants should be over. Colin has walked into storerooms that looked like the last scenes of the film National Treasure - rows of expensive stuff, some going back to the time of the Pharaohs. That might be a slight exaggeration.

- **Regular review of contracts:** There should be a process of rolling review of contracts to ensure best value, and the procurement team should undertake ad-hoc reviews based on intelligence and expertise as to where opportunities may be arising. Some hospitals in South Africa regularly review and renegotiate service contracts, ensuring competitive pricing and service quality.

- **Centralise procurement where optimal:** Suppliers are very good at getting the best price for their products and selling as much as they can. To even the odds, you need a lot of good people to make sure that you aren't overbuying or overpaying. Centralising procurement skills allows for the team to put their best people on keeping non-pay prices under control. The UK's NHS centralised procurement strategy has led to significant savings in medical supply costs, sometimes up to 30%.

- **Strategic partnership with suppliers:** We talk a lot about seeing suppliers as money-grabbing entities that we need to "beat" (and, let's face it, we all know a few suppliers who need this...) but there is an alternative. Establishing long-term partnerships with suppliers, a practice we've seen in Canada, can lead to more favourable pricing and better service terms, resulting in cost savings.

- **Group Purchasing Organisations (GPOs):** Joining or forming GPOs can leverage collective buying power for better pricing on supplies and equipment. This is taking centralisation of procurement as far as you can – acting in groups (even with competitors) to bring down prices for all.

THEME 4.2
Energy

Managing energy costs can produce significant reductions in countries where energy is expensive. This theme focuses on minimising energy costs through engagement, control and specific interventions. It includes six ideas

- **User charging:** Individual areas within the organisation should be monitored and charged for their actual use of gas and electricity supported by sub-metering and appropriate reporting.

AI's Role in Improving Value-Based Procurement

- Analysing past procurement decisions: By examining vast amounts of data, AI can identify patterns and lessons learned from previous procurement decisions. For example, a study by the World Economic Forum found that AI- driven procurement analysis reduced costs by 15% and improved outcomes in 75% of cases. Additionally, AI can identify potential areas of cost savings and efficiency improvements that were previously overlooked due to human biases.

- Mimicking key decision-makers: AI can learn from the behaviour of CPOs and CFOs, helping to align incentives and create more evidence-based decisions. In a pilot project at a major hospital, AI-driven decision-making resulted in a 20% reduction in procurement costs. Furthermore, AI can help bridge communication gaps between stakeholders by synthesising their needs and preferences into unified procurement strategies.

- Simulating scenarios: AI can demonstrate the potential outcomes of various procurement decisions, guiding health and care providers towards better value- based choices. A recent study in the Journal of Health and care Informatics Research showed that AI-driven scenario planning could reduce treatment costs by up to 30%. Additionally, AI can help health and care providers identify potential risks and unintended consequences of procurement decisions, enabling them to make more informed choices.

Challenges AI Can Address

- Habits: AI can help overcome human resistance to change by introducing unbiased, evidence-based decisions. A 2020 study in Health Affairs found that human biases in procurement could lead to an average of 10-15% in cost inefficiencies. AI can also help break down organisational silos and foster a more collaborative approach to value-based procurement.

- Uncertainty: AI can help humans better understand the potential results of different procurement decisions, leading to more informed choices. In a trial at a large hospital network, AI-driven procurement analysis led to a 25% increase in accurate decision-making. Moreover, AI can enable organisations to adapt quickly to changing market conditions and emerging trends in health and care.

- Misaligned incentives: AI can help identify situations where procuring a product or service would deliver better overall value, even if it contradicts traditional payment structures. An AI-driven procurement program at a major medical centre found that by prioritising value-based procurement, hospital costs were reduced by 18%. AI can also facilitate the development of innovative payment models that incentivise value-based care and promote better patient outcomes.

- **Energy awareness:** Strong energy awareness measures could be put in place to reduce the unnecessary usage of energy around the organisation. This can include nominating energy managers or champions, adequate signage setting out how much things cost and the education of staff.

- **Use of renewables:** Utilising solar power and renewable energy sources reduces exposure to variable energy markets (and could even be good for the environment). While the initial setup cost can be high, transitioning to solar power and other renewable energy sources can offer substantial long-term savings and sustainability benefits.

- **Energy consumption audit:** The organisation should regularly conduct audits of energy consumption to identify areas where energy savings can be made, such as switching to energy-efficient lighting and equipment.

- **Best energy price:** The organisation needs to get the best price for its energy and utilities – in the short or long-term depending on your needs. Benchmarking energy costs, joining a procurement group or getting expert help in this area if needed could release significant savings.

- **Efficiency upgrades:** Bringing costs down by focusing on your old, heavy-energy use and investing in energy-efficient lighting, heating, and cooling systems is a basic approach but can substantially lower utility bills.

THEME 4.3
Tax

Who likes paying taxes? If you have a cost problem, you'll want to avoid losing all your hard-earned income to the government, so it is worth focusing on this area for some potential big results. Specific taxes depend on your country, but key areas to consider in this theme include taking advantage of any tax breaks (like "salary sacrifice" schemes in the UK), taking a proactive approach to managing sales or value added taxes, using tax-efficient third parties to provide medicines or equipment, or using Managed Service Providers (MSPs).

We have already considered a complete tax review in the early part of this book.

The specific ideas are:

- **Salary sacrifice schemes:** Countries sometimes have mechanisms by which benefits to staff can attract less tax – so that their take-home salary is reduced and everyone pays less tax. These are worth looking at – but to make them work the scheme has to be well communicated, with high levels of take-up based on strong education and marketing of the scheme.

- **Tax management:** The organisation should have a proactive approach to managing these taxes including identifying and addressing opportunities – as most organisations have some sort of financial advisor, they could engage specialist help to find examples of where they may save money on these taxes

- **Home care services:** Sometimes, tax savings can be made by moving the spend around the system. For example, in the UK it has been possible to make VAT savings using Home care services for drugs – where these do not attract tax when undertaken in this way. The organisation could look for opportunities like this.

- **Managed service provision:** Sometimes, tax savings can be made by outsourcing services through an MSP. Examples have included using them for sterile services or pharmacy.

THEME 4.4
Other Non-Pay

- **Preventative maintenance:** Undertaking preventative maintenance of medical equipment on a regular schedule is crucial for avoiding costly repairs and downtime. Or you can be data led - rather than traditional reactive maintenance, predictive maintenance tools can use data analytics to foresee and address equipment issues before they become costly problems.

- **Maintenance costs optimised:** Costs for ad-hoc repairs and maintenance for teams should be reviewed, and where teams identify high prices being charged, these should be appropriately investigated and discussed with users so that they can either be addressed or appropriately explained.

- **Water usage metered:** Water usage should be metered locally and monitored so that excessive use can be quickly identified and remedied.

- **Review of service contracts:** The organisation should regularly review and renegotiate service contracts and agreements to ensure they are getting the best value for services like maintenance, IT support, and clinical waste disposal.

- **Optimised catering:** The provision of catering across the organisation should be optimised so as to reduce the costs of maintaining multiple catering points etc.

- **Minimised mail costs:** Postage costs should be minimised by centralising mail and postage, reducing postage levels through alternative routes (email, etc), considering the use of a print provider, and pre-sorting mail to get reduced costs from mail providers.

- **Printing costs optimised:** Printing and photocopying costs should have been addressed, where it makes sense operationally, by standardising printers, centralising where possible, and monitoring usage.

- **Telephone charges controlled:** Telephone costs should be minimised by a central team being responsible for overall minimisation, front-line teams having individual responsibility, and information being available on the use of telephones. Home phone rental reduction can also be considered.

- **Taxi costs controlled:** Transport should be charged with reducing overall taxi costs based on mix, price and volume. Front-line teams should hold budgets and their performance against each is monitored centrally. The overall aim should be to optimise usage and price together. Where this is an issue, you might consider putting central controls in place on authorisation.

- **In house van fleet efficient:** All in-house transport should be as energy and repair efficient as possible and its use should be minimised through monitoring and proper route planning so as to share duties (moving notes, tests, etc).

- **Transport assets controlled:** In-house transport maintenance costs should be minimised through appropriate planning, negotiation of contracts, identification of poor practice by drivers etc. The actual physical assets themselves should be tracked and monitored to ensure they don't go missing...

- **Patient transport costs minimised:** Transport should be charged with reducing overall patient transport costs based on mix, price and volume. Front-line teams should hold budgets and their performance against each monitored centrally. The overall aim should be to optimise usage and price together.

- **Planned patient transport:** The use of patient transport and taxis should be planned in advance as much as possible, rather than ad-hoc, to reduce cost. This could be done through an electronic system.

THEME 4.S1
Medicines

With more than forty individual ideas to consider, this theme covers everything to do with the control of spend on medicines and drugs. The ideas focus on strong processes, using the cheapest and most effective option, engaging staff in optimising spend and technological support in the form of cabinets and electronic medicines management. These ideas are not just for the pharmacy department - they are for any area delivering front-line care as well.

- **Generic drug substitution:** Wherever possible, replace brand-name drugs with their generic counterparts, which are cost-effective and equally efficacious. You should review all current opportunities and implement a process to prepare for when new generics will become available. Encouraging the use of generic medications, as in the UK, offers significant cost savings without compromising efficacy. The U.S. FDA notes that generic drugs save the American health and care system around $1 billion weekly. A pharmacy team should be responsible for overall maximisation of generic drugs where appropriate, and service lines should have individual responsibility. Management information should be available on the use of generic products and benchmarked against national and peer group usage - and a system should be in place to flag availability of a cheaper alternative.

- **Formulary management:** Implement a controlled list (formulary) of approved medications, which guides prescription to more affordable options. Kaiser Permanente's formulary system ensures cost-effective medication use without compromising care quality. The formulary should be regularly updated and there should be a monitored policy in place to limit off formulary prescribing. The pharmacy team should support this by producing regular reports on prescribing off formulary.

- **Bulk purchasing agreements:** Where you are able, you could negotiate with drug manufacturers to buy medications in large quantities at discounted prices. The UK's NHS effectively uses bulk purchasing to lower drug costs.

- **Therapeutic interchange programmes:** In certain circumstances it is possible to substitute a prescribed drug with a therapeutically equivalent alternative to reduce costs, especially where prescribed drugs are not having the required effect. The US Veterans Health Administration employs this approach to combine savings with effective patient outcomes.

- **Step therapy protocols:** These protocols are when you begin treatment with the most cost-effective and safest drug therapy, and then advance to other treatments only if necessary. Organisations or areas can examine their drug use and build a library of these protocols where they will have the most impact. U.S. insurers often use step therapy to manage medication costs efficiently.

- **Prescription management software:** The organisation can use advanced software like Epic Systems or Cerner for optimal drug prescribing. These and other systems offer real-time data on drug interactions, allergies, and cost-effective alternatives to support prescribing decisions. This can reduce cost, improve outcomes and reduce errors.

- **Drug Utilisation Review (DUR):** Costs can be controlled by regularly evaluating prescribing patterns to ensure appropriate medication use and reducing unnecessary drug expenses. The approach can be used to consider high spend areas or areas of high variations in practice to consider opportunities to reduce cost. This practice has significantly lowered drug spending in many health and care settings.

- **Patient education programmes:** Organisations should focus on educating patients on the importance of medication adherence and the effective use of generics. Not only will this improve outcomes, but it should reduce cost through swifter improvements in health, reduction in unnecessary visits and diagnostics. The Mayo Clinic's patient education initiatives have helped in reducing unnecessary medication use and costs.

- **Pharmacy Benefit Management (PBM) partnerships:** PBMs are designed to combine the buying power of all that join to bring down drug prices, as well as manage the formulary etc. Where they exist, organisations can collaborate with them, to manage drug benefits effectively – and focus on reducing cost. PBMs use tools like mail-order pharmacies and tiered formularies to lower costs.

- **Value-based pricing models:** Where able, you could look to link drug prices to their clinical effectiveness – paying a price depending on the impact that they have, This allows for drugs to be used more widely, with the risk sitting with the pharmaceutical company or intermediary rather than the health and care organisation. This model, used in countries like Germany, aims to align drug spending more closely with patient outcomes, promoting cost-effective treatments. In countries where such opportunities do not exist, you could still consider understanding how much cost medicines have in the patient pathway, and how much each contributes to the outcomes to see where less drug-intensive approaches might be better.

- **Centralised medicines management:** Centralising medicines management allows for the costs associated with drugs to be more closely controlled. Australia's centralised systems enhance efficiency in medication distribution, reducing errors and associated costs.

- **Automated dispensing cabinets:** These systems require identification of the person for whom the drugs are to be used and the person providing the drugs. This allows for a very accurate record of prescribing and can prevent allergic reactions and inaccurate prescribing. It is also possible that they can be used to reduce the permissions needed to provide drugs. Widely used in the US, these cabinets control medication dispensing, track usage, and reduce waste.

- **Regular medicine reconciliation:** Medicines reconciliation is the process of accurately listing a person's current medicines. It allows you to consider differences between what the record thinks they should be taking and what they are actually taking, and it should be done every time someone moves between health and care settings. In Canada, regular reconciliation of patient medications upon each health and care interaction minimises errors and redundant prescriptions.

- **Pharmacist-led medication reviews:** Experts generally know their stuff, so where possible you should engage them in reviewing the medication that patients are on. This is especially true where patients are on multiple drugs due to multiple co-morbidities. In Sweden, clinical pharmacists conduct medication reviews, optimising therapy and reducing unnecessary drug use.

- **Personalised medicine management:** Where patients have multiple co-morbidities, are on long-term medications, or are reporting issues, a personalised medicines management plan can improve adherence, reduce unnecessary prescribing and reduce costs. Programs in Germany focusing on personalised medication management have shown to improve patient outcomes and reduce costs.

- **E-prescribing:** Electronic prescribing, as in the Netherlands, improves accuracy and reduces the likelihood of medication errors through ensuring that the use of drugs is compared with the patient record, formulary, and drug combination databases.

- **Data-driven formulary management:** Formulary management can be turbo-charged by using data analytics to identify the most effective (and cost-effective) drugs for each condition. This approach for formulary management has been used in France, to help in selecting the most cost-effective and beneficial medications.

- **Real-time drug utilisation review:** When working across systems or large organisations, you can put in place a real-time utilisation system, possibly through the use of a clinical command centre. This can be used to identify individual and wider issues in real time allowing for faster intervention than historical reviews. In Spain, real-time review systems monitor drug utilisation, preventing overprescription and identifying potentially problematic drug interactions.

- **Practice by practice review:** Whether you are working in a system, an organisation or in a large team, reviewing the use of drugs between different clinicians, teams or Primary Care practices can help to identify good and bad practice which can then be addressed to reduce unnecessary prescribing.

- **High drug use reviews:** It is well worth reviewing the use of the largest drugs by cost to identify opportunities to reduce cost and usage. This is where you are likely to find the biggest bang for your buck, and it might give you the chance to solve your drug cost issues in one go.

- **Drugs in cupboards:** This is one of the largest perception problems with prescribing in many cases - kitchen cupboards full of unused medications due to patients stopping using them or not completing courses. If you put in place an amnesty and a programme of identifying unused drugs in peoples homes (e.g. by getting ambulance staff or community staff to check (with patients' permission of course), and then adjust practice based on the learning.

- **Review returns:** Drugs get returned in all sorts of situations, and many come into pharmacies for disposal. Putting in place a more mindful process for getting drugs returned, and analysing why they haven't been used can allow you to review returned drugs from all sources and adjust practice based on the learning.

- **Predictive, automatic ordering systems:** Predictive, automatic ordering systems can streamline drug ordering and eliminate paperwork when used at an individual, team or organisation level.

- **Pharmacy budgets distributed:** Where individuals or teams are responsible for the cost of medicines that they prescribe (or use) then there is less chance that they be used wastefully. Service lines (clinics, teams and organisations) should have pharmacy budgets and an awareness of cost and wastage impacts.

- **One-stop dispensing:** When drugs are prescribed in a hospital or other bed-based setting, the quantity of the medication dispensed should be sufficient for both the inpatient stay and for the patient to take home (based on expected date of discharge (EDD)). This reduces the need for additional dispensing. All patients in hospital should have POD lockers.

- **Self-medication at all times:** Whenever they are in an inpatient setting, patients should be educated where possible to provide their medication themselves to aid compliance after discharge.

- **Pharmacy staff deployed in service lines:** Pharmacy staff should be deployed within a service line structure in which each line determines its usage, but governance remains central. These pharmacy staff should have responsibility for minimising ineffective drug spend and are monitored accordingly. The impact that these staff can have should more than account for their costs, and they should also help improve outcomes.

- **Pharmacy accounting drives right behaviour:** Service line teams define how many drugs are used, but a central pharmacy team are charged with reducing overall drug costs based on mix, average price, volume, outpatients spend, wastage, use of patients' own drugs and use of cheaper alternatives. Service lines should hold the budget and performance against each is monitored centrally. Service line reporting information can show clinicians where they are spending above peers and where their junior doctors are spending.

- **Lean pharmacy process:** Pharmacy processes should be subject to Lean review so as to be able to respond quickly to the needs of the wards in the provision of drugs to patients.

- **Drug cost benchmarking:** Drug usage and costs should be benchmarked against other organisations to identify opportunities to improve prescribing.

- **Non-approved spend has to be pre-authorised:** All non-approved spend (e.g. anything not approved by NICE in the UK) must be pre-authorised through the formulary and its decisions compared to other organisations to identify where there are inappropriate decisions being made.

- **Pharmacy spend and usage data reviewed:** There should be a cascade of information with clear data available to the executive against benchmarks, expected performance and previous years with drill-down capacity to understand variations. Service lines and individual prescribers should have specific reports for their pharmacy use benchmarked externally and internally.

- **Hospital-only drug use reviewed:** Hospital-only drugs should be regularly reviewed and reduced where appropriate. Only hospital-only drugs should be prescribed at outpatient appointments, unless there is an urgent clinical need to start treatment without delay, as these decisions may best be left to the GP/family physician. Levels of outpatient prescribing above hospital-only drugs should be reported on and reviewed.

- **Patients own medicines:** There should be a policy on patients' own medicines in place in inpatient settings so that patients routinely bring in their own medicines, and where appropriate these are used in all service lines in line with organisational policy. The usage of patients own drugs should be reported on, and areas of non-use (or GP / family physician patches where patients not coming in with their own drugs) should be identified and addressed.

- **Default generic prescriptions:** Making generic prescriptions the default option in EHR systems, as practiced in Australia, nudges physicians towards more cost-effective prescribing habits.

- **Transparent price negotiation:** As practiced in the UK, transparent negotiation of drug prices between health and care providers and pharmaceutical companies helps ensure fair pricing.

- **Prescription refill reminders:** Automated reminders for prescription refills, as implemented in the US, can help nudge patients to adhere to medication schedules, reducing hospital readmissions. If you can also implement feedback so that patients can record if they are no longer taking them, if they have stocks, or if they are experiencing issues, then even better.

- **Messaging for adherence:** In France, pharmacies use subtle messaging in packaging and dispensing to encourage patients to adhere to their medication regimens, reducing complications and repeat visits, and thus reducing costs.

THEME 4.S2
Health & Care Facilities

- **Patient specific meal ordering system:** Adopting a patient-specific meal ordering system, similar to the Netherlands, can reduce food waste and associated costs by ensuring that meals are ordered only when they are needed.

- **Patient meal cost review:** The cost of patient meals should be appropriately controlled. Cook / chill or sous-vide should be considered and implemented where cost effective, and patient meals are monitored for wastage levels / meal times are adjusted to keep wastage down.

- **Optimised waste management:** Implementing more efficient waste segregation and disposal methods can significantly reduce costs, particularly in areas with high disposal fees. Waste disposal costs should have been minimised by maximising use of patients' own drugs, proper marking of bins (and proper placing of clinical waste bins,) streaming confidential and non-confidential waste, use of fluid disposal systems etc. The organisation should negotiate the best prices for disposing of waste, including participation in local schemes across the system.

5.6 Improve Efficiency

This should be the absolute core of any cost control and efficiency programme. So much cost is based on inefficient processes, demand in the wrong places and a failure to build innovations into practice. Process improvement can be targeted at efficiency, and at reducing the need (or changing the type of staff and consumables needed).

Again, this has been split between generic ideas sets, and those that will apply to a subset of health & care organisations.

THEME 5.1
Admin & Clerical

This theme includes a long list of individual ideas in this very varied part of delivering health and care. It includes some generic ideas for administration as a whole, centralisation, use of pathways, standardised processes and technology changes of various sorts. As an area, administration should be a core part of any cost control plan as it can simultaneously reduce cost and increase the efficiency of the front line through a laser-focus on automated slick processes.

Specific ideas include:

- **Administration director:** Ensuring that an executive director has responsibility for all administration staff across the organisation will help ensure not only that the staff's needs are better catered to, but will also provide a single point of focus to lead service improvement and technological improvement of the work of the administration staff.

- **Administration issues monitored and resolved**: All issues faced by administration staff or caused by administration process should be recorded and collated so that they can be appropriately dealt with by an improvement team, rather than remain as issues that arise time after time.

- **Administration customer behaviour addressed:** Excessive letter lengths, inaudible dictation, long delays for review of letters, lack of referral letters, poorly completed referral forms, not using appropriate referral routes – there are lots of behaviours that administration "customers" exhibit that should be addressed to reduce the workload of admin staff. These issues should be collated, reported on and addressed.

- **Centralised admin:** For greater control and reduction of costs through economies of scale and reduction of silos, administration functions can be centralised either at organisation or system level. Hospitals in Canada have centralised administrative functions like billing and human resources, achieving economies of scale.

- **System administration pathways**: Pathway administration should be designed to operate across the whole system, rather than just for individual organisations. For example, family physicians should be included in the redesign of admin processes in hospitals, so that efficient referral processes are followed, and information can be electronically transferred to primary care.

- **Standard processes:** There should be a clear set of standard processes for all administration within the organisation or system, rigorously adhered to and supported by appropriate training and source material. This will ensure that new staff have a clear set of instructions to work to, and that people can swap between areas without having to learn new processes.

- **Outsourcing non-core admin:** Administration is an area that should be easier to outsource than many other areas, as you can define the requirements more clearly. With strong service level agreements, you could outsource much of the administration of the organisation.

- **Paperless systems:** Adopting completely paperless systems for administration as a strategy should significantly reduce cost. Some organisations we have worked with in Singapore have done this for all patient intake and records, minimising paper-related costs and improving efficiency. This also includes having an Electronic Patient Record (EPR).

- **Referral management:** Referrals should be managed so that they all come in through a single electronic referral route where possible. Referral management centres (if used by commissioners) should be engaged with to streamline the referral process and there should be an agreed and enforced protocol with Primary Care that governs what referrals will be accepted and what will be rejected.

- **Centralised booking:** A centralised team could be put in place for the booking of all appointments. This would be based centrally, but would have core teams aligned with the service lines in the business. An alternative version of this is that there could be governance centrally rather than complete centralisation. Centralisation reduces silos, allows greater control and creates efficiency through standardisation.

- **Admin telecommuting:** Allowing non-clinical staff to work from home, as seen in Australia, cuts down on facility and utility costs. Any role that does not need direct engagement with service-users could be done remotely – and with video conferencing facilities, this definition can be extended further.

- **AI and automation:** Robotic Process Automation (RPA) and AI are very much at home with repetitive administration processes. Use them where you can to reduce costs.

- **Standard templates:** Only new information should be added when processing anything the organisation does. All the rest of it should be pre-filled in a standard template to minimise admin time.

- **Automated billing and coding:** The organisation should have systems in place that create bills for each service-user, whether they are directly billed or not. By building an accurate picture of all costs, the organisation is much more likely to get the right amount of income, and can identify areas where income is not enough to cover costs – which can be addressed with commissioners or referrers. Where service-users are directly billed, this entire process should be completely automated, with manual review to ensure all is working appropriately.

- **Standard pathway monitoring:** Sometimes organisations can focus on teams rather than on service-users and patients. Within large organisations there should be specific and standard pathway monitoring in place across the organisation, with responsibility clearly defined within service lines. Service-users should not get lost between departments or organisations on a pathway.

- **Administration technology:** Where possible, introduce technology to reduce the amount of administration required.

THEME 5.2
Resource Usage

- **Organisational capacity and demand model:** The organisation can clearly show the requirement for all resources used within the organisation for each activity or service-user type. This can be held in a capacity and demand model, linked to the workforce model.

- **Utilisation monitoring of all resources:** Every resource that the organisation has should be used as much as possible to bring down the variable cost. Optimal utilisation provides optimal efficiency. This utilisation needs to be measured, reported on, monitored and addressed if it is sub-optimal.

- **Monitoring of unnecessary usage of all resources:** If you don't get paid when your resources are used, then you want to make sure that every use is needed. Access to resources needs to be controlled to eliminate unnecessary use.

- **Monitor productivity of all resources:** Organisational capacity and demand models are the first step - but you do need to make sure that you are getting the levels of productivity that you expect at all times - especially early on so that you can adjust things.

- **Duplicate use of resources identified:** If someone has already used the resource, and you don't get paid for multiple uses, then you need to minimise events when the resource is used more than once. This can be done through (electronic) access controls, and review of incidents when it has occurred.

- **Usage variation monitored:** If some parts of your business, or some commissioners, are using your resources more than others, it is worth understanding why, so you can address any unnecessary variations (increasing use if you are paid per use, decreasing use if you are not).

- **Effectiveness of resources:** If this part of the process is not adding value to a particular group of service users, then we need to be freeing up its use for others.

- **Profitability of resources and each use measured:** We need to understand how much money we are making on every part of the process where possible, even where there are multiple resources being used as part of a paid pathway. If we aren't making money, we need to find a way to make money, or to stop doing it.

- **Electronic productivity management:** Electronic systems should be used to record, communicate, review and manage usage, utilisation and productivity information for all resources, to allow issues to be immediately addressed operationally, rather than waiting for irregular reviews.

THEME 5.3
Process Improvement

- **Users billed for use of all resources:** The use of all resources should be allocated to service-users so that we can assess profitability of complex pathways, and ensure that individual resource elements can be evaluated. It also makes sure that we can recover all money from service users or commissioners, if we are a provider.

- **Direct access:** Allowing people (service-users, other professionals, etc) to access services directly could be more efficient (as long as there is the right information and control to ensure that their use is profitable and effective).

- **Centralising or system wide provision of resources:** Lots of individual resource "puddles" could be brought together into a resource pool - leading to greater efficiency (in certain cases).

- **Experts at the front:** For complex processes it can sometimes be beneficial to deploy your most senior decision makers right at the front of the process so that they can quickly diagnose and stream people into less complex streams.

- **Automatic reporting to next step:** Once a process, or sub-process, has been completed, we need to make sure that it definitely gets to the next part of the pathway, and that it does it with the minimum of effort. We don't want things going missing,

- **Clear pathways:** Where there are pathways, everyone operating a process or sub-process needs to know where their bit fits in the whole thing, so they know what is important.

- **AI / automation used to optimise efficiency**: If there is any way to automate or bring in electronic systems to reduce cost and improve outcomes, then give it a go. These will be very specific to the process, but many apps, computer systems, AI, bots and equipment will be out there for you to use.

- **Physical environment fit for purpose:** The buildings should support your process, not be something your processes need to fit in. How can you change the buildings to reduce travel time and steps, locate the right staff together and help the flow of service-users.

- **Minimised travel times:** Can we reduce steps within the process, movement between sub-processes, or travelling between locations.

- **Remote working where possible:** Where can we reduce the travelling that service-users and staff need to do to get to the delivery point. One-stop services and remote working can reduce the footfall in your sites and improve efficiency.

- **Process designed around user journey:** Make sure that user-journey mapping is used to build the right process for all service-users. This can eliminate low value-added steps, improve the customer experience and drive efficiency.

- **Staff only used when needed:** Optimise when you need to involve staff to reduce cost and free people up for other tasks.

- **Process agreed with staff:** Preferably redesign processes with staff so that they are involved from the start - but when they have been in place for a time, make sure that all staff understand the process and agree that it makes sense, to improve buy in to quality delivery.

- **User cancellations minimised:** Last minute cancellations and no-shows can reduce efficiency. Put in place controls to prevent them, and review their levels to learn lessons and reduce further incidences.

- **Checklist based delivery:** Checklists are a great way to ensure standard processes are followed, and that staff know what they are doing. Build as many as you can to drive efficiency.

- **Known improvements made:** You may well find that there is good practice, or that processes have been reviewed before. Find these previous studies and reports and make sure that they have been implemented (or you may re-implement them if things have slipped).

- **Users used within process:** Where possible, get service-users to do the work themselves to reduce the need for staff to do the work - and get more buy-in from your service-users.

- **Eliminate rework/mistakes:** Identify where mistakes are being made or re-work is necessary, learn lessons and improve the process to remove these. Looking at service-user complaints can also help identify these issues, and possible solutions.

- **Eliminate fines for work not done properly:** Try to prevent them, but when you get them make sure that they are valid, and then put in controls to prevent them in future.

- **Value stream mapping:** Applying value stream mapping to identify and eliminate non-value-adding steps in patient care and administrative processes is often overlooked. This should be done regularly as new steps often sneak into processes to deal with issues, that may no longer actually be a problem. We should design pathways to be as efficient as possible if we need to improve productivity.

- **Data driven analysis:** Use analytics to assess where the highest costs are and where reductions can be made without compromising patient care. Analysing patterns and trends in data can reveal key areas for cost savings. Start with the biggest cost areas, or use benchmarking to identify the potentially biggest wins.

- **Benchmarking:** Compare your organisation's performance and spending with similar institutions. Benchmarking against industry standards can help identify areas where costs are higher than average.

- **Interdisciplinary care teams:** Implementing interdisciplinary teams, as seen in Sweden, enhances patient care efficiency, reducing unnecessary tests and procedures. This can be particularly effective for service-users at home, who may have visits from multiple teams - single teams with cross-trained staff can significantly reduce costs. And stop people having to keep getting up to answer the door...

- **Centralised communication:** Utilising centralised communication platforms ensures all team members are on the same page, saving time and resources. Again, this can work very well across pathways with multiple providers and teams.

- **Team based incentives:** Incentive programs based on team performance, as seen in U.S. healthcare systems, encourage teamwork and cost-effective care.

- **Regular team meetings and reviews:** Regular meetings and case reviews, as practiced in France, keep all team members updated and involved, leading to more coordinated and cost-effective care.

THEME 5.4
Estates and digital change

This theme includes "buildings-led" and "technology" changes like: reducing office space, centralisation of clinic space, charging for space, including space as part of the capacity plan, shared reception areas, patient physical journey mapping, stores centralisation, building for energy efficiency and creating healing environments. Specific ideas are included below, but health & care ideas specific to a subset of organisations are also included in later themes - especially for technology, where ideas tend to be very specific.

- **Estate consolidation:** The organisation can consolidate onto fewer sites to reduce travel times and maintenance costs. Multiple sites also create silos (which can adversely affect efficiency).

- **Hot desks:** The organisation can look to significantly reduce the amount of administration and clerical space by removing individual desks and introducing hot desks where appropriate. Assuming that you still have A&C staff actually coming into work.

- **Centralise operational space:** Clinical spaces can be brought together - e.g. clinics or theatres can all be centralised, stores and operational space brought together or manufacturing units consolidated - and the space shared by multiple teams rather than everyone having their own space.

- **Space part of capacity plan:** The requirements for operational and support space should be built into the capacity plan so that space reductions can be planned when things change.

- **Shared reception areas:** Administration areas, like reception space, can be brought together so that they are shared by all teams in an organisation. This removes the need for multiple teams and can ensure 100% cover for all times that clinics are on. It also helps bring about standard practices.

- **Stores centralised or minimised:** Storage areas can be removed from individual areas and centralised in an area which will help reduce wastage as well as be more efficient in space. Of course, just-in-time materials management could significantly reduce the amount of storage space needed.

- **Incorporating energy-saving building designs:** Investing in energy-efficient building designs and systems, though initially costly, can lead to significant long-term savings in utility costs (and reduce exposure to global energy markets).

- **Design for efficiency:** You can design buildings with efficiency in mind. From minimising walking, reducing unused space and optimising your environment, this area can encompass anything you do to create the most efficient environment. Some hospitals in China have utilised Feng Shui principles in their design to create a healing environment, reportedly leading to faster patient recovery and reduced costs. Designing environments for children or those with dementia can also improve care and reduce costs.

- **Optimise your processes through digitalisation:** Almost any part of a process can be supported by digital solutions in some form or another. Consider how it can support every part of your process

THEME 5.S1
Health Specific Admin

- **AI Driven and automated clinic admin:** Robotic Process Automation and Artificial Intelligence are very much at home with repetitive administration processes. Clinic admin – including booking, handling cancellations and undertaking post clinic actions – could all be automated.

- **Standard templates for end of clinic:** End of clinic administration can be minimised by using standard templates for letters, working with clinicians to optimise letter lengths and engaging with referrers to provide information to surgeries in electronic format where possible.

- **Check in kiosks and other tech:** Clinics could be as automated as possible. All clinic booking staff should have access to a hotelling system (for live clinic room booking), text messaging for reminders and cancellations, automated booking, automated clinic attendance kiosks and a paperless process.

- **AI Driven and automated theatre scheduling:** Robotic Process Automation and Artificial Intelligence are very much at home with repetitive administration processes. Theatre admin – including booking, scheduling, handling cancellations and undertaking post-surgery admin – could all be automated.

- **Automatic cancellation and rebooking:** With the right mechanisms to communicate with service-users supported by the right technology in the organisation, clinic and theatre cancellations and rebooking could be completely automated.

- **Rebooking minimised:** We just seem to accept that we need to cancel and rebook appointments, counselling sessions and operations. In some countries and organisations it just seems the norm. But it shouldn't be – these are inefficient and bad for service-users. We should be designing systems and workforce structures to minimise these, and should be reporting on the volume of cancellations and rebooking as a key performance indicator.

- **Electronic health records:** Every health organisation should have implemented electronic notes within the organisation through a process of engagement with staff and service users, backed up with a planned programme of scanning old information or notes with appropriate indexing and the phasing out of any sort of paper notes.

- **Medical records process streamlined:** The processes for any medical records (either paper or electronic) should be subject to Lean review or similar to help ensure that it is as fit for purpose, and as efficient, as possible.

- **Typing automated:** Why do we spend so much time typing up the results of meetings and clinics etc? There is no excuse for it in a modern health and care system – it can be replaced with voice recognition, or can be replaced with more efficient communication methods with referrers (such as discharge summaries) etc.

- **Remaining typing optimised:** If we must keep typing, then this can be done by specialist typists, preferably centralised rather than in separate silos across the organisation – and even better, it can be outsourced elsewhere rather than be done in the organisation. And letter lengths should really be a focus to avoid the voluminous masterpieces that can be produced by some clinicians…

THEME 5.S2
Service-user safety

If we do things right first time, then we will be much more efficient than if we are constantly paying for addressing our errors. And at the same time we will be providing an excellent service to our users - so what is not to like about this theme? It is another large theme that covers more than twenty individual ideas from the generic, to specific ideas around clinical areas of focus (cardiac, maternity etc). It's hard to quantify this as we tend to assume in our models that we are already perfect. We probably aren't.

- **Patient safety programmes:** Programmes focusing on patient safety, like ones in

Sweden, have been shown to reduce medical errors and associated costs by improving clinical practices. A safety programme includes reviews of previous issues and clinical risks, putting in place mechanisms to address them and ensuring that there are appropriate communication channels for staff and patients to report issues.

- **Patient safety leadership:** The leadership of the organisation and team should obviously show that patient safety is top priority by doing things like undertaking planned safety walk rounds, following up on actions and having review of safety top of their meeting agendas. They should prioritise safety considerations over everything else – because not doing that is bad for the organisation, bad for staff and bad for service users. And it is bad for efficiency in the long run.

- **Patient safety information:** Information should be available at executive level and cascaded through the organisation as part of a balanced scorecard. Information should be available on all aspects of patient safety, and issues identified should be addressed.

There are a range of individual areas where safety and quality can be reviewed and enhanced. These include:

- **Cardiac arrest safety:** The organisation can target cardiac arrest and mortality rate through a managed programme of recognition of deteriorating patients (track and trigger, improved reporting, education on understanding of changes).

- **Critical care safety:** The organisation should reliably apply care bundles to critical care patients including reduction of harm from ventilation (bed elevation, daily sedative interruption, relevant prophylaxis etc) and prevention of central line infections.

- **Surgical patient safety:** The organisation could implement improved care for surgical patients packages including reducing surgical site infections (appropriate use of prophylactic antibiotics, use of recommended hair removal methods, etc) and use of WHO safety checklist.

- **High risk medicine safety:** The organisation can implement approaches to reduce harm from high risk medicines including policies, staff guidance, standardisation, monitoring, labelling and storage, monitoring of effects on patients and effective record keeping.

- **CVC bloodstream infection safety:** The organisation can put in place approaches to reduce CVC bloodstream infections.

- **Medicine safety:** The organisation can focus on medicine safety through implementing approaches to improve medication safety including reducing harm associated with unsafe use of insulin, anticoagulants and neuro-axial devices. Efficient medication management systems, as employed in France, have minimised medication errors and associated costs.

- **Hospital acquired infection control:** Implementing rigorous infection control measures like in the Netherlands, which reduced HAIs by up to 30%, significantly cuts treatment costs.

- **Enhanced chronic disease management:** Australia's integrated approach to managing chronic diseases has reduced emergency hospitalisations, thereby cutting down health and care costs.

- **Data-driven safety:** Using big data analytics to inform clinical decision-making, as seen in the UK, can lead to more effective treatments and cost savings. Data can show us where patient safety is being adversely affected by some clinical decisions and provide retrospective or real-time information to clinicians to allow them to adjust their practice if required.

- **Preventive health:** Preventive health initiatives focusing on lifestyle changes, like those in Singapore, have shown to reduce long-term health and care costs by reducing the incidence of chronic diseases.

- **Reducing falls:** The organisation should implement specific responses to reducing falls (bed guards, slippers, medicines use etc), appropriate monitoring and remedial action. All falls or near-misses should be reported so that the organisation can address systemic issues.

- **Reducing pressure ulcers:** The organisation can implement specific responses to reducing pressure ulcers, put in place appropriate monitoring and investigate incidents.

- **Making childbirth safer:** The organisation should proactively monitor its maternity services to ensure that it is operating at the top of its game in terms of patient safety for mother and child and has implemented recommended actions related to making childbirth safer.

- *Standardised clinical guidelines:* Standardised guidelines, as used in the UK, ensure consistency in care, reducing variations and unnecessary costs. However, these need to be used, so should be actively monitored to ensure that clinical guidelines are followed. The organisation can introduce clinical guidance monitoring and reporting back to clinicians and areas to highlight variations and assess the impacts of those variations.

- *Standardised Clinical Pathways:* Clinical pathways in Australia streamline patient care processes, reducing hospital stays and associated costs. With evidence-led health and care, there are many pathways that can be standardised much more than they are, and we can standardise them, and monitor adherence – identifying where any variations are taking place and assessing the impacts of those variations.

- *Safety and quality improvement collaboratives:* Collaboratives, like those in the Netherlands, bring together multiple health and care providers to share best practices, leading to improved care and cost reductions. Using these groups as a focus to improve patient safety can bring good practice from multiple sources together.

- *Performance and outcome monitoring:* We often talk about patient outcomes, but how much monitoring of that do we actually do? We can often focus more on doing a quality job in the moment, but there is less monitoring of the impact on the service user. We could build a rich picture of the activity, outcomes and impacts of health and care interventions to make sure that care is effective – although that may not help efficiency on an organisation by organisation basis, it would make a large difference on the efficiency of health and care for a system or country. Monitoring performance and patient outcomes, as practiced in Germany, helps identify areas for quality improvement and cost reduction.

THEME 5.S3
Diagnostics

Another large theme, focusing on anything diagnostic in an organisation. These teams typically work across service lines, providing a service directly to service users as part of a pathway. As such, you can get disconnection and stress between teams - and you also get wastage. Tests that don't need to be done, impacts of delayed tests - and that's before you get onto the efficiency of tests themselves in often very stressed environments. This theme has a range of ideas to reduce cost - again focussing on such things as communication, monitoring, improved processes and improved technology.

Specific ideas in this theme are:

- **Diagnostic capacity and demand model:** The capacity for each type of diagnostic test is based on planned demand. The capacity and demand should be captured and modelled in an electronic system. Like all capacity and demand models, these allow for finance and operational teams to agree on the link between capacity and demand – how long each test should take - and it provides the basis for making sure that you are getting the capacity that you expect (and have agreed with diagnostic teams).

- **Diagnostic utilisation monitoring:** The utilisation associated with each test or intervention should be understood, monitored and optimised. Diagnostic utilisation identifies late starts, early finishes, delays between tests and cancellations on a service line/customer basis so that you are able to identify the amount of time lost – time that could be spent on more tests (possibly). A "cost per minute" diagnostic is measured and used as a KPI.

- **Diagnostic usage monitoring:** Strong management information should be available, at a user, team and organisation level. Diagnostic information from Ordercoms or similar) systems or RIS can feed Service Line Reporting Information and should be available on number and type of tests per patients, service usage, cost per patient etc. With this level of information, an organisation can clearly understand the opportunities to reduce unnecessary tests.

- **Diagnostic productivity managed:** The productivity of diagnostic staff should be monitored against the capacity model. This should cover the actual test, and the reading and reporting of results, so that we know that we are getting enough tests to meet the capacity plan. We should also monitor not only the number but the speed of reading/reviews of tests, so that we now that they are happening in a timely fashion.

- **Diagnostic PACs and RIS systems used:** PACS and RIS systems should be used in all diagnostic areas and the benefits should be realised in auxiliary services as well as film costs. Ordercoms systems such as should in place with all benefits realised - making sure that all tests are visible to all relevant parties to avoid additional tests being requested. These systems need to be fit for purpose and look to drive efficiency – and should be reviewed regularly to ensure that they remain efficient.

- **Diagnostic processes optimised:** All diagnostics processes should be subject to a "Lean" review or similar to help ensure that they are efficient. Diagnostic processes operate across multiple service lines, so there are lots of opportunities for inefficiency, so this needs to be closely looked at.

- **Users billed for diagnostic use:** Service-users or teams should be billed for the diagnostics and capacity that they use. Diagnostic teams should focus on keeping the unit costs as efficient as possible, and can provide expert advice on testing, but it is difficult for them to completely ensure that tests are appropriate as they don't know everything about the service-user. If the teams that request the tests are billed for it, then they are less likely to commission unnecessary tests.

- **Direct access to diagnostics:** Providing open access to diagnostic tests for all users as required can increase efficiency through removing delays. Access to diagnostics should be based upon a strong knowledge of costs to help reduce unnecessary interventions.

- **Income takes diagnostic costs into account:** The organisation should keep cost and profitability at the forefront when analysing the price of its block contracts, and includes diagnostic costs into that analysis – so that adjustments can be made to how many tests can be undertaken within funding envelopes or to negotiate higher contracts.

- **System-wide diagnostic provision:** The provision of diagnostic services should be considered on a wider basis than the individual organisation, so that efficiencies can be identified by working across the system or even the region.

- **Duplicate tests minimised:** Duplicate tests can be dangerous at times, but are also inefficient. To reduce the cost and danger to the patient of multiple duplicated tests, then potential duplicated tests should be highlighted automatically and the requester referred to the results via an electronic system. Where tests are duplicated outside of expected timescales, information should be available to teams and to the organisation as a whole so that issues and patterns of issues can be investigated.

- **Streamlined reporting:** The process for reporting test results should be streamlined with clinical and admin staff. Depending on the controls, potentially only abnormal tests are reported to clinicians for signing etc.

- **AI used to support diagnostic scanning:** Modern scanners can support the placement of patients to reduce scanning times. The organisation should consider the technology available, especially through AI, to reduce scanning times as much as practicable.

- **AI used to optimise diagnostic reporting:** Artificial Intelligence can be used to read or support the reading of diagnostic reports, identify the next steps, and communicate the findings to the right places. The organisation should consider the technology available, especially through AI, to reduce reporting times as much as practicable.

- **Tests done together to minimise swaps:** Batching tests to simplify the processes is a great way of reducing costs and increasing efficiency. When scanning, having lists that target the same body part, and/or don't require coil changes in between. When undertaking pathology tests, the more of the same type you can put together, the more efficient it often is. So batch where you can.

- **Support contracts for equipment ensure low downtime**: If an important piece of equipment is unavailable, then efficiency is going to be severely disrupted. Cancellations and rebooking, staff unable to scan, interrupted pathways all over the place – you don't want this to happen. So you want your equipment maintenance supplier to focus on making sure that the equipment is always available – bonuses for uptime or payments per test could help this happen.

- **Effectiveness/use of tests optimised:** The effectiveness of tests as part of each pathway are reviewed to ensure that they make sense within it. Where they do make sense they should be part of protocols, but where they don't, we should look to reduce these ineffective interventions.

- **Systems default to optimal tests:** Protocols can be a great help in ensuring that the most effective tests are ordered, but it is even better if you are able to build this into a system that suggests the most optimal test to clinicians. Yet again, AI can be your friend here as it can help suggest optimal tests in complex cases where protocols may not be available.

THEME 5.S4
Emergency units

Emergency units are characterised as "non-elective" events where people come into the organisation for care unexpectedly usually due to an accident or an emergency requirement. Emergency units can quickly become overwhelmed, and the people they accept into a process can require care from multiple parts of the organisation subsequently, so it is an important area to get right. It is another large theme, including more than twenty ideas including specific interventions around improved communication, benchmarking, processes and technology.

- **Hospital frequent flyers managed:** Staff in the organisation, and preferably across the health & care system, work to minimise attendances at emergency units through identifying "frequent flyers" – those people that regularly attend emergency units – and put in place plans to reduce these admissions.

- **Care planning for long term conditions:** Staff in the organisation, and preferably across the health system, work to minimise attendances through developing plans for those with long-term conditions that put them at risk of emergency admissions. This should include planning to avoid going into emergency units in certain circumstances (do not admit requests, etc).

- **Primary care at front door:** Attendances are minimised through appropriate engagement with family physicians. This can include having primary care clinicians at the front door but can also include having clear information available on things that ER staff should know about patients that are being actively managed by primary care clinicians.

- **Emergency provision on a pathway:** Appropriate arrangements should be in place to ensure that work is being undertaken in the best setting. That can include having a range of interventions from phone services to community settings for less serious conditions through to full trauma centres for the worst conditions. The streaming for patients is aided by clear information and integration with ambulance services and primary care so that people arrive in the best place as soon as possible. The US has effectively integrated urgent care centres to divert non-life-threatening cases from ERs, reducing overcrowding and costs.

- **GP practice variation managed:** Variations in the pattern of emergency attendances by family physician / GP practices should be understood and communicated (adjusted for the demographics of each area). Attendances minimised by investigating and acting on variations.

- **Staffing levels matched to predicted demand:** Staffing levels should match to patient demand patterns so as to reduce waits (delays generally cause cost) and avoidable admissions. It is possible to predict demand in Emergency units, and it is worth ensuring that we have enough staff to solve issues quickly and stream people to the right next steps as quickly as possible, as well as treat people. Hospitals in Germany use AI tools to predict patient influx, helping in resource allocation and reducing unnecessary expenses.

- **Innovative and useful IT in place:** Emergency units need to be supported with the latest technology to aid efficiency. This includes capacity planning software, information dashboards, hospital command centres, decent (and enough) computers etc.

- **Emergency processes optimised:** Processes have been subject to Lean, Six Sigma or similar review to ensure that all processes, including admin, have been streamlined to be as efficient as is possible. Regular reviews should take place to ensure that these processes continue to stay efficient over time.

- **Physical environment fit for purpose:** The emergency unit needs to have enough space and the right environment to ensure efficiency. This means having everything from enough bays, visible from central staffing areas through to helipads that do not require ambulance transfers.

- **All emergency income collected:** The organisation needs to ensure that it has controls and processes in place that make sure that all activity is recorded and that all income is received.

- **Ambulance links to minimise unnecessary transfers:** Systems should be in place so that, when ambulance staff are attending people's homes, that their care plans (including do not admit status) are communicated to avoid unnecessary transfers to emergency units. Communication systems should also allow streaming to the right unit for the needs of the patient first time, to avoid unnecessary transfers which can be expensive and impact patient care.

- **Fast-track minors:** Implementing fast-track lanes for non-critical cases, as seen in the UK, reduces wait times and improves overall ER efficiency. Where possible, the flow through this fast-track area should not be affected by issues in the majors area.

- **Post-ER care management:** We want to be able to ensure that we deal with patients once where possible. The organisation should have a post-care approach, policy programme and team to ensure that patients have support post care. This can include self-management steps, with appropriate support, or quick routes to return to get support if related issues arise. Singapore's care coordination programs post-ER visit help in managing follow-up care, reducing readmission rates.

- **Effective triage:** Adopting advanced triage protocols, similar to those in Australia and the UK, ensures patients receive the appropriate level of care promptly, reducing congestion. All people coming into the emergency unit should be appropriately triaged - and the quality of the initial triage should be recorded and reviewed to identify opportunities to improve its effectiveness.

- **Non-emergency telemedicine:** Many attendances at ER do not require an attendance, and are instead due to concerns that people have when other health and care settings are either not available or too busy. Phone (like 111 in the UK), or video consultations can reduce pressure on physical units. In Canada, telemedicine is used to handle non-emergency consultations, reducing physical ER visits significantly.

- **Streamlined admission and discharge:** The organisation should look to find the most efficient way to admit and discharge patients. The administration needs to be minimised and the authorisations need to be only those required in order to move people through the unit as quickly as possible. Efficient admission and discharge processes, as practiced in France, reduce ER stay duration, freeing up resources.

- **Mobile medical units:** The use of mobile units to provide care in the community can help deal with issues before they become so serious that people are prepared to travel to more central, fixed units. In parts of India, mobile units provide community-based care for minor health issues, reducing ER visits.

- **Primary care led ER:** Many people that attend emergency units are being managed on care plans by primary care physicians. Ensuring that primary care are involved in the care being given in emergency units so that they can takeover after the person leaves the unit, can help improve care and efficiency. In Sweden, improved communication between ERs and primary care providers ensures continuity of care and prevents unnecessary ER visits.

THEME 5.S5
Clinics

Clinics include hospital outpatients, GP practice appointments, counselling sessions and home visits - basically anywhere where you are working with people. It's a big area, and it is relevant to all organisations from voluntary sector community groups through social workers to hospitals. It is a very big theme, covering a wide range of ideas including helping people to help themselves, streaming and checking demand, technical solutions, improved processes, clear scheduling and booking and changing the way they are delivered (and who delivers them).

- **Clinic start and end times agreed with staff:** We should ensure that the staff running clinics start and end on time if we want to optimise efficiency in clinics – so a great place to start is to engage with the delivery staff to ensure that they are happy with the times and are not delayed by potential issues (such as ward round overruns for medics).

- **Clinic management information monitored:** A suite of management information needs to be made available to service-deliverers, to managers and to the organisation's senior management on clinic performance (these include such things as DNAs, capacity used, utilisation, prescribing, follow up rates, planned slots against actual used slots and/or planned time against used time). The information should be reviewed, and issues addressed.

- **Clinic productivity monitored:** Clinic productivity (and the productivity of delivery staff in clinics) should be monitored and performance managed to help ensure that there is an appropriate balance between efficiency and patient care and that the clinics are delivering the expected sessions as per the capacity model.

- **Clinic processes optimised:** All clinic processes should have been subject to a "Lean" review or similar, to help ensure efficient processes. This covers the whole process from referral to the end of the pathway. Review considered the administration, in-clinic and operational processes, and these are standard across the whole organisation.

- **Outpatients' physical environment is fit for purpose:** Purpose built facilities should be in place, aimed at putting the clinic in the right place (rather than where there is space) and allowing for efficient processing of service-users through the facility.

- **Profitability of clinics managed:** Profitability information should be available at service-deliver and team level (split by clinic types such as new and follow up) for all clinics. Information should be shared with service-deliverers, preferably in a graphical fashion and they should proactively use this information to improve profitability within clinic settings.

- **Follow-ups optimised:** Follow up appointments should used be only where appropriate, with most service-users instead referred back to their GP or family physician (preferably immediately, or when a follow-up threshold has been reached if required). The number of follow ups should be enshrined in pathways that have been agreed with primary care and robust performance management of follow up levels in should be in place.

- **DNAs minimised:** If people do not turn up for clinics, this creates a potential issue for adhering to the capacity plan. These are complicated situations as we really should have wanted the person to be there – otherwise why book the appointment. There are things we can do to manage DNAs including:

  - Using predictive systems to identify who will not attend.
  - Specific targeting of likely non-attenders to try to ensure attendance.
  - Overbooking to reduce the impact (vs predicted levels of DNAs).
  - Service-users can be referred back to the GP or family physician (where applicable) if they have missed an appointment. This should be part of an agreed policy that is rigorously enforced in most cases.
  - Specific feedback from DNA patients can be used to understand their main reasoning for lack of attendance.
  - Countermeasures such as a text reminder system can be put in place.

- **Virtual clinics used where possible:** The organisation should use multiple clinic types such as telephone, webcam and face to face, with the income for each agreed up front with commissioners. Virtual clinics should be used where practicable to reduce travel time and service-user traffic on physical sites.

- **Patient outcomes monitored:** The organisation can analyse the effectiveness of each clinic on patient outcomes and look to identify ways or reducing the number of appointments per patient. How many times are appointments used as little more than checks or sign offs that just don't need to be used? Yet someone books these, notes are prepared, the clinic session is run, the person takes a day off work and travels to the site…

- **Group clinics:** The organisation should systematically consider how it can deliver clinics through radically different models. One method is to help service-users through group sessions, where time with each can be reduced, yet all gain from the discussions – and a group can then help with support after care.

- **Clinic income optimised:** The organisation should put in place measures to identify what appointments they will not be paid for and to reduce or eliminate demand or activity for this type where possible. There should be a clear plan to identify what will not be paid for, to monitor "overtrading" against commissioned amounts and for addressing it where identified.

- **Clinics in most applicable setting:** The system or organisation should identify what appointments are more appropriately undertaken in different settings or that can be undertaken by other providers and should have a plan in place to redefine the capacity required within secondary care sites, so as not to be left with overcapacity.

- **Clinics on a pathway:** The use of clinics should not be a default option – there should be clear pathways in place that note when, and how many, clinics are necessary as part of care – and what each clinic should achieve.

- **Real time decision support systems:** Clinics can be used to diagnose an issue, to provide direct care (e.g. in mental health, physiotherapy or pain management) or to adjust the level of care. To support these steps, real-time decision support systems should in place to aid the service-deliverer in making the right decision in each case, including artificially intelligent systems or simple checklists.

- **Expand ambulatory care services:** How about redefining what can be done in a clinic setting? We do many things now in clinics that we used to do in theatres, so considering what else can be done in this setting, could drive significant efficiencies. In Sweden, expanding ambulatory care for procedures traditionally done inpatient has significantly reduced costs. You do need to check that payments won't change when you do this and ensure you manage profitability. New Zealand's innovations in performing more complex procedures on an outpatient basis have shown significant cost savings.

- **Centralised referral and triage systems / gateways:** "Inappropriate demand" is a phrase that is generally unpopular, but we all know what it means – it means that someone has turned up to a clinic and they should have gone somewhere else. Whenever that happens, we have inefficiency. So, approaches that allow us to ensure that people are directed to the right place first time should help improve efficiency. Having all potential service-users pass through a gateway service that can check and route effectively is one such approach. In Singapore, centralised systems ensure patients are directed to the most appropriate level of outpatient care, optimising resource use.

- **Routine follow-ups – tele-health or patient led:** Where routine follow ups form part of a pathway, we should consider not scheduling routine follow ups, but instead asking people to schedule a follow up if they feel it is necessary, based on education as to what is normal or not in their recovery. They can then schedule support when it is needed, rather than being called in. Where we need to schedule these ourselves, we should use tele-health options where possible. In Australia, tele-health services for routine follow-ups save costs on physical infrastructure and staffing.

- **Primary care led clinics:** Where primary care clinicians are "owning" the health and care of patients, the lines between secondary and primary care can be blurred if primary care are engaged in the provision of outpatient clinics. In some cases, primary care can undertake some of the work that would be done in secondary care, reducing the need for secondary care clinics – and as the work can be combined with other visits, this should not increase the costs in primary care by as much as is saved. Canada's integrated care models, coordinating outpatient services with primary care, lead to better resource utilisation and cost savings.

- **Challenge staff model:** The staff model in clinics can be challenged significantly, not using expensive service-deliverers as the default. Advanced Practice Practitioners may be able to deliver clinics, perhaps with support from more senior staff when needed (who could then work across multiple clinics). In the U.S., employing nurse practitioners and physician assistants in outpatient clinics offers high-quality care at a lower cost than physician-led care.

- **Patient self-management:** Are we providing care that the service-user would be better off doing themselves, with guidance, information, and support? The organisation should look to identify the opportunities for self-management in its pathways – especially for chronic conditions. In Germany, patient self-management programs for conditions like diabetes reduce the need for frequent outpatient visits.

THEME 5.S6
Theatres or treatment rooms

Theatres and treatment rooms as a theme covers forty different ideas in this wide ranging area. As an area we need to consider not just the theatres of the hospitals, but also anywhere where people are being provided elective (as opposed to emergency) treatment. The ideas include everything about a theatre from its initial booking and scheduling to discharge, as well as infrastructure, staffing, process and technology improvements that can be made to drive efficiency.

- **Standardised surgical protocols:** Where possible, the organisation should look to standardise surgical protocols, meeting best practice, so that all surgeons (or others) operate the same way. Standardisation should include a consideration of efficiency – but just by being standard it can help other areas be efficient - staffing. Use of non-pay etc. Implementing these standardised protocols, like those in Germany's Asklepios Kliniken, has also been shown to reduce surgery time by up to 15% through efficient processes.

- **Advanced surgical training:** Investing in training and development (especially on standard protocols) for surgeons and clinical teams can significantly increase efficiency. Some hospitals in Japan focus on intensive surgical training programs, leading to more efficient surgeries and reduced time in the operating room.

- **Appropriate pre-operative planning:** Various techniques can be used to plan for efficient operations. Customised surgical planning, based on patient-specific data and widely used in South Korea, has led to more precise surgeries and fewer errors. Utilising 3D modelling for pre-operative planning, a practice again adopted in South Korea, can significantly reduce surgical time by improving precision. In Sweden, multidisciplinary meetings before complex surgeries have significantly lowered the risk of surgical errors.

- **Efficient surgical team coordination:** In emergency rooms and theatres especially, team communication can make the difference between an ultra-efficient process and a confused mess. Spending time developing excellent surgical teams, and supporting them with the communication skills they need whilst in the room, can ensure that sessions are more on the efficient end of the spectrum. The Netherlands employs real-time communication tools in the OR, reducing surgery time by enhancing team coordination and efficiency.

- **Minimally invasive surgery where possible:** Surgery time, and of course the recovery time and outcomes, can be significantly improved by ensuring that as many pathways as possible include less invasive surgeries. In Brazil, the adoption of minimally invasive surgeries has resulted in a 20-30% reduction in surgery time compared to traditional methods.

- **Optimised use of robots:** We're probably a long way from all surgery being done by completely autonomous robots, but more and more are being developed that can assist in theatres. Hospitals in Sweden using robot-assisted surgical systems report a reduction in surgery time due to increased precision and efficiency.

- **Real-time data analytics:** Canadian hospitals utilise real-time data analytics to continuously improve surgical processes, reducing average surgery times. Hospitals in Singapore use AI-driven decision support systems in the OR to provide real-time guidance and reduce errors.

- **Checklist-Based Approaches:** Standardisation is important for efficiency, and there are many tools to ensure that the key elements are followed - checklists being a good example of a simple system that can help ensure that all steps are done. Following the WHO's Surgical Safety Checklist, as practiced in the UK, ensures efficiency, and reduces time spent on preventable errors.

- **Enhanced Recovery After Surgery (ERAS) Programs:** Whilst this might sound like it's more of an inpatient idea than a theatres one, the ERAS approach, widely adopted in Scandinavian countries, includes strategies that reduce surgery as well as recovery time.

- **Utilisation monitored and managed:** It's an old favourite for theatres process improvement – the monitoring of utilisation. Theatre utilisation has various definitions, but it's really about recording how much of the time is actually spent operating in theatres to maximise the use of expensive clinical team time. It includes the time spent before the first case starts (late starts), the time after the last case finished (early finishes) and the time between cases (turnaround time). This information should be collected and made available on a clinician, team and organisation basis to allow for common issues and outlier behaviours to be addressed.

- **Start and end times agreed with teams:** Sometimes we have early finishes because the service-deliverer needs to be somewhere else, and quite often we have late starts because they were engaged somewhere else. Start and end times for theatres should be discussed and agreed with clinicians to reduce the likelihood of late starts due to overrunning ward rounds or known/likely problems.

- **Wider theatre productivity managed:** There should be management information available on cancelled patients, budget usage etc, with managers receiving timely reports on each. The productivity of theatre sessions should be monitored and managed and there should be effective planning in advance to ensure that the theatre time is being used with minimal lost time at the end of the procedures.

- **Clinicians engage with booking staff:** The theatre scheduling team should engage with the service-delivery teams to ensure that all its assumptions are accurate, and to challenge the amount of work that can be done in any session. Average theatre times should be calculated by an automated system, based not only on the main service-deliver, but on the combination of personnel.

- **Theatre system in place:** There should be a good electronic theatre system in place, preferably one that everyone can work with. The system should require minimal input, and be able to produce detailed management information easily.

- **Theatre processes optimised:** Theatres processes should have been subject to a "Lean" review or similar to help ensure efficient operation. This should cover the whole process from list booking to the end of the pathway and should consider the administration, in theatre and hand off to the wards elements of the pathway. The "Golden Patient" approach should be used where applicable to help ensure that lists start on time.

- **Daily theatres meeting has been put in place:** One area of good practice is the daily theatres meeting, whereby all staff involved in the theatre session get together to identify what went well and what could have gone better, and then work to improve things for the following day and beyond. Where actions require support, a project is put in place, but many issues can be dealt with quickly. The organisation should have a system in place that ensures that meaningful meetings are taking place in every theatre suite every day. Conducting regular surgical audits and feedback sessions, a practice common in Canadian hospitals, helps identify and reduce recurrent errors.

- **All ideas implemented:** Any existing local or national reviews should have been implemented where they make sense to do so. The Productive Theatre initiative should be used fully, and recent checks should be done to ensure that its changes are still in place.

- **Theatres' physical environment fit for purpose.** The estates available to the theatres teams should be designed for efficiency and be completely fit for purpose. There should be purpose built day case facilities, and all theatres located in the area that makes the most sense - rather than just where they fit.

- **Theatre costs attributed to the service line:** If there is a central theatres team, their costs should be attributed to the area/team that booked or uses the space. The financial model for this should be designed in such a way as to improve performance on the part of theatre teams and clinicians.

- **Theatre information direct to coding / billing:** Information on the treatments received, and the items used in theatres should be provided directly and electronically to coders so as to help ensure that coding takes account of all appropriate procedures, and that patient bills are completely accurate with no additional effort on the part of the clinical teams.

- *Day cases optimised:* The use of day cases, and other non-inpatient interventions, should be optimised so as to reduce surgery costs. The scheduling process should challenge where possible day cases are scheduled as inpatients. The organisation should ensure that, where it is efficient to do so, all day cases conducted in day case theatres (sometimes, day cases can be used as "fillers" in main theatres, but the streaming of day cases separately does tend to drive efficiency).

- *Location of theatres optimised:* Theatres work is not done in isolation, so they should be located for efficiency – to ensure that patients and staff can get to and from theatres quickly and consistently with the minimum of effort.

- *Theatre consumables use optimised:* We want to minimise wastage and the unnecessary use of consumables, without restricting the needs of the service users and delivery teams. Where theatres are centralised, service lines should be in control of the budget for theatre consumables and the performance of theatre staff in this area should be reviewed against key criteria. Where possible there should be standards or protocols for the amount of key equipment that is needed for each type of intervention.

- *Theatre protocols focus on efficiency:* The organisation should look to improve efficiency through making standard surgery changes, including double-bedding, use of floating OPs, use of all day lists and the introduction of AHPs into recovery where required.

- *Pre-operative assessment optimised to reduce cancellations:* Processes should be strengthened to reduce cancellations due to avoidable reasons (including patient no longer wanting the operation). Thus the pre-operative assessment needs to be timely and comprehensive so as to ensure that everyone wants the operation to go ahead, and everyone is in the right condition for it.

- *Electronic pre-operative assessment system used*: To improve the efficiency of pre-operative work, an electronic system like EPAQ should be used. These systems allow people to pre-complete information to reduce time within face to face pre-op sessions, to further streamline pre-operative assessment.

- *Procedure effectiveness managed:* There is no waste like doing something that doesn't need to be done – or that makes things worse. The organisation should focus on ensuring that all surgical interventions are improving patient lives enough to outweigh the risks and the long-term effects. The organisation should consider the effectiveness of procedures with patients, primary care and commissioners after the event to understand patient outcomes.

- *Income from surgery and inpatient episodes managed:* The organisation should put in place measures to identify what inpatient episodes they will not be paid for and to reduce/eliminate demand or activity in these areas where possible. There should be a clear plan to identify what will not be paid for, to monitor "overtrading" and for addressing it where identified.

- *Intra operative diagnostics optimised:* Using intra-operative diagnostics can reduce the amount of time in surgery in certain cases. In Germany, the adoption of advanced imaging technologies like intra operative MRI has reduced errors related to tumour removal surgeries.

- **Enhanced OR environmental controls:** Japan's focus on optimal OR environments, including controlled lighting and noise levels, has been shown to reduce errors caused by environmental factors.

THEME 5.S7
Beds and wards

Currently the largest single theme, with more than 45 individual ideas, this theme covers any circumstances in which a service-user is in a bed. This includes hospitals, care homes, step-down provision in communities and virtual wards in people's homes. The long list of ideas can be subdivided into those that focus on flow, getting people better faster, discharge and interventions that prevent readmission.

The specific ideas are:

- **Patient flow optimised by Lean review:** All patient flow and ward processes should be subject to Lean review or similar to improve efficiency. Virginia Mason Hospital has used Lean to improve patient flow, leading to more efficient bed utilisation. In Germany, streamlined processes for admission and discharge enhance patient experience by reducing wait times and administrative hassles.

- **Bed allocation predictive analytics/Command centre:** Organisations across the world are using powerful predictive analytic tools to aid bed allocation for ER admissions, combined with knowledge of theatre scheduling combined with expected length of stay information. Predictive analytics tools are used, for example by the Cleveland Clinic, to forecast patient admissions and optimise bed allocation. This has been taken to the next level by hospitals and systems in the US (Johns Hopkins for example) and UK that have large-scale command centres to manage patient flow.

- **Scheduled elective planning:** If the organisation has flexible booking systems that operate across the organisation as a whole, it may be possible to actively manage bed occupancy in each ward by timing elective admissions based on length of stay expectations whilst also keeping theatres at capacity. Command centre systems would make that a whole lot easier than doing it on paper…

- **Post-acute care coordination:** In the UK, the lack of availability of post-acute beds is currently one of the biggest reasons for poor flow and high lengths of stays in hospitals. Collaborating with post-acute care facilities to ensure timely patient transfers as soon as patients are ready, could produce significant efficiency gains. Such collaboration could include:

    - Understanding the availability of post-care beds in real time via an electronic system where possible.

    - Capacity planning with post-care providers.

- Predicting when patients will be ready for post-acute care in advance.
- Streamlining process.
- Shared governance teams aiming to reduce delayed transfers, supported by clear information on issues.

The Geisinger Health System in the US has effectively used post-acute collaborations to improve bed efficiency.

- **Enhanced recovery protocols:** Adopting Enhanced Recovery After Surgery (ERAS) Protocols and ensuring that they are implemented consistently can significantly reduce length of stay, although may require more intensive support during the stay. Implementing ERAS, as done by hospitals in Sweden, has shown to reduce length of stay by up to 30% by streamlining preoperative and postoperative procedures.

- **Ambulatory care for chronic diseases:** Where possible, pathways should reduce reliance on inpatient stays. This can work best for chronic conditions where patients are better able to understand their own condition and may not need a stay. Introducing ambulatory care pathways and units can assist with the implementation of this. Denmark, ambulatory care units for chronic diseases manage patients without admissions, significantly reducing the length of hospital stays.

- **All reviews, including Productive Ward implemented:** The findings of all local and national reviews should be fully implemented across the organisation. This should include Productive Ward - which is supported by materials and good practice to aid implementation. Unless monitored, this may need to be re-implemented if it has been a while since it was introduced.

- **Interaction across pathways:** The organisation should operate its wards/beds as part of a wider pathway – and should interact with Primary Care, Social Care and Secondary Care to aid discharge or reduce admissions via pathway planning for all areas. No matter what beds or wards you operate, understanding likely demand (admissions) and/or being able to facilitate discharges should be valuable.

- **Real time management information:** Management information (e.g. information against benchmarks, expected performance and previous years and specific LoS benchmarking reports for service lines) should be available, reviewed and acted upon. Bed management systems should be used across the Trust to proactively identify bed requirements based on historic and other data (e.g. planned OP attendances) and a visual management package used so that real time information on bed state can be viewed.

- **Wards designed to optimise productivity and care:** All wards and beds units should be built for efficiency. Where there are nurse stations they should be situated so as to maximise access. The locations of key elements (e.g. sluices, day rooms and toilets should be designed so as to minimise time spent travelling). Note that single rooms are likely to be less efficient in nurse time than Nightingale wards.

- ***Clear protocols in place:*** There should be very clear and documented protocols in place for beds/wards activity and steps e.g. in maternity, clear advice on reducing N12s (or equivalent), caesarean rates, induction rates, number of pre/post natal appointments etc. This should also include a clear view on length of stay and the expected sub-steps that need to be in place in order to hit expected date of discharge. Standardising care pathways for high-volume procedures, similar to methods in Japan, streamlines care and reduces unnecessary hospital days.

- ***Predictive analytics for bed management:*** Hospitals in France use predictive analytics to anticipate patient discharges, thereby reducing delays and shortening the length of stay. These are also part of command centre technologies, providing the added benefit of being able to prompt when steps are in danger of being missed that might otherwise delay discharge.

- ***Telehealth integration:*** The organisation could integrate inpatient care with telehealth engagement with patients following discharge (perhaps allowing people to go home but call in if there are certain issues) or instead of admitting them at all. Kaiser Permanente do this, to manage certain health issues remotely and reduce unnecessary hospital admissions.

- ***Internal rapid response teams:*** Building Rapid Response Teams within organisations or across systems to quickly address patient needs before they get worse, thus reducing transfers and length of stay, a strategy successfully used by hospitals like Johns Hopkins.

- ***Patient centred care models:*** Adopt patient-centred care models, which focus on holistic and efficient treatment of the service user, rather than undertaking a general series of tasks to inpatients, thus reducing readmissions and length of stay, as demonstrated by the Cleveland Clinic.

- ***Ward utilisation monitored:*** An old favourite of any modelling or cost control plan, organisations should monitor and manage the utilisation of wards. This should be done especially well for more expensive areas like critical care. Utilisation should be monitored across time, as well as in average, as over-utilisation versus model assumptions can be as bad as under-utilisation.

- ***Leadership management of ward efficiency:*** People need to care about ward efficiency if it is to be focused on by staff. Thus, ward efficiency should be reviewed at all levels of management, including at the executive, and issues and opportunities to improve addressed.

- ***Length of stay performance management:*** The amount of time that people spend in beds should be managed through a specific central programme as well as clearly defined individual responsibility aimed at bringing length of stay into the top quartile. Modelling should make assumptions about length of stay that are based on organisational reality, but the organisation should look to improve performance every year.

- ***Users charged for their use of beds:*** Directorates should be recharged for their use of beds outside of their budgets to encourage them to balance demand and capacity better. Outliers – where patients are not in the beds assigned to the specialty – should be reported on daily, and payments should be higher than costs to penalise this behaviour.

- **Patient safety impact on LoS:** The organisation should understand the impact of patient harm to length of stay, monitor its impact and address individual concerns and themes.

- **Multidisciplinary team rounds:** It may be that a single consultant or other lead, visiting beds every day, may not be able to accurately define the next steps for each patient on their own. Introducing daily multidisciplinary rounds, similar to practices in Australia's health and care system, has been proven to reduce length of stay by facilitating coordinated care plans.

- **Rapid diagnostic centres:** Sometimes people remain in hospital so that they can gain access to diagnostic tests more quickly than if they were sent home. Providing rapid access to diagnostics can reduce length of stay by providing quicker diagnosis and treatment plans.

- **Outpatient drugs:** Not everything needs to be done in staffed beds. Programs like OPAT (OP Parenteral Antibiotic Therapy), successfully implemented in New Zealand, allow patients to receive IV antibiotics at home, reducing hospital days.

- **Early mobilisation programs:** Initiatives such as early physical therapy, started within 24 hours of surgery, have shown to reduce length of stay, as evidenced in Canadian health and care settings.

- **Pet therapy programmes:** Incorporating animal-assisted therapy, as seen in some US hospitals, has surprisingly reduced patient stress and shortened recovery times, leading to cost savings.

- **Sleep optimisation programmes:** In Australia, initiatives to optimise patient sleep in hospitals, using techniques like soundproofing and light control, have improved recovery rates and reduced the length of hospital stays.

- **Laughter therapy:** Hospitals in India have experimented with laughter therapy sessions for patients, which have been linked to quicker recovery and reduced medication use.

- **Telemedicine for specialist consultations:** Where patients have complex needs, rather than sending them to the experts, the experts could come to them. Using telemedicine to consult with specialists can reduce the costs associated with patient transfers and in-person specialist visits.

- **Discharge communication:** When someone leaves the bedded unit/ward, electronic summaries should immediately be sent to Primary Care Providers, in a manner that allows them to understand what they need to do to help keep the person well (and out of the beds).

- **Patient given an expected date of discharge:** All patients should be given an Expected Date of Discharge (EDD), preferably including indications of key dates / times within their stay for different elements of the process. There should be clear management information on adherence to this, and areas that do not provide EDDs should be helped to provide it every time.

- **EDD is managed to make it a reality:** EDD Information should be shared with their family as required, with primary care provides, with post-acute providers and enshrined in the PAS system so that it can be reported on and monitored.

- **Excess bed days minimised:** Variations to expected date of discharge or expected lengths of stay (Excess bed days) should be proactively avoided with a plan to address any patients with EBDs and the reasons for them known.

- **Infrastructure elements in place:** The organisation should have access to facilities that help reduce length of stay as much as possible. This can include:

    - A patient hotel (whereby patients do not need to be admitted before surgery, or can be discharged when well).

    - Admission lounges.

    - Discharge lounges.

    - Step down beds.

- **Comprehensive discharge planning:** There should be clear policies for discharge so that patients are not waiting for staff availability before being discharged. There should be a range of responsible individuals with enough patient time to be able to discharge at the earliest moment. This includes "nurse-led discharge". The organisation should develop comprehensive discharge processes that begin at admission, similar to the Mayo Clinic's approach, ensuring timely discharge and bed availability. The Netherlands uses a multidisciplinary approach to discharge planning, ensuring all patient needs are addressed, thereby reducing readmissions. Singapore's hospitals use a structured discharge checklist to ensure all necessary steps are taken before a patient leaves the hospital, minimising the chance of readmission due to oversight.

- **Real-time bed management systems:** Organisations can use real-time bed management software, similar to the systems used in Singapore's public hospitals, for up-to-date information on bed availability. Again, command centres can assist with providing the most accurate view of actual available bed stock.

- **Post-discharge follow-up calls:** Organisations can still be responsible for service-users that have left the bedded unit/ward, and should look to reduce re-admissions. Contacting patients post discharge can help identify issues. In the US, some hospitals have implemented follow-up call systems to address any post-discharge complications early, preventing readmissions. Utilising telemedicine, like in Singapore's tele-health pilot programs, helps monitor patients post-discharge, reducing readmission rates and subsequent hospital stays.

- **Transitional care between settings:** Transitional care models, as seen in Germany, bridge the gap between hospital and home care, significantly lowering readmission rates. As people head towards discharge, their details are made available to transitional care teams who can help people remain at home, addressing issues as they arise.

- **Re-admissions penalties minimised:** Overall, unnecessary re-admissions need to be minimised, as they represent additional cost and represent a quality issue. However, all readmissions should be analysed, as not all can be considered the fault of the discharging provider - so the organisation should aim to have an open and honest dialogue with commissioners around performance to reduce "unfair" fines.

- **Patient and family education programmes:** At some point, service-users have to look after themselves again, hopefully with some family support especially over an interim period. Educating patients and families about post-discharge care, as practiced in Germany, can lead to a decrease in length of stay by ensuring better at-home care (and should also reduce readmissions).

- **Medication reconciliation:** Medicines issues can cause a lot of re-admissions. Hospitals in Canada emphasise medication reconciliation at discharge to prevent medication errors, and educating patients and providing reminders by text to take medicines can help reduce these issues.

- **Use of patient portals for post-discharge communication:** Let's keep talking, especially in the period immediately after discharge. Reminders to take medication, access to hot-clinics, identifying issues and providing education - all of these things require communication with the service user so recently discharged. A decent system can be put in place to help make this an efficient and well-used part of the care pathway. In Sweden, patient portals allow for ongoing communication between patients and health & care providers post-discharge.

- **Home health services referral:** The referral of patients to home health services, as practiced in France, ensures continued care post-discharge, reducing the likelihood of readmission.

- **Community resource engagement:** Hospitals in India engage with community resources to provide support for patients after discharge, particularly in rural areas. You can also engage with voluntary organisations for certain service-users or conditions.

THEME 5.S8
Technology

Whilst many digital ideas have been included in other parts of this list, based on specific needs, this group of ideas focuses on taking an innovation and making it happen across the organisation. It includes: AI, tele-health, remote monitoring, electronic health records,

Digital Health in Value-Based Health and care Examples

Digital health technologies, such as electronic health records (EHRs), telemedicine, mobile health (mHealth) applications, wearable devices, remote monitoring systems, artificial intelligence (AI), and big data analytics, are pivotal in enhancing health and care delivery, patient outcomes, and system efficiency across the world.

Digital health solutions hold transformative potential for health and care systems globally, including high-income countries and low- and middle-income countries (LMICs). The innovation in LMICs often leads to creative, cost-effective health and care solutions, demonstrating universal lessons and models that can be adapted in various contexts.

Global Success Stories in Digital Health include:

- **Kenya's M-TIBA Platform:** M-TIBA is a mobile-based health wallet that revolutionised health and care access in Kenya, enabling over 4 million people to afford health and care. It exemplifies how mobile technology can bridge financial barriers to health and care access, a model that can be replicated in other settings to improve health and care affordability.

- **India's National Health Stack:** This initiative aims to create an integrated digital health infrastructure, streamlining health and care delivery across India, especially in rural areas. The project underscores the importance of a unified digital platform for health and care management, which could be beneficial in other countries to enhance health and care coordination.

- **Brazil's SI-PNI:** Brazil implemented an electronic immunisation registry, improving the efficiency of vaccination campaigns and increasing coverage rates. This digital platform showcases how technology can streamline public health programs, applicable in managing similar health initiatives globally.

- **South Korea, the United Kingdom, and the United States:** These countries have made significant strides in digital health implementation. South Korea's "Digital Health Development Plan" encourages innovation and collaboration, the UK's NHS has advanced in telemedicine and AI, and the US has seen growth in AI-driven diagnostics and patient care models.

mobile health, automation of patient monitoring, digital therapeutics, 3D printing and smart tech.

- **AI-based diagnostic tools:** More and more decision support tools are coming onto the market to help clinical diagnosis. AI systems, like those developed in Israel, offer quick and accurate diagnoses, reducing the need for multiple tests and subsequent costs.

- **Telehealth services:** Telemedicine platforms, widely used in Australia, have significantly reduced patient visit costs and improved access to care, especially in remote areas.

- **Remote patient monitoring:** In the US, wearable devices for chronic disease management have decreased hospital readmissions, cutting down long-term health and care costs.

- **Electronic health record:** EHR systems, such as the ones in Singapore, streamline patient information management, reducing administrative costs and improving care coordination.

- **Automated patient monitoring:** Hospitals in Germany use automated monitoring systems in ICUs, leading to decreased need for constant manual monitoring and reducing staffing costs.

- **Mobile health applications:** In India, mobile health apps have been effectively used for patient education and monitoring, reducing the frequency of in-person visits.

- **3D printing:** The Netherlands has seen cost savings in custom prosthetics manufacturing through 3D printing technologies, compared to traditional methods.

- **Digital therapeutics:** Digital therapeutic platforms in the UK, offering cognitive behavioural therapy, have proven to be a cost-effective alternative to traditional therapy models.

- **Smart beds:** In Canada, smart beds equipped with sensors have been utilised to monitor patient vital signs and movements, reducing the need for manual checks and improving patient safety.

5.7 Align the Back Office

A lot of controllable spend sits outside the direct delivery of health and care - and corporate, support and back office spend can often get out of control through a lack of alignment to the core operations of the organisation. A key part of a cost control programme should be the review of the added-value of these functions, their strengthening where they can help the front-line be more efficient and their removal when they are in the way. Specific themes under this heading include the consideration of spend in all main corporate areas (finance, HR, executive teams etc) as well as a focus on billing, business development, outsourcing and compliance.

THEME 7.1
Corporate staff

This theme is relevant to all corporate staff, focusing as it does on such things as ensuring that there is a corporate workforce plan based on workload, that there are defined and relevant job descriptions, that productivity is evaluated, that they are linked to the front line and that they work together to serve the delivery units as well as ensuring that processes and IT are fit for purpose, challenging for automation where possible. This area also considers the size of the executive team.

- **Corporate workforce plan based on workload:** We should ensure that we have a clear picture of what corporate staff we need, rather than one based on historic levels minus cost improvement requirements. The rationale regarding staff levels should be clearly set out and transparent and linked to activity and required tasks – it should be recorded in a workforce model.

- **Corporate staff work to defined job descriptions:** Sometimes, the role of corporate staff can be a little unclear, which actually doesn't help the organisation or the staff member. Job descriptions should be accurate, should be kept up to date and should link to the workforce plan, so that extraneous or low value tasks can be removed and the impact identified, and so that extra time is made available for extra tasks (otherwise they won't have to do it properly, and if they can't do it properly, why ask for it to be done at all?)

- **Corporate staff productivity evaluated**: Why do we just check that the front-line staff are productive? We should do this for everyone. Corporate staff productivity, at a departmental or individual level (where it makes sense to do so and can be done) should be monitored and evaluated and actions taken to address issues.

- **Corporate functions enablers for performance:** Corporate team like HR, Finance, Estates and Communication should aim to modernise their operations so as to be real enablers for organisation performance. They should analyse and challenge the amount of work done for regulators or "head office" of various sorts, and ensure that the work they do for the organisation is aimed at making life efficient for everyone, not just making their own bit of the process easier for the corporate team.

- **Corporate meetings minimised:** Meetings (internal and with others) are:

    - Only put in place when needed and removed when not.

- Kept to the optimum length.
- include only those participants needed.
- Reviewed for effectiveness as part of the agenda (and regular reviews of meeting schedules should be undertaken).

Staff that actually have jobs to do should be encouraged to have large swathes of time to actually do stuff, rather than be on Teams, Zoom or in meetings.

- **Corporate functions aligned to users at a single point:** All frontline teams should have a single point of contact with the corporate teams to ensure that information is consistent and that the division is not overrun by queries from multiple sources. This corporate contact should shield the front-line from unnecessary requests, as they should understand what life is like on the front-line, and working in corporate. They should be a link that helps drive understanding.

- **Corporate processes are "fit for purpose":** Corporate processes should all have been subject to Lean review to ensure that they are as required to run the organisation effectively and efficiently. They should not be too lax, so that there is little control over productivity etc, but should also not be "over the top" in their controls and their attitude. They need to help, not hinder.

- **Executive team size optimised:** The size and responsibilities of the Board and executive team should be regularly reviewed to ensure that there has not been a "creep" in the size of the team, and there should be regular opportunities to refresh the accountability of each member to ensure there is efficient leadership and no areas missing or overlapping.

- **Function for cross-organisation working:** The trouble with corporate functions is that they each have a boss that directly works on the Executive team. This can lead to each one championing their own little fiefdom, which leads to inefficiency and difficulty in making any changes across corporate function. Believe us when we say that trying to cost control corporate functions is the hardest job in the world, because none of the executive likes you. Someone, typically working for the CEO, should take an overall view on cross-organisation working that operates across individual corporate areas, so that synergies can be identified and acted upon.

- **Departments have minimised "transactions":** In the old days, corporate functions were responsible mainly for doing lots of transactions – recruiting processes, payroll, expenses, financial entries etc. Much of this work can be removed or automated these days, so the whole corporate function should look to implement direct entry systems (e.g. from rostering, ESR within divisions) and automate the rest. The use of IT solutions for billing and coding in India has shown to reduce administrative costs by automating routine tasks.

- **Corporate staffing and structure optimised:** The staffing structure of the corporate functions should be reviewed periodically to see where there are opportunities to outsource or remove whole functions, share locations, share staff/process, share management etc.

- **Corporate costs benchmarked:** Various organisations and clubs exist that allow you to benchmark your corporate function costs against similar organisations (e.g. within the English NHS), other public and private providers in health & care, and against other industries. A regular review of benchmarks may identify opportunities to improve.

- **Telecommuting for Administrative Staff:** If staff don't need to be in the office, then why can't they just work from home, thus reducing the need for car parks, offices, and energy? Allowing non-clinical staff to work remotely, as some Australian health and care providers do, can reduce facility costs and increase staff satisfaction.

THEME 7.2
Finance staff

This theme includes two individual ideas focusing on: Review of high spend areas and supporting them to address costs and simplifying finance processes where possible to reduce overheads on the front line. It is about being less transactional and more strategic in the way in which finance supports the business.

- **High spend area review:** The finance team should undertake a rolling, risk-based, review of high spend areas or areas that are over budget so that savings can be identified or potential overruns avoided. They should also look at ones that are under-budget to look at opportunities to take costs out in the short term.

- **Simplified finance:** The team should look for opportunities to simplify the finance (and finance / HR) activities across the Trust that the individual front-line teams have to operate, to see where costs can be reduced. They should only engage with the front-line when we are actually going to use what they provide, and requests should have minimal impact. They should also look to simplify their own processes with. For example, fast month/year end close approaches, etc.

THEME 7.3
Information and IT

In an environment where will likely see increased IT costs (due to increased automation etc), IT is an interesting area to consider when looking to control costs, Specific ideas in this area focus on reducing unnecessary demand for their services, on reducing spend on unnecessary licences, controlling spend on IT assets and ensuring that the organisation is getting best value on the technology that it already has.

- **Licences controlled:** The IT team should maintain a complete view of licences and ensure that they are re-used rather than new ones purchased. This could include charging the user teams for their licences to encourage them to cancel old ones, or automated means to do the same. We shouldn't be paying for stuff we don't use.

- **Reporting optimised:** Reports provided by the information team should be optimised to include those that are absolutely required and used, and should only include the information that is needed. Systems should be designed so that users can generate reports themselves.

- **IT assets rigorously controlled:** We should know what we have got across the whole organisation, and ensure that it isn't going missing, and is actually being used. Where we haven't used assets (software and hardware) that we have purchased, then reports should be available to the organisation on what, why and how much – and these should be acted on to avoid issues in future.

- **Technology utilisation review:** The IT team should support the business by evaluating current technologies and systems used within the organisation to identify tools that are underutilised or not cost-effective and consider alternatives. It should also act as an expert in helping areas to understand, select, implement and use new technologies. Investing in the right technology can lead to long-term savings.

THEME 7.4
Governance

This theme includes a few ideas, but with insurance spend increasing, it is an important one to consider. Specific ideas include a mapping of governance resources to reduce duplication and confusion between teams, ensuring that feedback from service users is acted upon to provide a source of improvement opportunities and that, crucially, insurance premiums are minimised.

- **Governance resources mapped:** There should be a clear view within the organisation of the resources deployed on governance, within the service lines/teams and corporately. Levels should be optimised by eliminating duplication and placing resources where they have most impact.

- **Patient complaints analysed:** If people have taken the bother to write to us then there are either real or perceived issues that we should be dealing with, which should help us be more efficient. All complaints should be reviewed and acted upon where they reveal the opportunity to improve the value of services or eliminate waste.

- **Insurance premiums minimised:** All insurance premiums and legal costs should be (e.g. CNST) minimised through an appropriate programme of improvement. We should be looking at what makes these costs so high, and addressing the highest areas of concern.

THEME 7.4
Human resources

This theme includes a a mix of HR specific ideas including the centralising of training (and training budgets) so as to optimise its use, the control of staff overpayments, ensuring that tax is being appropriately handled (and recovered where possible) on staff expenditure and then one large idea around completely automating as much of HR processing work as is possible.

- **Centralised Training:** Training and development should be centralised to some extent – to at least include someone having a clear view on the costs and level of training across the organisation to ensure that the money is being used to best effect. It is important to invest in training – but only if the training is leading to development and improvement. Scare resource should be targeted at the highest value areas, and all training should be evaluated to ensure that it is having a positive impact.

- **Over-payment of staff controlled:** The organisation should have strong controls in place to prevent over-payment of staff. Where this happens, then we need to understand why and record it as a "never-event" as getting money back from staff members can be very distressing for some.

- **HR work automated:** The team should look for opportunities to simplify the HR activities across the trust that the individual front-line teams have to operate, to see where costs can be reduced. We only engage with the front-line when we are actually going to use what they provide, and requests should have minimal impact.

- **Tax recovery on staff costs:** The organisation needs to ensure that it is recovering all the tax it can on staff transactions including recovering taxes on staff that have been overpaid, and ensuring sales tax / VAT is handled correctly on expenses.

THEME 7.5
Other corporate

When considering the whole of the cost of the organisation, there are a range of corporate functions that bear a quick consideration for completeness. These include health and safety, research, marketing and comms, legal advisory, R&D and service improvement. In all these cases we want to optimise spend (which may include increasing it to drive efficiency elsewhere). This theme also includes ensuring that there is a clear view on corporate efficiency, that contracting is clear and that non-core areas are market tested:

- **Health and safety costs optimised:** All costs associated with this area, both corporate and within the service lines/teams, should be identified and optimised so as to reduce duplication and improve performance.

- **Non-core areas market tested:** The weird areas that some organisations do (and sometimes do really well,) but don't leap to mind when thinking health and care – like sewing rooms, although there can be many other areas should be identified and tested against the market so as to reduce management overheads.

- **Research costs optimised:** All costs associated with this area, both corporate and within the service lines/teams, should be identified and optimised so as to ensure that appropriate funding is being received and that activities fit the strategy of the organisation.

- *Marketing, engagement and communications spend optimised:* All costs associated with this area, both corporate and within the service lines/teams, should be identified and optimised so as to reduce duplication and improve performance. In cost improvement times, there should be clear messages, understood by all, on cost optimisation plans, and contingency plans for dealing with stakeholder groups and the press.

- *Legal advisory costs optimised:* All costs associated with this area, both outsourced and insourced should be identified and optimised so as to reduce duplication and improve performance. We should stop doing anything we don't need, and consider the balance between insourcing and outsourcing.

- *Service improvement teams optimised*: All costs associated with this area, both corporate and within the service lines/teams, should be identified and optimised so as to reduce duplication and improve performance. The work of service improvement teams should be assessed and market tested against external providers.

- *Clear and open contracting with commissioners:* When contracting with commissioners or similar, this should be done with clear links to the service lines/front-line teams so that undeliverable promises are not made, or clear financial advantage given away.

- *Research and development function costs optimised:* All costs associated with this area, both corporate and within the service lines/teams, should be identified and optimised so as to reduce duplication and improve performance.

- *R&D income opportunities maximised:* Corporate teams should be on the lookout for central money that can be grabbed and brought into the organisation. Research and development (and other) funding a should be maximised, perhaps through a team that can clearly show the additional value that it is bringing.

THEME 7.6
Estates and facilities

This theme is an eclectic mix of ideas for more efficient facilities spend, including patient meals, waste, maintenance, water usage, printing, postage, porters, domestics, and telephone charges across the organisation. This theme also considers ideas on lean facilities, user charging for facilities and market testing of all operations.

- *Patient specific meal ordering system*: Adopting a patient-specific meal ordering system can reduce food waste and associated costs by ensuring that meals are ordered only when they are needed.

- *Optimised catering:* The provision of catering across the organisation should be optimised so as to reduce the costs of maintaining multiple catering points etc.

- *Patient meal cost review:* The cost of patient meals should be appropriately controlled. Cook / chill or sous-vide should be considered and implemented where cost effective, and patient meals are monitored for wastage levels / meal times are adjusted to keep wastage down.

- **Optimised waste management:** Implementing more efficient waste segregation and disposal methods can significantly reduce costs, particularly in areas with high disposal fees. Waste disposal costs should be minimised by maximising use of patients' own drugs, proper marking of bins (and proper placing of clinical waste bins, streaming confidential and non-confidential waste, use of fluid disposal systems etc. The organisation should negotiate the best prices for disposing of waste, including participation in local schemes across the system.

- **Preventive maintenance:** Undertaking preventative maintenance of medical equipment on a regular schedule is crucial for avoiding costly repairs and downtime. Or you can be data led - rather than traditional reactive maintenance, predictive maintenance tools use data analytics to foresee and address equipment issues before they become costly problems.

- **Maintenance costs optimised:** Costs for ad-hoc repairs and maintenance for teams should be reviewed and where teams identify high prices being charged, these should be appropriately investigated and discussed with users so that they can either be addressed or appropriately explained.

- **Water usage metered:** Water usage should be metered locally and monitored so that excessive use can be quickly identified and remedied.

- **Review of service contracts:** The organisation should regularly review and renegotiate service contracts and agreements to ensure they are getting the best value for services like maintenance, IT support, and clinical waste disposal.

- **Lean facilities:** Like all areas, estates and facilities should look to review their processes using a Lean approach or similar. Hospitals in Japan adopting ILan principles in facility maintenance have reported a reduction in costs by improving efficiency and reducing waste.

- **Market tested services:** All in-house facilities services could be market tested against outsourced providers - gardening, security, waste disposal, linen, domestics, laundry and canteen for example.

- **Minimised mail costs:** Postage costs should be minimised by centralising mail and postage, reducing postage levels through alternative routes (email etc), considering the use of a print provider and pre-sorting mail to get reduced costs from mail providers.

- **Porter costs optimised:** Porter staffing costs should be controlled through effective workforce planning, and aligning them to front-line teams where possible. The amount of porters required should be based on a workforce model, which flexes with activity.

- **Domestics costs optimised**: Domestic staffing costs should be controlled through effective workforce planning, and aligning them to front-line teams where possible. The amount of domestic staff required should be based on a workforce model, which flexes with activity.

- **Printing costs optimised:** Printing and photocopying costs should have been addressed, where it makes sense operationally, by standardising printers, centralising where possible and monitoring usage.

- **Telephone charges controlled:** Telephone costs should be minimised by a central team being responsible for overall minimisation; front-line team having individual responsibility and information being available on the use of telephones. Home phone rental reduction can also be considered.

THEME 7.7
Transport

This theme considers all things to do with transport, so includes ideas on controlling taxi and patient transfer usage and pricing alongside appropriate control of the transport assets of the organisation. The theme also considers maintenance costs and the efficiency of the fleet. The specific ideas are:

- **Patient transport contract costs minimised:** Transport should be charged with reducing overall patient transport costs based on mix, price and volume. Front-line teams should hold budgets and their performance against each is monitored centrally. The overall aim should be to optimise usage and price together.

- **Taxi costs controlled:** Transport should be charged with reducing overall taxi costs based on mix, price and volume. Front-line teams should hold budgets and their performance against each is monitored centrally. The overall aim should be to optimise usage and price together. Where this is an issue, you might consider putting central controls in place on authorisation.

- **In-house van fleet efficient:** All in-house transport should be as energy and repair efficient as possible and its use should be minimised through monitoring and proper route planning so as to share duties (moving notes, tests etc).

- **Planned patient transport:** The use of patient transport and taxis should be planned in advance as much as possible, rather than ad-hoc, to reduce cost. This could be done through an electronic system.

- **Transport assets controlled:** In-house transport maintenance costs should be minimised through appropriate planning, negotiation of contracts, identification of poor practice by drivers etc. The actual physical assets themselves should be tracked and monitored to ensure they don't go missing…

THEME 7.8
User billing

This is an enabler in most cases to ensure that you get all the income that you should get, and don't do work for people that either won't pay, can't pay or are surprised by how much they should pay. This is equally important whether you get your money direct from service users, from commissioners or insurers. It includes transparent pricing, cost estimation tools, standard billing and regulated pricing, as well as counselling and support services for people that can't pay.

- **Clear pricing:** As seen in India, providing patients with clear pricing information for treatments and procedures helps in making informed health and care decisions and managing costs.

- **Online cost estimation:** Online cost estimation tools like those used in US health and care systems offer patients a transparent view of expected costs, reducing billing surprises and disputes.

- **Standardised billing:** In Germany, standardised billing statements have improved patient understanding of health and care costs, enhancing transparency and trust and leading to fewer disputes.

- **Public reporting of health and care Costs:** Countries like Australia have initiatives for public reporting of health and care prices, promoting transparency and competition.

- **Insurance plan cost transparency:** In the Netherlands, insurance companies provide detailed cost breakdowns for services covered, helping patients understand their health and care spending.

- **Regulated pricing:** Singapore's government-regulated health and care pricing ensures that patients are aware of the maximum costs for medical services.

- **Health and care cost navigators:** In Canada, some hospitals offer health and care cost navigator services to help patients understand and manage their health and care expenses.

- **Display of cost comparisons:** Hospitals in Japan display cost comparisons for common procedures, empowering patients to make cost-effective decisions.

- **Financial counselling services:** Financial counselling services in U.S. hospitals assist patients in understanding their health and care costs and insurance benefits, promoting cost transparency and patient satisfaction.

THEME 7.9
Business development

This theme is all about making as much money as you can from the stuff that you do well, or the potential sources that you have available. It is a long list of specific ideas that range from income on payroll services, retail, branded goods, self-pay areas, energy, consultancy or providing clinical services for other people.

- **Physical service provision:** Where the organisation runs physical services such as a Pharmacy Manufacturing Units (PMUs) or a laundry, it should optimise the opportunity through selling these services to other organisations. The organisation could also consider floating the service as a separate company.

- **Consultancy provision:** The organisation could sell consultancy to other organisations for services that it is good at. This should be done by "productising" what the organisation does so that it can be efficiently undertaken for multiple clients.

- **Appropriate profit margins maintained:** The organisation should understand the income and cost associated with all services, and where possible negotiate increased prices in each area where profit margins need to increase. Or just negotiate price increases everywhere…

- **Energy repayment:** Where the organisation generates energy through renewables or a generator, it should ensure that it sells energy back to the grid at peak times and is appropriately rewarded.

- **Clinical service provision:** The organisation could look for areas where it is providing new or cutting edge clinical services and sell these where possible.

- **Retail income optimisation**: The organisation should maximise potential income from retail opportunities, including pharmacy, food, general retail and gifts.

- **Branded goods sales:** The organisation could sell branded goods (clothing, etc.) to develop the brand of the organisation in the local area and raise funds.

- **Charitable income maximisation:** The organisation should maximise charitable income through a professionally run, and staffed, campaign of donation generation in order to update estate and equipment, etc.

- **Payroll provision:** Where the organisation runs payroll or occupational health services etc, it should maximise the opportunity to run these for other organisations.

- **Private patient provision for public entities:** Where the organisation is a public provider, it could maximise income from private patients - actively looking for opportunities to sell private work (examples include inpatient spells for procedures not paid for by commissioners, clinics for people going abroad, use of scanners to reduce need for autopsy, even scanning animals for vets…). There should be a proper business plan in place though.

- **ER legal payments:** The organisation could implement a scheme to generate money from ER attendees through links with solicitors on a no-win no-fee basis.

- **Income generation team:** The organisation could run an appropriately monitored team dedicated to driving income generation opportunities across the organisation.

- **Market share planning:** The organisation should have a clear idea of where it can take market share, or whole services, from other organisations and has a plan to win and deliver them where they will be profitable. There should be a proper plan to deliver this.

- **Training provision:** The organisation could consider selling training on services to the independent sector.

- **National or international opportunities**: The organisation could consider selling its services outside of the local area – either nationally or internationally.

- **Income repatriation:** The organisation could work to repatriate profitable work from other hospitals/areas through understanding market share and reasons for patients/ Gps / physicians choosing other hospitals.

THEME 7.10
Health & care compliance

The ideas in this theme are a checklist of the main elements of a compliance programme to ensure that you reduce the risks of fines and other costs due to lack of compliance. Such a programme consists of: Compliance training, leadership training, compliance management software, proactive policies, audits, engagement with legal experts, risk management, compliance metrics, employee compliance feedback and integrating the electronic health record with compliance.

- **Regular compliance training:** Implementing ongoing compliance training programs, as seen in Germany, ensures staff stay informed about current regulations, reducing the risk of costly violations.

- **Compliance-focused leadership training:** Training health and care leaders in compliance management, as practiced in the Netherlands, ensures a top-down approach to maintaining high compliance standards.

- **Use of compliance management software:** In the US, many health and care providers utilise software like Compliancy Group to streamline compliance tracking and reporting.

- **Proactive policy updates and reviews:** Regularly updating and reviewing health and care policies to reflect current laws and guidelines, a practice common in the UK, helps prevent compliance lapses.

- **Internal compliance audits:** Conducting internal audits, as in Australia, helps identify potential compliance issues early, allowing for timely corrections.

- **Engaging with legal experts:** Collaborating with legal experts in health and care law, a strategy used in Canada, ensures all aspects of health and care delivery comply with the latest regulations.

- **Risk management programmes:** Implementing comprehensive risk management strategies, similar to those in Japan, identifies areas vulnerable to non-compliance and mitigates risks.

- **Employee feedback mechanisms:** In France, health and care organisations encourage staff to report potential compliance issues, fostering a proactive compliance culture.

- **Compliance performance metrics:** Tracking compliance performance through specific metrics, as in Spain, helps health and care providers quantify compliance efforts and identify areas for improvement.

- **EHR integration with compliance guidelines**: In Singapore, electronic health record systems are integrated with compliance guidelines to ensure real-time adherence during patient care.

-

THEME 7.11
Outsourcing

Obviously, this theme is all about outsourcing - not always a popular area, and one that can increase costs if not appropriately managed, but one that can lead to large savings if done by someone who is used to doing things that you don't have the same expertise or economies of scale in. The three ideas in this theme are: Having an outsourcing strategy and plan, considering all areas for outsourcing and a focus on outsourcing non-core elements

- **Outsourcing plan:** There should be an overall plan for outsourcing within the Trust to identify opportunities and assist with making sure outsourcing actually works (proper contracts, penalties, contingency plans, costing etc).

- **All areas considered:** The organisation should consider all areas for outsourcing, such as:

    - Occupational Health.

    - Medical equipment (e.g. Through Managed Technology Solutions)..

    - Pharmacy manufacturing unit.

    - Pathology.

    - Transactional finance – accounts payable and receivable.

    - Payroll.

- **Outsourcing non-core Services:** The organisation could take the view to "stick to the knitting" – that is to say that it should concentrate on what it is good at and outsource the rest (it should also get good at outsourcing well…). Following Singapore's model, outsourcing services like laundry, catering, and cleaning can lead to cost reductions of up to 20%.

5.8 Transform

The transformation heading contains the bigger ideas generally, focusing on revolution in the approach to cost control. Specific themes under this heading include: Organisational approaches to transformation, system shape change to reduce secondary care involvement, transformational changes and focusing on prevention rather than care to reduce reliance on the health and care system. Any cost control plans should include some element of the transformational to give the plan some excitement, but bold change could be at the heart of truly transformative efficiency programmes.

THEME 8.1
Lean or organisational wide quality approach

This theme consists of three ideas: A focus on Lean as an organisational wide approach, use of other approaches like Clinical Microsystems or Theory of Constraints, and/or the use of an operational engagement method like Service Line Management, to build cost control into the ongoing operations of individual business units.

- **Lean approach:** The organisation could embrace "Lean" thinking, with most staff trained to an awareness level and with fully trained and supported Lean practitioners addressing the processes across the organisation. This would include building a culture of continuous improvement within teams.

- **Other approaches:** The organisation could implement an improvement methodology such as Clinical Microsystems, Six Sigma or theory of constraints across the organisation – teams should work to improve every aspect of care and reduce cost at the same time.

- **Service line management:** The organisation could implement Service Line Management (and Service Line Reporting) as a tool to drive authority and responsibility through the clinical layers of the organisation. The organisation would build clear structures and strong performance management, ensuring that all layers engaged in a clear annual planning process and are supported by strong information, including Patient Level Costing. Look this approach up online, it is a game-changer.

THEME 8.2
Shape Change

This is most appropriate for health and care systems, as it takes careful handling an the right money flows to ensure that this is cost effective for the "losers" of activity and funding, but it is inevitable and important as part of the management of an ageing population and ever growing health and care demands.

Specific ideas within this theme include: Ensuring people are in the right setting for care, that this is supported by electronic systems, financial flow planning, putting clinics in the community by default, ensuring ER is only for emergencies, implementing lead provider models and putting in place elective gateway systems

- **Right setting:** The organisation can consider its productivity within its system setting and build a clear understanding of what services should be delivered in which settings. There could be a clear view that only acute work should be done in the acute setting, with flow through into community and primary care, and the organisation can focus on the bit that it does and ensuring that that is profitable.

- ***Right setting electronic systems:*** When making sure that care is in the right setting, executive and front-line teams need information to help them understand the impact and how to do it on the ground. The use of an evidence-based system (such as MCAP or some population health management systems) can provide that.

- ***Financial flow planning:*** A clear plan should be in place across the economy to take account of where the activity and money is expected to be across the system. Whilst this does not aim to eliminate choice, this shows the boundaries within which each organisation should expect to work, setting out the activity and payment which can be used to build profitable (if efficient) capacity plans and workforce models.

- ***Outpatients in community by default:*** As the activity that is least likely to need hospital equipment, the system could move to largely delivered outpatient appointment in the community, with only those that are required still delivered in acute settings (e.g. access to acute care, specialist equipment).

  Examples of specific ways of making this happen are included across this book.

- ***ER only for emergencies:*** Non-elective care could be transformed, with only true accidents and emergencies coming through ER, with the rest identified in advance through monitoring of conditions and access through local responsive services.

- ***Lead provider models:*** Elective care could be transformed through the development of lead provider models for almost all elective pathways. Lead provider models involve a commissioner engaging one entity to take accountability for a pathway, bringing in others as necessary, but with the aim of providing improved outcomes and a reduced cost.

  Musculoskeletal models across parts of the UK take this approach.

THEME 8.3
Structure change

Specifically, this theme focuses on things we can do to radically change the way we deliver services. It considers: Can we merge or partner with others (and save costs through shared functions). Can we just stop doing things that are too expensive and start doing things that might be more profitable? Can we aggressively outsource almost all (or all) of our operations and become an organisation that contracts with each and brings them together to deliver?

- ***Merge with or acquire others:*** This is a tough area to get savings out quickly, but it is possible if you do it properly. Merging with or acquiring other organisations wholesale, or elements of their service, can lead to economies of scale, process efficiency and reduced overheads

- **Stop doing things:** The tough decision to close or consolidate units can face significant pushback but can lead to substantial cost savings by eliminating redundancy and underutilisation.

- **Outsourcing everything:** While potentially controversial due to concerns over job losses and quality control, outsourcing as many functions as you can, and just focusing on the core of what you do, could lead to greater efficiency.

THEME 8.S1
Transformational ideas

This is a list of nearly forty different transformational ideas, based on completely changing the way you work, or elements of it. What if we were to automate everything we could by default? Implement a value-based care approach? Run our supply chain like Amazon does? Completely integrate voluntary community providers into the system? Eliminate paper? Put in place a single user portal for all patients? Let patients decide what they need? The list is endless - but bold choices may reap great rewards.

In your organisation, some of these ideas may seem too grand, but you could consider what they mean for you if you apply the principles:

- **Global health data sharing platform:** Implementing a universal platform for sharing health and care data across borders to improve disease tracking, treatment outcomes, and facilitate global research collaborations.

- **Crowdsourced health and care solutions platform:** Developing an open-source platform for crowdsourcing health and care innovations, where ideas can be shared and developed collectively.

- **AI-driven personalised medicine:** Developing or using advanced AI algorithms for personalised medicine to precisely diagnose and treat conditions, reducing trial-and-error treatments.

- **Universal preventive care protocol:** Developing and using a global standard for preventive care focusing on lifestyle, diet, and early detection to decrease the incidence of costly chronic diseases.

- **Complete decentralisation:** Completely decentralise health and care delivery model using local clinics and telemedicine to reduce reliance on expensive hospital care. Start with what can be provided in homes, by the VCSE sector, by primary care, then community care and then, only then, secondary care settings.

- **Voluntary sector integration:** Completely integrate large parts of the voluntary sector to focus on community resilience first and foremost – funding the sector properly and on a long-term basis to help prevent a requirement for more formal health and care provision, and to allow people to return to their homes.

- **Completely renewable energy-powered health and care Facilities:** Transitioning all health and care facilities to renewable energy sources to cut operational costs, and maybe just save the planet.

- **Automated robotic surgery systems:** Working to automate surgery as much as is possible - developing robotic surgery systems for routine procedures to enhance surgical efficiency and reduce human error.

- **Revolutionising health and care with AI:** Extensive use of AI for diagnostics, patient care management, and predictive analytics, like AI integration in Tesla's autonomous technology. Employ AI to optimise hospital operations, from patient flow management to predictive analytics for health and care needs, similar to how Amazon uses AI to predict consumer behaviour.

- **Remote health and care delivery via drone:** Using advanced logistics and transport technology to deliver health and care services and supplies to remote locations efficiently. And why just remote - some supplies could be delivered to everyone this way.

- **Autonomous vehicles for patient transportation:** Using self-driving vehicles to transport patients, thereby reducing the costs associated with medical transportation services.

- **Reusable medical equipment:** Emphasising the development and use of reusable medical equipment, inspired by the reusable rocket technology of SpaceX.

- **Redesign health and care estate:** Redesigning health and care facilities for maximum efficiency and sustainability, much like Tesla's approach to vehicle design.

- **Blockchain health records:** Implementing blockchain technology for secure and efficient management of health records, reducing administrative costs and improving data accessibility.

- **Advanced logistics:** Utilising systems like Amazon's state-of-the-art logistics to streamline health and care supply chains, reducing costs related to procurement, storage, and distribution of medical supplies.

- **Telehealth first:** Expanding tele-health services, leveraging cloud computing and data processing capabilities, to provide efficient and cost-effective care. Expanding the use of tele-health services, inspired by Apple's emphasis on connectivity, to provide efficient and accessible care.

- **Customer-Centric service model:** Applying Amazon's customer service model to patient care, focusing on patient satisfaction and efficiency to reduce unnecessary procedures and readmissions.

- **Big data:** Examples in this area include:

- Analysing vast amounts of health data to identify trends and areas for cost savings, much like Amazon analyses consumer data to optimise its offerings and supply chain.

- Taking Apple's approach to data, applying advanced analytics to personalise patient care and predict health trends, potentially reducing costly interventions.

- Using big data analytics to predict patient health trends and prevent illnesses before they require expensive treatments.

- **Patient engagement platform:** Creating intuitive and user-friendly patient portals for scheduling, communication, and health record access, enhancing patient engagement and reducing administrative burdens.

- **Dynamic pricing:** Implementing dynamic pricing models for non-critical health and care services to optimise costs and resource utilisation.

- **Global health and care market:** Establishing a global online marketplace for health and care services and products, offering competitive pricing and a wide range of options for patients and providers.

- **Seamless ecosystems:** Creating a seamless ecosystem of care, akin to Apple's integrated product ecosystem, where all devices and services are interconnected for efficient patient management.

- **User-friendly integrated apps:** Developing intuitive health apps and tools for patients and providers, improving health monitoring and communication, thereby reducing unnecessary visits and tests.

- **Genius bars:** Setting up walk-in centres similar to Apple's Genius Bars for quick, efficient handling of basic health inquiries and minor ailments.

- **Prevention through technology:** Leveraging wearable technologies to encourage preventive health practices, reducing long-term health and care costs.

- **Public-private partnerships:** Encouraging collaborations between the public sector and private technology companies to fund and develop innovative health and care solutions that can reduce overall health and care costs.

- **Telemedicine for chronic care:** Expanding the use of telemedicine to manage chronic conditions and conduct consultations, saving on patient transportation and inpatient care costs.

- **Quantum computing:** Harnessing the power of quantum computing to accelerate medical research, potentially leading to more cost-effective treatment options and quicker drug development.

- **Universal health coverage model:** Promoting a health and care model that provides universal access to essential health services, preventing costly health emergencies by ensuring early and regular care.

- **Major overhaul of IT:** Investing in cutting-edge IT systems can be risky and costly upfront but can lead to massive long-term savings and efficiency gains.

- **Restructuring the entire workforce:** This could involve reshaping staff roles, salaries, and benefits, a move that requires careful handling due to potential morale impacts, but it can align staffing costs more closely with actual needs.

- **Radical shift to value-based care models**: Fully transitioning to value-based care requires a fundamental change in operational and clinical approaches but can significantly reduce costs by focusing on patient outcomes.

- **Eliminating paper:** Moving to a completely paperless system is a daunting task given the reliance on physical documents, but it offers significant long-term savings.

- **Aim to eliminate all admin tasks:** Can all administration be automated through a range of electronic systems, AI, Robotic Process Automation and data collection tools? One organisation we have worked with has a programme to do just that to eliminate anything done by administration staff in bands 2-4 in the UK.

THEME 8.S2
Focus on prevention and self management

This list could be almost infinite, but instead contains a selection of ideas that focus on prevention, on community resilience and on quick diagnosis, rather than on treatment. Obviously, you need to do both, but if you commit at least some resources to prevention, in a controlled way, you make a start on a journey that should deliver better outcomes for the money you are spending. Or you could just go whole-heartedly for thus as a system - this is supposed to be the transformational section...

- **Community gardening for mental health:** In the UK, community gardening projects have been used as a therapeutic tool, reducing the reliance on traditional mental health services and their associated costs.

- **Virtual reality (VR) for pain management:** Innovative use of VR in pain management, as trialled in France, has shown potential in reducing the need for pain medication and shortening hospital stays.

- **Music therapy:** Incorporating music therapy in patient care, as practiced in Canada, has shown to reduce anxiety and pain, potentially decreasing the need for certain medications.

- **Dance and movement therapy:** In Brazil, dance therapy sessions for patients, especially the elderly, have contributed to better overall health and reduced care needs.

- **Farming initiatives:** Hospitals in the Netherlands have started growing their own food to provide exercise and engagement for their service users (as well as getting great cheap food).

- **Energy healing and Reiki:** Some US hospitals offer energy healing therapies like Reiki as a complementary treatment, which patients report help in faster recovery and reduced reliance on medication.

- **Digital patient engagement platforms:** Platforms like MyChart, used in the US, offer patients easy access to their health information and care plans, improving engagement and satisfaction.

- **Enhanced communication and education:** In Australia, effective communication and patient education about treatments and expectations have led to higher satisfaction and reduced readmission rates.

- **Community health workers:** Employing community health workers for patient education and basic care, especially in underserved areas, can significantly reduce the burden on more expensive health and care resources.

- **Use of collaborative care models in chronic disease management:** The Netherlands uses collaborative care models for chronic diseases, which have been shown to reduce hospital admissions and overall treatment costs.

- **Developing patient education materials**: Creating tailored patient education materials can improve patient compliance and reduce readmissions, yet many organisations rely on generic materials.

- **Patient-Centred Medical Home (PCMH) Model**: The PCMH model, widely adopted in Japan, focuses on team-based care coordination, leading to improved patient outcomes and reduced health and care costs.

- **Co-management models:** Co-management models in patient care, used effectively in Germany, ensure collaborative decision-making, optimising resource use and reducing costs.

- **Community health fairs**: Organising health fairs with a focus on prevention and wellness education, reducing long-term health and care costs.

- **Work across the full system:** Focus on housing, education and policing to improve people's health generally.

There are literally thousands more things that can be done if you engage with community resources and VCFSE sector organisations to design a truly preventative and resilient culture for health and care.

The Bit at the Back

Glossary of Terms

Benchmarking: Comparing business processes and performance metrics to industry bests or best practices from other organisations to identify areas for improvement.

Bradford Index: A measure of absenteeism which weights short, frequent absences greater than fewer, longer spells.

Capacity and Demand Modelling: A method to match the available capacity (resources, services) with the demand (patients, cases) to improve efficiency and reduce costs.

CIPS (Cost Improvement Programmes): Structured initiatives undertaken by healthcare organizations to achieve financial savings and efficiency gains. These programs often involve a comprehensive review of spending, processes, and service delivery models to identify opportunities for cost reduction and quality improvement.

Clinical Pathways: Standardised, evidence-based multidisciplinary management plans which identify an appropriate sequence of clinical interventions, timeframes, milestones, and expected outcomes for a specific patient population or clinical condition. They are designed to streamline and coordinate care, enhance quality, and reduce variability in outcomes.

Cost Reduction: The process of identifying and implementing strategies to decrease expenses and improve efficiency within healthcare organizations, without compromising the quality of care provided to patients. This involves analyzing various aspects of healthcare delivery, including operational processes, resource allocation, and service provision, to find ways to reduce costs while maintaining or enhancing patient outcomes. Organisational vs System Cost Reduction:

Organisational Cost Reduction: Initiatives and strategies focused on reducing expenses at the level of individual healthcare facilities or provider organizations. These strategies may include operational efficiencies, workforce management, procurement savings, and technology optimizations that directly impact the organisation's bottom line.

System Cost Reduction: Efforts aimed at reducing healthcare costs across a broader system, such as a national health service, insurance system, or integrated health network. This includes policy reforms, payment model changes, care delivery redesign, and preventive health measures that address cost drivers across the entire healthcare ecosystem.

CRES (Cost Reduction and Efficiency Savings): Holistic strategies to reduce healthcare costs while enhancing operational efficiency and patient care quality.

CRPs (Cost Reduction Plans): Detailed plans developed by healthcare organizations to outline specific actions, timelines, and targets for reducing expenses. CRPs typically include both short-term and long-term strategies to manage costs effectively, ensuring that financial savings are achieved without negatively impacting patient care standards.

Economies of Scale: Cost advantages achieved by increasing the scale of production, leading to a lower cost per unit.

Evidence-Based Practice / Medicine (EBP/M): The conscientious use of current best evidence in making decisions about patient care. In healthcare, it involves integrating clinical expertise with the best available research evidence and patient values and preferences to improve outcomes and quality of care.

Financial and Resource Constraints: Challenges faced by healthcare organizations due to limited financial resources and constraints on available materials, workforce, and infrastructure. These constraints necessitate efficient resource management and strategic planning to optimize care delivery and ensure sustainability.

Gantt Chart: Designed by Henry Gantt, this is a project management tool that shows tasks, dependency between tasks, start and finish dates, who is undertaking tasks, etc.

Healthcare Policy Reform: Modifications to the regulations governing healthcare systems to improve public health, reduce costs, and enhance care quality.

Integrated Care: A coordinated approach to healthcare delivery that ensures patients receive comprehensive services across the continuum of care.

Lean or Lean Management: A methodology focused on reducing waste and enhancing efficiency, adapted for healthcare to improve patient care and value.

Operational Grip: The effective management and control of day-to-day operations within a healthcare organization to ensure optimal performance, efficiency, and cost-effectiveness. This involves closely monitoring operational processes, resource utilization, and performance metrics to make informed decisions and adjustments as necessary.

Patient-Centred Care: Care models that prioritise the preferences, needs, and values of patients in all healthcare decisions.

Performance Management: The practice of monitoring and managing employee performance to align with organisational goals and improve healthcare delivery.

Process Improvement: Methods to enhance healthcare processes for better efficiency, patient flow, and outcomes, often involving the elimination of unnecessary steps.

Rapid Improvement Events: Sometimes known as Kaizen are events in which staff spend 3-5 days analysing and solving a problem together.

Risk Management: Identifying and mitigating risks in healthcare organisations to protect patients, staff, and assets while ensuring regulatory compliance.

Sankey Diagrams: Chart showing flow of service-users between services, highlighting major flows and variations from it.

Service Line Management (SLM): An organisational approach that focuses on managing specific sets of related healthcare services, or 'service lines,' as distinct operational units. This model enables healthcare providers to enhance the quality, efficiency, and profitability of specific service lines (e.g., cardiology, orthopedics) by concentrating on performance metrics, patient outcomes, and cost reduction strategies specific to each service line.

Skill / training Needs Assessments: Identification of individuals current and needed skills.

Technological Advancements: Refers to the integration and utilisation of cutting-edge technology in healthcare to improve patient care, operational efficiency, and cost-effectiveness.

Transformation: Comprehensive and significant changes in healthcare organisations aimed at improving service delivery, efficiency, and patient outcomes.

Turnaround: A strategy used in critical situations to reverse a healthcare organisation's decline by focusing on cost control, process improvement, and restructuring. Can include the use of certified insolvency practitioners.

Unforeseen Consequences: Outcomes that were not anticipated as a result of specific actions or interventions in healthcare, potentially impacting patient care or costs.

Unintended Outcomes: Results occurring as a side effect of an action aimed at achieving a different goal, often highlighting the complexity of healthcare decision-making.

Value-Based Healthcare: A healthcare commissioning/purchasing and delivery model in which providers, including hospitals and physicians, are paid based on patient health outcomes. Under this model, payments are based on the quality of care provided, measured by patient health outcomes, rather than the volume of services delivered. This approach aims to enhance care quality, patient satisfaction, and cost-efficiency by aligning incentives with the achievement of health improvements.

Workforce Planning: Ensuring that there is enough staff with the right skills, behaviours and attitudes at the right place and the right time to meet the demand for excellent heath and care to the population. Preferably within a reasonable financial envelope.

Abbreviations

A&C	Administration & Clerical
A&E	Accident and Emergency Department (also known as ER)
AHP	Allied Health Professional
CIP	Cost Improvement Plans.
CLEAR	Clinically LEd workforce and Activity Redesign
CNST	Clinical Negligence Scheme for Trusts
CRES	Cost Reduction and Efficiency Schemes
CRP	Cost Reduction Plans
CVC	Central Venous Catheter
DIA	Diversity Impact Assessment
DNA	Did Not Attend
DUR	Drug Utilisation Reviews
EBD	Excess Bed Days
EDD	Expected Date of Discharge
EHR	Electronic Health Record
EPR	Electronic Patient Record
ER	Emergency Room
ERAS	Enhanced Recovery After Surgery
FOI	Freedom of Information
FT	Foundation Trust
GP	General Practitioner (a family physician) or General Practice
GPO	Group Purchasing Organisation
HAI	Hospital Acquired Infection
HVAC	Heating, Ventilation and Air Conditioning.
ICB	Integrated Care Board

ICU	Intensive Care Unit	
IT	Information Technology	
IV	Intravenous	
KPI	Key Performance Indicator	
LMIC	Low- and Middle- Income Countries	
LoS	Length of Stay	
MARS	Mutually Agreed Resignation Scheme	
MDT	Multi Disciplinary Team	
MRI	Magnetic Resonance Imaging	
MSP	Managed Service Provider	
MTS	Managed Technology Solutions	
NICE	National Institute for Health & Care Excellence	
OP	Operating Practitioner or Out Patients	
OPAT	Outpatient Parenteral Antibiotic Therapy	
OR	Operating Room	
OT	Occupational Therapist	
P&E	Productivity & Efficiency	
PA	Programmed Activity	
PACS	Picture Archiving and Communication System	
PBM	Pharmacy Benefit Management	
PCMH	Patient-Centred Medical Home	
PMO	Programme Management Office	
QIA	Quality Impact Assessment	
R&D	Research & Development	

RIS	Radiology Information System
ROL	Reorder Level
ROQ	Reorder Quantity
RPA	Robotic Process Automation
SLA	Service Level Agreement
SLM	Service Line Management
SMART	Specific, Measurable, Achievable, Relevant, and Time-bound
SPA	Special Programmed Activity
SRO	Senior Responsible Officer
VAT	Value Added Tax
VBHC	Value-Based Health Care
VCFSE	Voluntary, Care, Faith and Social Enterprise
VR	Virtual Reality
WHO	World Health Organisation

Links

It's a bit difficult to provide links in a physical document - so if you are reading the print version of this book, don't fancy typing all this lot in, and have no luck finding them online through normal searches, please just get in touch - colin.lewry@carados.com

King's Fund

https://www.kingsfund.org.uk/

World Health Organisation

https://www.who.int/

Service Line Management

https://www.gov.uk/government/collections/service-line-management-an-approach-to-hospital-managment

UK Model Hospital

https://model.nhs.uk/

Map of Medicine

https://russellgroup.ac.uk/policy/case-studies/medic-to-medic-and-the-map-of-medicine-developed-at-ucl/

Bumper Book of Health & Care Workforce Planning

www.carados.com

Health Education England STAR tool

https://www.hee.nhs.uk/our-work/hee-star

CLEAR

https://www.hee.nhs.uk/our-work/workforce-transformation/clinically-led-workforce-activity-redesign-clear

E-learning for Health

https://www.e-lfh.org.uk/

Productive series

https://www.england.nhs.uk/improvement-hub/wp-content/uploads/sites/44/2017/11/The-Productive-Series-generic-flyer.pdf

Printed in Dunstable, United Kingdom